Teachers' Work in a Globalizing Economy

Schools and their purposes are changing at a faster pace now than at any other period in the history of schooling. It is not just the pace of change that is important, the direction and the substance of these changes are also crucial. This is where the labour process of teaching becomes a vital focus.

This book locates what is happening to teachers' work in the global economy. Within the dramatically changed circumstances of globalization, schools are being required to act as if they were private businesses, driven by the quest for efficiency and operating in a supposed atmosphere of marketization and competition with each other for resources, students, reputation, and public support for their continued existence. Meanwhile, this ideology of schools as cost centres has become so pervasive that there has been little public debate on its desirability or its alternatives.

Teachers' Work in a Globalizing Economy addresses this imbalance and provides a major renovation of labour process theory in an educational context. Two case studies provide a tangible working expression of the labour process of teaching, showing how teachers are simultaneously experiencing significant changes to their work, as well as responding in ways that actively shape these processes.

John Smyth is Foundation Professor of Teacher Education at the Flinders University of South Australia, and Associate Dean (Research). He is also Director of the Flinders Institute for the Study of Teaching. **Alastair Dow** is Superintendent within the Department of Education, Training and Employment. **Robert Hattam** is Research Manager at the Flinders Institute for the Study of Teaching, Flinders University of South Australia. **Alan Reid** is Associate Professor at the School of Education, University of South Australia. **Geoffrey Shacklock** was Research Associate with the Flinders Institute for the Study of Teaching at the Flinders University of South Australia.

Teachers' Work in a Globalizing Economy

John Smyth
Alastair Dow, Robert Hattam,
Alan Reid and Geoffrey Shacklock

Preface by Michael Apple

London and New York

First published 2000
by Falmer Press
11 New Fetter Lane, London EC4P 4EE

Simultaneously published in the USA and Canada
by Falmer Press
Garland Inc., 19 Union Square West, New York, NY 10003

Falmer Press is an imprint of the Taylor & Francis Group

Typeset in Times by Taylor & Francis Books Ltd
Printed and bound in Great Britain by Biddles Ltd,
Guildford and King's Lynn

British Library Cataloguing in Publication Data
A catalogue record for this book is available from the British Library

Library of Congress Cataloging in Publication Data
Teachers' work in a globalizing economy / John Smyth ... [et al.].
    Includes bibliographical references and index.
    1. Teachers. 2. Education – Economic aspects.
    3. Postmodernism and education. I. Smyth, John.
    LB1775.T4184   1999
    371.1–dc21   99-39365
    CIP

ISBN 0–750–70962–6 (hbk)
ISBN 0–750–70961–8 (pbk)

Contents

Foreword

In a book that seeks to locate what is happening to teachers' work in the global economy, it is appropriate to stop and ask difficult questions about the wider forces. At the time of writing there is mounting evidence that the concept of globalization is under increasing attack and that there is something of a backlash emerging. It seems that even the most ardent advocates of the global economy are having second thoughts. For the past 20 years, 2000 world leaders have been gathering annually in January in the small Swiss town of Davos as part of the World Economic Forum to celebrate the unfettered market. The agenda seems to have gone awfully wrong in 1999. As the world economic crisis deepens, the only thing that seems certain is the unanimous feeling of a lack of clarity as to where the future might be headed, and no agreement about what needs to be done. The pace and extent of change is clearly beyond the ability of individual governments to control or manage, and the forces 'creating chaos in many parts of the world are only likely to continue growing ever more powerful' (Kitney, 1999, p. 19). Celebration seems to have given way to fear and apprehension as the world financial system proves incapable of managing the massive capital flows that can ravage economies overnight. The virtues of market liberalization and unlimited capital mobility which had been unquestioned articles of faith, are looking decidedly tarnished as the disciples of global capitalism undertake a reassessment of the uncontrollable forces they have unleashed.

In a set of comments that are far from comforting, Claude Samdja, the managing director of the World Economic Forum, frankly admitted that the process of international conformity, far from producing an agreed way of dealing with the problems, was having the reverse effect:

> What has developed instead is the first systematic crisis of the global economy, brutally exposing vulnerabilities and explosive structural weaknesses in the international financial system.... [The] crisis [is] beyond the control of elected governments...[and there is] also deep

alarm at spreading disillusionment among ordinary people with the economic policies which have lead to the crisis.

The concept of globalisation – thought of until now as an unstoppable trend – is under attack and reconsideration, leading today to a perception of global capitalism in retreat.

(Kitney, 1999, p. 19)

We can only wonder about the sincerity of the economic barbarians who have wreaked such havoc, and whether they are truly committed to a real change of direction. Reassessments like 'responsible globality', recognizing 'the social dimensions of the global market', and 'sharing the benefits of globalization more equally' sound like hollow platitudes and belated realizations for what has euphemistically been labelled the need for a 'new financial architecture' capable of regulating global markets.

What is equally worrying is that the policies that have so demonstrably failed in the economic arena are the same ones that have been used to relentlessly assail schools around the world over the past two decades, and in many instances have led to the decimation of once proud public education systems. Teachers' work has been in the middle of this economic maelstrom and we must hold grave fears for schools that are now wedded to economic policies that are possibly in terminal trouble.

The emergence of this book is a timely one in the sense that it begins to explore the wider forces shaping the work of teachers, what these mean, and how we might begin the process of reclamation from polices that have been extremely destructive.

Portions of this book began their life as doctoral dissertations I supervised, and were undertaken by Alan Reid, Alastair Dow and Geoffrey Shacklock within the Flinders Institute for the Study of Teaching. Other parts of this account are new and have been written by Robert Hattam and myself as we have struggled with a way forward in resuscitating the work of teaching.

'The Process of Economic Globalization' section in Chapter 1 is based upon Smyth (1998) 'Economic Forces Affecting Supervision'. In J. Firth and E. Pajak (eds) *Handbook of Research on School Supervision*. New York: Macmillan. The 'Teaching in the "New Work Order"' section in Chapter 1 is based upon Smyth (1996a) 'Evaluation of Teacher Performance: Move Over Hierarchy Here Comes Collegiality!' *Journal of Education Policy* 11(2), pp. 185–96. Chapter 2 is based upon Reid (1997) 'Controlling Teachers' Work: a Labour Process Analysis of Teachers' Work'. Unpublished doctoral thesis, Flinders University of South Australia, July. The first section of Chapter 3 'Introduction to the Nature of Critical Research' is based upon Shacklock (1995) 'A Socially Critical, Ethnographic, Work-storied Account of Teachers' Work'. Unpublished doctoral thesis, Flinders University of South Australia, July. The second section of Chapter 3 'Critical

Ethnography' and Chapter 4 are based upon Dow (1996) 'Collaboration and Resistance at Gallipoli High School: the Work of Teaching in a Post-Fordist Era'. Unpublished doctoral thesis, Flinders University of South Australia, December. The last section of Chapter 3 'Critically Ethnographic Work-storied Account' is based upon Shacklock (1995) 'A Socially Critical, Ethnographic, Work-storied Account of Teachers' Work'. Unpublished doctoral thesis, Flinders University of South Australia, July. Chapter 5 is based upon Shacklock (1995) 'A Socially Critical, Ethnographic, Work-storied Account of Teachers' Work'. Unpublished doctoral thesis, Flinders University of South Australia, July, and all quotes in Chapter 5 come from this work.

I wish to express by appreciation to my co-authors, to Anna Clarkson of Falmer Press, to the two anonymous reviewers, and to Michael Apple for writing the Preface. Solveiga has been a constant support in all phases of the writing of this book, and cheerfully undertook the mammoth job of producing a consistent format and bringing together the references.

John Smyth
February 1999

Preface

In his influential history of curriculum debates in the United States, Herbert Kliebard has documented that educational issues have consistently involved major conflicts and compromises among groups with competing visions of 'legitimate' knowledge, what counts as 'good' teaching and learning, and what is a 'just' society (Kliebard, 1986). That such conflicts have deep roots in conflicting views of racial, class, and gender justice in education and the larger society is ratified in even more critical recent work as well (see, e.g. Rury and Mirel, 1997; Teitelbaum, 1996; Selden, 1999). While I believe neither that these competing visions have ever had equal holds on the imagination of educators or the general citizenry nor that they have ever had equal power to affect their visions, it is still clear that no analysis of education can be fully serious without placing at its very core a sensitivity to the ongoing struggles that constantly shape the terrain on which education operates.

Today is no different than in the past. A 'new' set of compromises, a new alliance and new power bloc has been formed that has increasing influence in education and all things social. This power bloc combines multiple fractions of capital who are committed to neo-liberal marketized solutions to educational problems, neo-conservative intellectuals who want a 'return' to higher standards and a 'common culture', authoritarian populist religious fundamentalists who are extremely powerful in the United States in particular and who are deeply worried about secularity and the preservation of their own traditions, and particular fractions of the professionally oriented new middle class who are committed to the ideology and techniques of accountability, measurement, and 'management'. While there are clear tensions and conflicts within this alliance, in general its overall aims are in providing the educational conditions believed necessary both for increasing international competitiveness, profit and discipline and for returning us to a romanticized past of the 'ideal' home, family and school (Apple, 1993; Apple, 1996).

In essence, the new alliance has integrated education into a wider set of ideological commitments. The objectives in education are the same as those which guide its economic and social welfare goals. They include the dramatic expansion of that eloquent fiction, the free market; the drastic reduction of government responsibility for social needs; the reinforcement of intensely competitive structures of mobility both inside and outside the school; the lowering of people's expectations for economic security; the 'disciplining' of culture and the body; and the popularization of what is clearly a form of social Darwinist thinking, as the recent popularity of *The Bell Curve* (Herrnstein and Murray, 1994; see also, Apple, 1999 and Kincheloe and Steinberg, 1996) so obviously and distressingly indicates. The seemingly contradictory discourse of competition, markets and choice on the one hand and accountability, performance objectives, standards, national testing and national curriculum have created such a din that it is hard to hear anything else. As I have shown elsewhere (Apple, 1996), these tendencies actually oddly reinforce each other and help cement conservative educational positions into our daily lives.

While lamentable, the changes that are occurring present an exceptional opportunity for serious critical reflection. Here, I am not speaking of merely the accumulation of studies to promote the academic careers of researchers, although the accumulation of serious studies is not unimportant. Rather, I am suggesting that in a time of radical social and educational change it is crucial to document the processes and effects of the various and sometimes contradictory elements of what might best be called 'conservative modernization' (Dale, 1989) and of the ways in which they are mediated, compromised with, accepted, used in different ways by different groups for their own purposes, and/or struggled over in the policies and practices of people's daily educational lives (Ransom, 1995, p. 427). For those interested in critical educational policies and practices, not to do this means that we act without understanding the shifting relations of power that are constructing and reconstructing the social fields of power in which education goes on. While Gramsci's saying, 'Pessimism of the intellect, optimism of the will', has a powerful resonance to it and is useful for mobilization and for not losing hope, it would be foolish to substitute rhetorical slogans for the fuller analysis that is undoubtedly required if we are to be successful.

It is here where *Teachers' Work in a Globalizing Economy* enters. That the book provides us with one of the clearest syntheses of the long tradition of work on teaching as a labour process would be enough to warrant its publication. However, it goes significantly further. It reworks this material in creative ways and applies it to the current economic and political forces that are having such a profound impact on teachers' work in so many nations. Not content to 'only' make interventions at the theoretical level, however, the authors apply their critically reworked approaches to the daily life and experiences of teachers in schools that are in the midst of these changing economic, ideological and political conditions. This is a rarer accomplishment than we might like to admit, since the critical literature is often filled with (sometimes overly) theorized and rhetorical analyses of 'the post-modern condition' that ignore structural realities or seem to believe that the economy and the state do not have real material effects and consequences. Or it is characterized by reductive, essentializing, and overly structural accounts that treat people as if they were puppets. Or, finally, it is equally filled with empirically detailed but undertheorized studies of individual schools or sets of teachers in which nothing exists outside of the local setting.

Teachers' Work in a Globalizing Economy goes beyond these limits. It combines both neo-Gramscian and 'post' positions; it provides empirical detail while at the same time situating these details in their larger context; and it recognizes that 'bearing witness' to the negativity of the current situations in which teachers find themselves is important but insufficient. That is, it grapples with the crucial question of 'What is to be done?' Let me say more about this last point, since it is of considerable import. Perhaps I can illuminate the significance of this through an example in which I have been personally involved.

In many nations, critical educators are devoting considerable efforts to building counter-hegemonic movements to provide both space and legitimacy for policies and practices that are alternatives to those being proposed by conservative modernization's new hegemonic project. Smyth, Dow, Hattam, Reid and Shacklock rightly propose a number of conceptual and policy-oriented interruptions to those offered by the dominant bloc, interruptions that they hope will provide elements of a revitalized tool-kit for more progressive work. These kinds of things are very valuable; and they can and must be connected to even more proximate interruptions by practising teachers. These are in fact happening. In a number of nations, teachers at all levels of the educational system are teaching each other about their successes and struggles. Important aspects of how this joint teaching can be strategically accomplished are found in the following example, an example that is based on understandings that are very similar to those so nicely documented in this book.

At the same time as these larger critical movements are being built, critical educators are also attempting to occupy the spaces provided by existing 'mainstream' publication outlets to publish books that provide *critical* answers to teachers' questions about 'What do I do on Monday?' during a conservative era. This space has too long been ignored by many theorists of critical pedagogy, for example Carlson and Apple (1998). Some of these attempts have been remarkably successful. For instance, one very large 'professional' organization in the United States – the Association for Supervision and Curriculum Development (ASCD) – publishes books that are distributed each year to its more than 150,000 members, most of whom are teachers or administrators in elementary, middle, or secondary schools. ASCD has not been a very progressive organization, preferring to publish largely technicist and overtly depoliticized material. Yet it has been concerned that its publications have not sufficiently represented socially and culturally critical educators. It, thus, has been looking for ways to increase its legitimacy to a wider range of educators. Because of this legitimacy problem and because of its large membership, it became clear to a number of people who were part of the critical educational traditions in the United States that it might be possible to convince ASCD to publish and widely circulate material that would demonstrate the actual practical *successes* of critical models of curriculum, teaching and evaluation in solving real problems in schools and communities, especially with working class and poor children and children of colour.

After intense negotiations that guaranteed an absence of censorship, a colleague of mine and I agreed to publish a book – *Democratic Schools* (Apple and Beane, 1995) – with ASCD that provided clear practical examples of the power of critical approaches at work in classrooms and communities. It was, expressly, an overt attempt to counter the deskilling logics that increasingly dominated the lives of teachers (and students and parents) that are so clearly documented in Smyth and his co-authors' book. *Democratic Schools* was not only distributed to all 150,000 members of the organization, but it has gone on to sell an additional 100,000 copies. Thus, nearly 250,000 copies of a volume that tells the practical stories of the largely successful struggles of critically oriented educators in real schools are now in the hands of educators who daily face similar problems.[1]

This is an important intervention. While there is no guarantee that teachers will always be progressive (nor is there any guarantee that those who are progressive around class and union issues will be equally progressive around issues of gender, sexuality and race), many teachers do have socially and pedagogically critical intuitions. However, they often do not have ways of putting these intuitions into practice because they cannot picture them in action in daily situations. Due to this, critical theoretical and political insights, then, have nowhere to go in terms of their embodiment in concrete pedagogical situations where the politics of curriculum and teaching must be *enacted*. This is a tragic absence and strategically filling it is absolutely essential. Thus, we need to use and expand the spaces in which critical pedagogical 'stories' are made available so that these positions do not remain only on the theoretical or rhetorical level. The publication and widespread distribution of *Democratic Schools* (a new and revised edition specifically for the UK, Australia and New Zealand has just been published; see Apple and Beane, 1999) provides one instance of using and expanding such spaces in ways that make Freirian and similar critical educational positions seem actually doable in 'ordinary' institutions such as schools and local communities.

I raise this example to show how important it is to follow up on the powerful analysis offered in *Teachers' Work in a Globalizing Economy*. If the authors' points are correct – as I believe they are – then we are faced with a choice. Do we lament the situation, simply saying that teachers are not immune to the globalizing logics that infect so many other aspects of paid labour? Or do we do what Smyth and his co-authors begin to do in the concluding section of their book? Do we build collective responses based on the recognition that a deskilled and intensified labour process of teaching leads to 'training', not an education worthy of its name? In answering these questions in a time of conservative modernization, we can be guided by Raymond Williams' advice. He rightly reminded us about the immense resilience of people in unfavourable conditions and the remarkable diversity of the ways they express their autonomy, even in very unfavourable economic, political and cultural circumstances. As he put it, 'We must speak for hope, as long as it doesn't mean suppressing the nature of the danger' (Williams, 1989, p. 322). The authors of this book clarify where many of these dangers lie. It is up to us to show our resilience.

Michael W. Apple
University of Wisconsin, Madison

Note

1   Translations of this volume have been or will be published in Japan, Argentina, Brazil, Spain, Portugal, and elsewhere. Thus, it is clear that providing critical answers to the pressing issues of 'What do I do on Monday?' is seen as crucial in a number of nations. This gives even more salience to Smyth, Dow, Hattam, Reid and Shacklock's analysis, since it demonstrates the truly global nature of the processes and dangers they critically discuss.

References

Apple, M.W. (1993) *Official Knowledge: Democratic Education in a Conservative Age*. London and New York, Routledge.

Apple, M.W. (1996) *Cultural Politics and Education*. New York, Teachers College Press.

—— (1999) *Power, Meaning, and Identity*. New York, Peter Lang.

—— (2000) *Official Knowledge*. 2nd edn. New York, Routledge.

Apple, M.W. and Beane, J.A. (eds) (1995) *Democratic Schools*. Washington, DC, Association for Supervision and Curriculum Development.

Apple, M.W. and Beane, J.A. (eds) (1999) *Democratic Schools: Lessons From the Chalk Face*. Buckingham, Open University Press.

Carlson, D. and Apple, M.W. (eds) (1998) *Power/Knowledge/Pedagogy*. Boulder, CO, Westview.

Dale, R. (1989) 'The Thatcherite Project in Education'. *Critical Social Policy* 9 (3).

Gramsci, A. (1971) *Selection from the Prison Notebooks of Antonio Gramsci* (translated and edited by Hoare, Q. and Smith, G.). New York, International Publishers, p. 175.

Herrnstein, R. and Murray, C. (1994) *The Bell Curve*. New York, Free Press.

Kincheloe, J. and Steinberg, S. (eds) (1996) *Measured Lies*. New York, St. Martin's Press.

Kliebard, H. (1986) *The Struggle for the American Curriculum*. New York, Routledge.

Preface

Ransom, S. (1995) 'Theorising Educational Policy'. *Journal of Education Policy* 10, 427–48.

Rury, J. and Mirel, J. (1997) 'The Political Economy of Urban Education'. In Apple, M.W. (ed.), *Review of Research in Education*. Washington, DC, American Educational Research Association, 49–110.

Selden, S. (1999) *Inheriting Shame*. New York, Teachers College Press.

Teitelbaum, K. (1996) *Schooling for Good Rebels*. New York, Teachers College Press.

Williams, R. (1989) *Resources of Hope*. New York, Verso.

1 Deindustrialization, Global Capital and the Crisis in Teachers' Work

Introduction

All political processes require a narrative or convincing story to carry them, and because teaching is a political process, recent worldwide reforms of teaching have had their own unique hallmark which has tended to coalesce around the notion of crisis. The narrative about teachers' work that we want to unmask in this book is around teaching as an occupation being subjected to, resisting and accommodating to, forces of globalization bent on transforming teaching into something quite different from what it was even a decade ago.

The genesis of the changes in teachers' work lie within the identifiable socio-cultural and geopolitical paradoxes that are restructuring societies and economies to conform to a particular global view of the way some interests want the world to be. Within the dramatically changed circumstances of globalization, schools are being required to act as if they were private businesses driven by the quest for efficiency, pursuing concrete specified outcomes, and operating in a supposed atmosphere of marketization and competition with each other for resources, students, reputation and public support for their continued existence. So pervasive has this ideology of schools as cost centres become, that there is negligible public debate and discussion on whether this might be a desirable path to follow or not – it has become an unquestioned and unchallengeable article of faith. Teachers are increasingly expected to follow directives and become compliant operatives in the headlong rush to encase schools within the ideology, practices and values of the business sector – never mind that they have histories, aspirations and professional cultures that make them decidedly different to car plants, breweries or fast-food outlets.

We believe Waters (1995) provides some sage advice as we struggle to make sense of the social, economic and political changes referred to as globalization. He defines globalization as 'a social process in which the constraints of geography on social and cultural arrangements recede and in which people become increasingly aware that they are receding' (p. 3). He offers a 'guiding theorem' that traces globalization as it operates in three arenas of social life – the economy, the polity, and culture:

1 The economy: social arrangements for the production, exchange, distribution and consumption of goods and tangible services.
2 The polity: social arrangements for the concentration and application of power, especially insofar as it involves the organized exchange or coercion and surveillance (military, police, etc.), as well as such institutionalized transformation of these practices as authority and diplomacy, that can establish control over populations and territories.
3 Culture: social arrangements for the production, exchange and expression of symbols that represent facts, affects, meanings, beliefs, preferences, tastes and values (pp. 7–8).

We agree with Taylor et al. (1997) that globalization is not an amorphous or homogeneous entity. In fact it is a very complex phenomenon (see Smyth and Shacklock, 1998) in which simultaneous processes of 'global integration' and 'national fragmentation' are at work. For instance, in the case of the former: 'New politics associated with social movements such as feminism, green politics and the peace movement operating transnationally have destabilised traditional political organisation within nation states' (Taylor et al., 1997, p. 59).

On the other hand, in respect of the latter, there has been: 'the disintegration of some nations into..."ethnic tribalism".... In various ways...the links between ethnicity and the nation, which forms the artifice of "the nation" are being challenged and rearranged through these contrary pressures for integration and disintegration' (p. 59).

Elsewhere we have argued (Smyth and Shacklock, 1998) that this more complex view of globalization:

> acknowledges hybrid identities and the manner in which the technicisation of educational policy works to efface difference. Keyman (1997) proposes that we take a critical reading of postcolonial criticism 'by placing the question of identity/difference at the centre of critical analysis by stressing the importance of culture' (p. 194). According to Keyman (1997) we need 'to dismantle the signifying practices of global modernity' (p. 195) through approaching the question of identity/difference not at an abstract/philosophical level, but rather in terms of the concrete discourse in which it is situated/located: 'This shift is necessary...for the assertion and affirmation of a denied, silenced subjectivity' (p. 195). It is, Keyman (1997) argues, 'in this sense that the situated/located notion of difference constitutes a precondition for "engendering" and "decolonising"' (p. 195) the notion of globalization. Only by doing this will it be possible to 'create an ethical space for the

Other not to be spoken of but to speak and assert its subjectivity'
(emphasis in the original, p. 195).

(Smyth and Shacklock, 1998, p. 14)

Having said this, we want to start our analysis by giving primary attention
to aspects of 'economic globalization', and pick up in considerable detail on
the cultural and symbolic aspects in Chapter 6, as they operate to shape
(and are shaped by) teachers' work.

The Process of Economic Globalization

Worldwide forces are dramatically changing the way we think and conceive
of schooling. Vastly improved forms of information technology, instantaneous communication, and a capacity of international capital to move
around the world at short notice to take advantage of local circumstances
(most notably, cheap labour), has meant that corporations as well as governments are faced with unprecedented levels of volatility, uncertainty and
unpredictability demanding quite different kinds of responses – both in
terms of work organization as well as workplace skills.

These new circumstances are characterized by:

1   flexible post-Fordist forms of production and restructured workplace
    organization;
2   a greater reliance on market forces as a mode of regulation, rather than
    rules, regulations, and centralized bureaucratic modes of organization;
3   more emphasis on image and impression management as a way of
    shaping consumers;
4   a re-centralization of control in contexts where responsibility for
    meeting production targets is devolved;
5   resorting to increasingly technicist ways of responding to uncertainty;
    and,
6   a greater reliance on technology as the preferred means for resolving
    complex and intractable social, moral and political problems.

For schools as industrial enterprises, these changes constitute quite a
different regulative framework for the exercise of social control. We are
experiencing a dramatic shift in the boundaries of control from direct, overt
and bureaucratic forms of surveillance, to much more covert forms that take
expression in the nature of the way in which work itself is being restructured. The 'just-in-time' (Sewell and Wilkinson, 1992; Conti and Warner,
1993) and 'total quality management' (Sayer, 1986) processes touted in the
management literature are a particular case in point. The very success of
processes like these relies on somewhat more self-regulative procedures that
are predicated on an intensification of work practices brought about by the

harnessing of peer pressure through 'team work' and 'partnerships' aimed at responding to 'customer needs', eliminating waste and generally promoting a culture of continuous improvement (Delbridge et al., 1992). We are experiencing the emergence of these trends in schools through so-called processes of 'empowerment' and the creation of schemes like 'lead teachers' (Ceroni and Garman, 1994; Ceroni, 1995) and Advanced Skills Teachers (Smyth and Shacklock, 1998).

Decisions and steerage in contemporary capitalism, therefore, is increasingly being removed from the control of national (and democratically elected) governments, and placed in the hands of transnational economic forces that operate largely outside the scope of any single government and which are accountable only to their head offices in London, New York or Tokyo. This process of global economic rearrangement is producing a new international economic order as well as generating a new international division of labour and new and unstable settlements and sets of social forces that are time specific.

Castells (1989) argued that there are really three identifiable aspects to this wider economic restructuring: (1) a fundamental realignment of the relationship between capital and labour, such that capital obtains a significantly higher share in the benefits of the fruits of production; (2) a new role for the state in the public sector, which is not so much about reducing the role of government intervention in the economy, but a changing of its style; and (3) a new international division of labour in which low cost labour is profoundly shaping what is happening in the 'developed' world.

There are a number of outcomes occurring regarding the first of these contemporary trends that might best be summarized in terms of: higher productivity through technological innovation; lower wages, reduced social benefits, and less protective working conditions; decentralization of production to regions of the world with more relaxed labour and environmental restrictions; greater reliance on the informal economy – i.e. unregulated labour; and, weakening trade unions, which is the single most important factor in restoring the level of profits (Castells, 1989, pp. 23–5).

As to the second, Castells (1989) argues that we are not witnessing the withdrawal of the state from the economic scene; rather we are witnessing the emergence of a new form of intervention, whereby new means and new areas are penetrated by the state, while others are deregulated and transferred to the market (p. 25). He sees this emerging redefinition of the role of the state as embracing: deregulation of many activities, including relaxation of environmental controls in the workplace; shrinkage of and privatization of productive activities, in the public sector; regressive tax reform favouring corporations and high income groups; state support for high technology research and development and leading industrial sectors; priority and status for defence and defence-related industries; shrinkage of the welfare state; and, fiscal austerity, with the goal of a balanced budget.

These changes have implications for the way in which schools are organized and administered, and these along with their implications for teachers' work, will be addressed in later sections of this book.

Third, the opening-up of new markets through global expansion (or 'internationalization') has been possible as a consequence of several noticeable developments: industry taking advantage of the most favourable conditions anywhere in the world; capital taking advantage of 'around-the-clock capital investment' opportunities; homogenizing markets, and making up market loss in one area through increases in another (pp. 26–8).

All of these have quite pronounced implications for schools, how they are organized, and what constitutes teachers' work within them.

The Crisis in Teaching

Seddon (1997) summarized the package of changes occurring to teachers' work across several Anglo-Saxon countries in the following way:

> unions are under pressure as a result of changes in industrial relations; salaries have declined; teachers' work has intensified as social and organisational demands have increased; teachers feel less valued in the community; teachers' work has become more routinised and subject to accountability; and, as a result of cuts in education funding, teachers work in increasingly poorly resourced workplaces.
>
> (p. 230)

The crisis in teachers' work can really be summarized as a crisis in confidence around the purposes for which schools exist – as annexes of industry, spot welded on to the economy, rather than autonomous, dialogical or interpretive communities committed to enthusing the young with the tools and critical sensibilities necessary to interrogate society. An analysis of Australian schools by Susan Robertson (1994) concluded that: 'It is essential...that observers begin the process of tracing out in detail what the theoretical arguments are, and that they seek to make sense of these by linking them to changes in the workplace' (p. 144).

In a similar vein, speaking of Canadian schools, Heather-Jane Robertson (1998) argues that the changing rules of the game for schools closely mirror or follow the wider shift towards the tendencies of transnational capital as it rearranges and restructures itself in order to take advantage of the cheapest possible option for enhancing profits.

We don't want this to be interpreted as yet another book that rails against the forces of globalization; our task is both more expansive and complex than that. We certainly want to establish a connection between the forces that are working to rearrange global capital and the effect that it is having on teachers' work. But, in the process, we want to go beyond critique and suggest that the way out of the situation we find ourselves in is through attempting to restore social capital in schools, with a vision that might lead to the wider resuscitation of notions of civil society in our culture generally.

If we can return to the notion of crisis for a moment. Talk about a crisis in schools, teaching and education and you can almost be guaranteed to draw a crowd. We don't want to appear to be adding to the circus that regularly manufactures these crises, but on the other hand, neither do we want to resile from our responsibility of accurately reporting on what is happening to the culture of teachers' work, which is under intense and immense pressure worldwide. Public schooling, and within it the work of teachers, is undergoing dramatic changes at the moment, and mostly for reasons that reside a long way from classrooms, curriculum, pedagogy and learning. We believe that to understand what is happening, any analysis must get inside the culture of teachers' work (Carlson, 1992) and regard teaching as a form of 'cultural work' (Anyon, 1998). Michael Apple (1996a) has written extensively of the importance of directing our attention to the various elements of this perspective: 'economic goals and values; visions of both the family and race, gender and class relations; the politics of culture, difference and identity; and the role of the state in all of this' (p. 18). Connell (1995) situates the issue of what is happening to teachers' work when he locates its genesis in 'rational choice theory' within social theory, or 'economic rationalism' and 'market-driven policy' in the area of social and economic policy. More specifically: 'The school system is seen as the producer of human capital needed by the economy, in the form of a trained and differentiated workforce. Teachers are then readily seen as the specialised workforce producing the larger workforce' (p. 94). According to Connell (1995) this is 'unquestionably the most influential theory of teachers in the advanced capitalist world at present' (p. 94).

In order to advance our understanding we need, therefore, to simultaneously focus on the forces of commodification of our culture that are so vociferously insisting on schools being dutiful annexes of industry, at the same time as we consider the countervailing forces of resistance operating from within teachers' own interpretation of their work lives.

It is something of a cliché that teachers are living in a sea of educational change. Schools and their purposes are changing at a faster pace now than at any other period in the history of schooling. But, it is not just the pace of change that is important, but the direction and the substance of these changes that is also crucial. To advance this we need to focus somewhat more sharply on the labour process of teaching and show what is happening to it. Connell (1995) argues that teaching is a form of work that embodies a 'capacity for social practice' (p. 98). At one level, in conservative human capital terms, this can mean something as technical as teaching the ability to learn spelling, which can represent nothing more than a thinly disguised code for 'diligence, orderliness, and obedience to rules' (p. 99). At another level, teaching operates 'on the terrain of culture, identity formation, and communication' (p. 99) – which is another way of saying teaching is a cultural process where the 'final determination of meaning [is] always deferred' (p. 100) in circumstances that are always changing. At a third level, teaching embodies a 'capacity for power' (p. 100) in that unless it develops an understanding of the culture of power at work in the school then students will be forever condemned to living and working 'in an authoritarian institution that gives them no real responsibility' (p. 100). As Connell (1995) put it: 'there is a sense in which virtually everything about teaching is political.... [T]eachers cannot choose to be non political' (pp. 101–2).

Cookson and Lucks (1997) have recently described teaching as 'a dangerous activity' (p. 971) in the sense that it is always straddling the boundary of being a conserving force versus being quietly revolutionary. As they put it:

> Historically, teaching has been a dangerous activity because the transmission of ideas and the acquisition of literacy invites critical reflection. Whatever the dailyness of teaching, its underlying purposes remain quietly revolutionary, although few teachers think of themselves as change agents. The evolution of the teaching profession is the story of the dynamic tension between conservation of culture and the development of critical consciousness.
>
> (p. 971)

Susan Robertson (1994) locates the increasing unease being expressed by many teachers within 'a virulent economic rationalist model [with] its penetrating ideological themes of flexibility and skills for the workplace' (p. 145) which operate, she argues, 'to undermine any opportunity for the development of critical citizenship' (p. 145). Robertson's (1994) analysis of what is happening to teachers' work led her to the conclusion of a cascading wave of reforms with associated outcomes:

> A process of destabilisation has rapidly been followed by the implementation of a new set of exploitative and alienating regulatory controls over teachers' labour, with the precise purpose of extracting increasing levels of surplus value and hitching teaching firmly to the global economic agenda.... [A]n exploratory analysis of the outcomes of this shift is revealing. The first outcome is a growing tendency towards the integration of the variety of tasks constituting teachers' work. This process has highlighted teachers' managerial role (e.g. management of students and other education workers) and de-emphasised their pedagogical one. The process of integration has also dramatically intensified teacher's labour. A second outcome has been the shift towards a process of reprofessionalisation. This has resulted in the establishment of a new

set of regulatory controls over professional behaviour and competence, to be closely supervised by the state. The third outcome is the shift toward deregulation of teachers' unions, along with the diminishing wages and award conditions.

(pp. 144–5)

One way into the discussion about what's happening to teachers' work is through the 'deprofessionalization' and 'reprofessionalization' of teaching. Seddon (1997) argues that the contemporary changes occurring in respect of teaching are not a simple matter of deskilling and reskilling teachers as individuals. She says that 'the more significant changes are occurring at the level of the school, in the organisation of work and the reconstruction of teachers' identities' (p. 237). The argument, drawing from Lawn and Mac an Ghaill (1996, p. 237), is that the 'social space' of schools is being reconstituted:

through marketing processes as 'enterprises', individualised units of educational service provision with a distinctive and defining social space. Within the school, the relations of work are being reorganised. The traditional private domain of the classroom is being opened up to public scrutiny and to the inter-supervisory monitoring by teachers who take up both teaching and managerial roles within the school.

It is this redrawing of the social, economic and cultural 'geography of schooling' (Seddon, 1997, p. 237) that is contributing to the reconstituting of the school as a 'social technology' (Lawn and Mac an Ghaill, 1996). But as Smyth (1980) put it, 'the term "technology" assumes a wider meaning than the electronic gadgetry and mechanical devices normally alluded to in educational discussions. The sense in which technology is used here applies to the totality of the work processes employed…' (p. 68).

One of the more pervasive elements operating around the changing social technology of teachers' work and the shift in the cultural geography of the school has been the marked shift from educative to economic imperatives as the underpinnings of schooling. There is an increasingly cynical public, fed by a media bent on simplification and misrepresentation, prepared to accept quick-fix solutions like testing, league tables, and performance indicators offered by politicians who continually propagate the same ideologically worn-out policies that are argued to be in line with nebulous notions of 'international best practice'. Far too much reliance is placed upon proposals from the 'failed' captains of industry, to the exclusion of the voices of teachers and educators about what is likely to work in education. This has meant a dramatic shift in the discourse of schools from being primarily about curriculum, teaching, and learning – to canons of efficiency, effectiveness, competencies and accountability as governments jostle to try and resolve the problem of the collapse of the youth labour market with policies that end up producing forms of forced retention in schools. Along with unfounded claims that technology will solve all of the problems afflicting schools and society we have pronouncements that amount to forced partnerships between schools and industry, indicative of a wider fiscal retreat of the state from its responsibility for funding public education. To cap off this fanciful scenario we are supposed to accept that devolution and charter schools based upon an unproven individualistic competitive ethos, will somehow supposedly fix the problems of schooling and wider society – altogether a huge and totally untested leap of faith.

Teaching in the 'New Work Order'

It is becoming increasingly clear that the old hierarchical, reductionist ways of thinking and acting to control work (teaching included) are certainly breaking down and giving way to new and apparently more enlightened, flexible, democratic and empowering forms. We are hearing much these days about cultures of learning, learning organizations, partnerships, teamwork, coaching, and collaboration. These are the new genres within which the world of work is increasingly being described. Gee and Lankshear (1995) put it in these terms:

> The logic of the new work order is that the roles and responsibilities of the middle will pass to the 'front line workers' themselves (formerly, the bottom line of the hierarchy). Workers will be transformed into committed 'partners' who will engage in meaningful work, fully understand and control their jobs, supervise themselves, and actively seek to improve their performance through communicating their knowledge and their needs clearly.
>
> Such 'motivated' workers (partners) can no longer be 'ordered' around by 'bosses', they can only be 'developed', 'coached' and 'supported'. Hierarchy is gone, egalitarianism 'in'.
>
> (p. 7)

None of this is to suggest, of course, that the apparent withering away of hierarchical forms of control is meant to equate with a disappearance of control over the work of teaching, or even a democratizing of schools as workplaces, for that is not the case. The terrain is shifting dramatically. Hartley (1994) described this phenomenon in terms of mixed messages (even contradictions) in education policy, and suggests that it may be 'a sign of the times':

> But these contradictions to some extent express the tensions which have become apparent in an age of transition: that between the modern and the post-modern, or between Fordist and 'disorganised' forms of

capitalism. A new mode of regulation is being established...at the level of the pupil, the teacher, the parent and the school. [It gains expression in] the management of consent, and whose justification appeals to the culture of consumption.

(p. 230)

At the level of the school, Mac an Ghaill (1991) found that far from this new discourse being liberating that the language of 'enterprise culture' was producing: 'a strong sense of confusion and resentment among the teachers concerning the changing structure and status of their work, the restructuring of state education, the vocationalization of the curriculum and the narrowing of opportunity for subordinated groups of students' (p. 300).

We want to argue here that the new work processes and paradigms, while grappling sensibly and sensitively with more enlightened and participatory ways, are nevertheless still a form of surveillance and control over the work of teaching – albeit, of a style and a form that is not regarded as being especially hurtful or harmful in comparison to the forms they seek to replace. We need to be gracious in acknowledging that they are in many respects decidedly for the better. However, as Gee and Lankshear (1995) note, much of what we are coming to learn and absorb into reconfigured forms of teaching, is coming from a paradigm which is only partially understood. It is emerging from the new 'keywords' of the business texts that employ the new genre of the 'enchanted workplace...where hierarchy is dead and "partners" engage in meaningful work amidst a collaborative environment of mutual commitment and trust' (p. 5). But, what is being portrayed in this new so-called 'participative' mode is far from the complete picture. There is something of the surreal about such portrayals, because for most of us, such representations fail to square with our reality of schools as places that are highly politicized, and where forms of knowledge, culture, curriculum, pedagogy, administration and evaluation are continually being contested, confronted, resisted, and at least to some degree, reconstructed.

Gee and Lankshear (1995) describe the genesis of these new and progressive ideas as being linked to the shift from so-called Fordist to post-Fordist forms of capitalism, and in particular, to 'fast capitalism' – the notion that old modes of production that relied heavily on hierarchical, overt and punitive forms of control, are giving away to more flexible, responsive, market and niche-driven forms of production in which design, customization and timely delivery come much more sharply into focus as 'quality', 'excellence', 'productivity' and 'competition' become the organizing icons, rather than old-fashioned coercion, supervision, standardization and compliance. The claim is that flatter forms of hierarchy are capable of producing workers who are not only able to engage in reflection and higher order thinking about the nature of work and the human benefits of this, but along the way, they are also able to generate greater profits.

But, this new paradigm can only work as long as workers are effectively insulated from being empowered to the point where 'they might question the very ends and goals of fast capitalist businesses themselves' (Gee and Lankshear, 1995, p. 8) – for to do that would be to 'make them very poor fast capitalists indeed' (p. 8). There is a major tension within empowering paradigms:

> Fast capitalism is strong on encouraging and enabling 'critical reflec-tion' on the part of employees at the level of understanding relations and processes *internal* to the organisation's systems.... Fast capitalists do not, however, want to promote critical reflection in the sense of ques-tioning systems as wholes and in their political relations to other systems. On the contrary, they are keen to pre-empt this....
> (Gee and Lankshear, 1995, p. 17, emphasis in the original)

There are still very large unanswered questions as to whether the alternative participatory conceptualization of teaching is genuinely committed to allowing teachers to frame their own discourses of learning and the 'ability to frame up [their] own learning ideals, to make explicit [their] own theories and goals, to identify and contest competing constructions, and to insist always that spaces for such contestation be maintained within educational settings' (Gee and Lankshear, 1995, p. 15).

The warning we offer is that the 'new work order', as Gee and Lankshear (1995) term it, which underpins the collegial school culture of professional growth, may need to be monitored carefully, if the signals from industry where this has been tried, are any indication. There are some dire forebod-ings that the kind of partnerships and paradigms teachers are being urged to embrace, are far from innocent. It may turn out to be the case as Lawn and Ozga (1986) argue, that teachers are at risk of being 'unequal partners' in a context of 'indirect rule' (p. 225). What appears to be a shift in the direction of teacher self-management and autonomy, may turn out (as it has in the past), to be a case of 'teachers' acceptance of a limited or licensed profes-sionalism' (Lawn and Ozga, 1986, p. 225). This is not to suggest that there is somehow 'a hoax of teacher autonomy' (Lawn and Ozga, 1986, p. 227), for that would be to largely miss the point that what we are dealing with here is far more complex and contradictory than that. Grace's (1985) conceptual-ization of 'structural', 'occupational' and 'workplace' autonomy is a useful signifier of the shifting contexts within which teachers possess degrees of independence – variously, in relation to the structures of the state and the economy; with regard to the form and substance of admission to and the construction of self-governance of teaching; and, with regard to 'teachers' autonomy in relation to curriculum, pedagogy, assessment and evaluation of pupils and their own assessment and evaluation' (Lawn and Ozga, 1986, p. 227).

To take one illustration of where the shift of control is at an advanced stage, we need only look to the JIT (Just-In-Time) and TQM (Total Quality Management) techniques originating in the manufacturing industry in Japan in the 1980s. According to one set of commentators, these are processes that are quite literally 'pushing back the frontiers of management control' (Delbridge et al., 1992) with a marked set of changes that usher in quite a different life world.

There is a façade of 'decentralizing work' that is a deception because it is within a 'framework of centralised surveillance' (Delbridge et al., 1992, p. 100). While the rhetoric of this system is of 'work autonomy' (p. 97), 'team ownership' (p. 100) and 'worker empowerment' (p. 98) the reality is one of increased central surveillance within a 'neighbour-watch system' of 'employee peer surveillance' (p. 100). Regimes of 'real autonomy [are] largely cosmetic' because all 'product decisions' and 'targets' are 'dictated either by management-decreed goals and regulations, or working to "satisfy customer needs"' (p. 102). The system is one that relies on 'demand pulling' products through the system (i.e. what the 'customer wants'), rather than 'production pushing' (turning out products, which the customer then elects to purchase) with work being organized around 'product groups' who are responsible for 'quality', so that quality is built into the process rather than having to be 'inspected' for. The social relations of work undergo dramatic changes particularly through 'group pressure' to 'cover for workers' during absences, or ensuring that colleagues meet targets. The real significance of 'team work' and 'team relationships' is to facilitate peer pressure. Workers have to 'perform for' and be 'controlled by' fellow workers (p. 103). Under this regime, there is 'a very strict control of the workforce behind the façade of granting autonomy and increased discretion' (p. 102). There is a carefully designed 'management information system' capable of pinpointing deviations from the norm accurately and speedily (p. 99). Indeed, the whole basis of JIT/TQM is to produce 'what the customer wants, when it is wanted' (p. 103) with faults being able to be readily traced back to the 'culprit', and any deviation from quality or quotas is able to be quickly detected and 'sanctions meted out' (p. 100). The number of supervisors, quality checkers and other layers of middle management is reduced, and give the appearance of a 'flatter hierarchy' (p. 98). These appearances are sustained by making the 'visibility' of the production process more transparent, especially with regard to production 'targets' (p. 98), with the removal of job demarcations and an emphasis on 'multi-skilling' (or more accurately, 'multi-tasking') producing workers who are interchangeable and, therefore, dispensable (p. 100–1).

These kind of processes are making noticeable incursions into schools (see for example: Hannaway and Carnoy, 1993 in the USA; Ball, 1994, and Bush et al., 1993 in the UK; and Smyth, 1993a in Australia) as 'bad' old bureaucratic structures are rapidly being dismembered and replaced by the new genre of 'freedom', 'empowerment' and 'liberation'.

Why Labour Process Theory?

The kind of teachers' work perspective we adopt in this book is based upon an understanding that since any educational workplace is made up of unequal social relations, then conflict is always present. It is inevitable that the more powerful will seek to control the less powerful. Thus, an understanding of control is central to a study of teachers' work. As Connell (1995) argues, a focus on work is more likely than any other approach to uncover the complexities of what shapes educational practice because it recognizes the messiness of the politics of teachers' work:

> What happens in education is the result of partly intersecting, partly independent struggles around industrial and economic issues over the curriculum, and over the institutional shape of education. Changes in the labour force, such as the 'feminisation of teaching', respond to the same mixture of social forces as changes in the industrial labour force or in office work.
>
> (p. 95)

The sociology of work implicit in this kind of perspective covers an enormous field of study. The challenge is to select the approach which is most likely to yield an understanding of why, how, and with what effect teachers are controlled. We argue that labour process theory offers that approach.

It is clear that teachers sell their labour power to the state, and work for a wage in a specified place with specified students under a set of conditions that can be modified. The object of their labour is, to use Connell's (1995) words, 'the development of the capacity for social practice' (p. 97), by which he means that students acquire learning strategies, for themselves and for their society, which are used in and sustained by, the social world into which they enter. This happens through the interaction between teacher and student which constitutes their labour process, the main specification of which is the curriculum. Thus, the joint labour process of students and teachers is an important component of any process of social change which can be shaped by changes to the curriculum, as it can also be affected by changes to the conditions under which students and teachers labour.

Since the 'capacity of social practice' is a social and cultural, rather than a technical construct, its definition and achievements are clearly a political act. That is, curriculum aims and teaching practices will be the subject of contestation involving those groups who have an interest in the outcomes of the labour process of students and teachers. The stakes are high since capacities for social practice have an impact on capital accumulation and the distribution of wealth, and this makes education and its labour process a highly political activity. It should come as no surprise therefore that if powerful groups believe in purposes and practices of education that are at odds with the beliefs of those involved in the production of social capacities, that is teachers, then efforts will be made to ensure that the interests of the powerful are preserved. This involves ensuring that teachers, at the level of their labour process, will conform to educational purposes defined by dominant groups. It is crucial to understand the labour process of teachers in order to appreciate the origin, forms and effects of the mechanisms that are used to control it. This understanding is certainly enriched by the use of other work perspectives such as labour market analysis, industrial relations and the culture of the workplace, since these also shape what teachers do in their work. But it is a focus on the labour process that best emphasizes the socially constructed and conflictual character of work relations in educational sites. As such, it lies at the heart of the politics of education and so provides the clearest view into the purpose, form and effects of controls on teachers. The purpose of the next chapter is to explain how the labour process of teachers has been understood.

Conclusion

What we are attempting in this volume is a major move to renovate labour process theory in an educational context. The two case studies provide a tangible working expression of the labour process of teaching, showing how teachers are simultaneously experiencing significant changes to their work, as well as responding in ways that actively shape these processes. The framing of in-school experiences by the wider sets of forces producing pedagogical change also provides the opportunity of seeing how the complex processes of seduction, entrapment, accommodation and resistance are worked out in school contexts; in Alvesson and Willmott's (1996) terminology, there is a space here within which to investigate how practitioners identify and utilise opportunities for 'micro-emancipation'.

2 Towards a Labour Process Theory of Teachers' Work

Introduction: Why Study the Labour Process of Teaching?

In the previous chapter we outlined the manifestations of what we called a crisis in teaching which is apparent in so many countries. This grim picture is more than a background to what is happening in education: it is a reality that teachers live with and through in their daily professional lives. It establishes the conditions of education work, and so structures the nature of that work and the ways in which it is experienced. It determines largely whether or not teachers enjoy their job. For this reason alone it is important that we understand what is happening.

But there is an even more fundamental reason for wanting to engage in a study of teachers' work at this juncture of our history. If education is central to the development of a decent civil society, healthy polity and productive economy – and such rhetoric pervades the official discourse of political parties throughout the world – it is axiomatic that teachers are the key to achieving that aim. It also follows, however, that if teachers are alienated, disillusioned, angry, disempowered and overworked, then it is unlikely that educational practice will ever match political rhetoric. That is, questions about how education work is structured and with what effects must lie at the heart of any project which is seriously interested in the contribution that education can make to the building of a better world. Our shared concern in this book is to contribute to the development of a theoretical framework which can bear the burden of explaining what is happening to teachers' work, and which can point to the sorts of political strategies and educational policy reforms which are needed to address the crisis in teaching. The purpose of this chapter is to start that process by developing the educational lens which is to be used in this task.

So what is happening? How can the 'crisis' in teaching be understood? Governments have tended to explain it in two ways, both of which individualize the problem. One relatively benign approach is to suggest that the many disillusioned or stressed teachers possess some psychological or skill deficit which needs fixing. Thus, teachers are introduced to stress management programmes which are designed to help them handle their 'problems' more efficiently than they have been doing; or they are sent to training courses to develop skills that are deemed to be lacking. Another more authoritarian explanation is that the problem stems from recalcitrant and uncooperative teachers who need to be pulled back into line through various mechanisms of appraisal and accountability. Both of these explanations have one thing in common: they accept the way in which teachers' work has been structured and organized, and they locate the problem with the individual teacher. It is the educator who must change, not the structure and organization of the work itself. This is a useful way for governments to understand the issue, because it allows blame to be located in places other than in the educational policy, resources and structures for which they are responsible. It allows them to divert the blame to individual workers.

These responses from governments are destructive, not only because they misapprehend the causes of the problem and so exacerbate it, but also because they continue to hamper the best efforts of teachers and principals to deliver educational programmes which maximize the individual potential of all students, and which are socially transformative. If governments are wrong, how else might the problem be explained? The analysis of the 'problem' and its causes is very different when the structure and organization of work is made the suspect, rather than the individual teacher. Put another way, when the focus is on the labour process of teaching, rather than on individual teachers, the causes of low teacher morale and stress take on a very different aspect.

Now, at this point, the thing to do would be to refer to the labour process literature in education, and to build from that. Unfortunately, such literature is very thin on the ground. After a brief flurry in the early to mid 1980s, labour process theory in relation to teachers' work appears to have run into a cul-de-sac, not least because some unresolved theoretical and methodological issues left it exposed as an archetype of the modernist project. It made easy pickings for post-structuralist critique, redolent as it was of grand narratives and the construction of people as passive bearers of structure. As a consequence, labour process theory was abandoned as interest turned to the micro-politics of institutions, and away from macro-analyses. All that remains in the education literature are remnants of its language – concepts such as 'deskilling' and 'intensification' are examples here – usually employed without reference to, or understanding of, the theoretical tradition from which they derived. Even the term 'labour process' has come to represent little more than a fancy way of saying 'work'.

Given all of this, is a labour process lens capable of offering the sorts of insights necessary to the task we have set ourselves in this book? In this chapter we will argue that not only is a labour process perspective useful, it is central to a more complete understanding of what is happening to teachers' work. Labour process theory has been consigned to a premature grave in education, and its body needs to be exhumed to allow for an examination of the causes of its demise. It will be argued that one of the contributing factors has been an all too unproblematic transfer from the industrial sociology literature which was its original home. There, a labour process research programme has been building and refining labour process theory over the past 20 years. The challenge for this chapter will be to engage in a task of theoretical renewal by returning to the mainstream labour process debates, identifying the core characteristics of labour process theory, and adapting these to the special contexts and circumstances of education. We start this process of theoretical renewal by returning to the source of contemporary interest in labour process theory.

The Rebirth of Labour Process Theory

In 1974, Harry Braverman published his famous book: *Labour and Monopoly Capital*. For the first time since Marx made it central to his understanding of class struggle a century before, this work reopened the labour process as a serious area of enquiry. Braverman accepted the central components of Marx's understanding of the labour process: that the gearing of labour power to the accumulation of capital creates a fundamental conflict of interests between workers and capitalists. Like Marx, he argued that since workers cannot be relied upon to work in the best interests of capital, then control is necessary for capital to realize the full potential of the labour it employs. It is this need for coercive control which determines the structure and experience of work in a capitalist society, and which produces class struggle. Braverman sought to update this understanding to the conditions of twentieth-century capitalism. His work had a dramatic impact, and almost overnight labour process theory became a burgeoning field of investigation in industrial sociology.

Specifically, Braverman argued that the desire for profit determines the organization of the capitalist labour process, and in particular the tendency for labour to become progressively fragmented and deskilled, and for the work of conception (mental labour) to be separated off from the work of execution (manual labour). These processes occur because of the tremendous savings in the cost of labour that capital can thereby obtain. However, dividing and deskilling labour, coupled with the ever increasing concentration and centralization of capital, brings to the fore the problem of coordination, management and control of labour. Braverman argued that it is essential for the capitalist that control over the labour process pass from the hands of the worker into the hands of the capitalist. Thus, subordination of the autonomy of manual workers is engineered through simultaneously decreasing the level of skill in production tasks and increasing managerial control over their execution. According to Braverman, this has been achieved in the twentieth century through the application of F.W. Taylor's theory of scientific management (Taylor, 1911).

17

The central concept of scientific management is the distinction between conception and execution, that is between designing tasks and carrying them out. Labour is divided and subdivided to the extent that each task is fragmented into its smallest constituent units which can be timed and measured. Jobs are deskilled, both to further facilitate the employment of cheaper labour, and to eliminate the restrictive practices then used by employees on the basis of their monopoly over knowledge. For Braverman, Taylorism in action divorced mental from manual work and reduced the jobs of the mass of workers – including white-collar workers – to degrading tasks lacking any responsibility, knowledge or interest. The degradation of work to which Braverman referred can be seen to encompass a number of processes, namely:

1   the loss by the ordinary worker of the right to design and plan work;
2   the fragmentation of work into meaningless segments;
3   the redistribution of tasks among unskilled and semi-skilled labour, associated with labour cheapening;
4   the transformation of work organization from the craft system to modern, Taylorized forms of control.

Braverman argued that Taylorism was not only compatible with, but would in fact expand with, increasing mechanization. This would increase its pervasiveness as a form of managerial control and deepen worker deskilling and task fragmentation. He recognized, however, that there would be contradictions within this general trend. For example, in some work areas, deskilling brought about by job restructuring might be accompanied by reskilling of a smaller number of workers through say, an increased involvement in planning. Nevertheless, he maintained that the general tendency for deskilling and increased managerial control would persist through changes in technology and work organization. The all-pervasiveness of Taylorism would, according to Braverman, appropriate all attempts to introduce alternatives to it. For example, the application of social science such as the human relations theory developed since the 1930s, would serve only to habituate workers to the dictates of Taylorist systems. There is thus a big gulf between the rhetoric and reality of modern 'human relations' whose significance is essentially ideological: 'Taylorism dominates the world of production, the practitioners of "human relations"…are the maintenance crew for the human machinery' (Braverman, 1974, p. 87).

While the bulk of Braverman's work focused on industrial workers, he also examined clerical, technical and managerial labour which are described as a range of intermediate categories (he included teachers in these categories) and as enjoying a 'privileged market position' (Braverman, 1974, p. 407). These middle layers of employment, Braverman argued, cannot sensibly be included among members of senior management who act professionally for capital or any 'part of the class that personifies capital and employs labour' (1974, p. 405); neither can they be classified as members of the class whose labour they 'help to control, command and organise' (1974, p. 405). However, because the dynamics of capitalist development demand that their work is subjected continuously to a process of fragmentation and degradation, it is anticipated that workers in these growing intermediate categories will increasingly experience their work in ways that will strengthen their affinity with 'the mass of working class employment' (Braverman, 1974, p. 408). In short their work is being proletarianized:

> In such occupations, the proletarian form begins to assert itself and to impress itself upon the consciousness of these employees. Feeling the insecurities of their role as sellers of labour power and the frustrations of a controlled and mechanically organised work-place, they begin, despite their remaining privileges, to know those symptoms of disassociation which are popularly called 'alienation' and which the working class has lived with for so long that they have become part of its second nature....
>
> (Braverman, 1974, p. 408)

Braverman's work has been the central reference point of the labour process debates which have raged ever since its publication. Within these debates, scholars have variously embraced or attacked the Braverman interpretation. For the purposes here, we will identify four important ways in which the post-Braverman debates have enriched his insights. First, many scholars (Friedman, 1977; Edwards, 1979; Gospel, 1992) dispute Braverman's contention that scientific management is as widespread as he implied, and argue that Taylorism is only one among many forms of control. Once this view became widely accepted, it followed that deskilling is not inevitable, but is only one of a number of possible consequences of control. This understanding accommodated critiques from those who maintained that labour process theory was irrelevant in a new industrial environment of post-Fordist work practices. New organizational forms of working, including increasing flexibility, the disintegration of institutional hierarchies, and democratization of the workplace do not obviate the need for control.

Second, it is argued that, by focusing on coercive control, Braverman had omitted the ways by which worker consent is organized within the capitalist labour process. Workers regulate themselves, as well as being regulated by others (Burawoy, 1979, 1985; Sakolsky, 1992). Control of the labour process can be understood through discursive work practices, as well as material practices. Third, a number of writers point out that by implying that workers are the passive recipients of managerial control, Braverman had ignored the many ways in which workers resist various forms of control. And finally, it is argued that by privileging class, Braverman had been blind to the ways in which the experience of work is shaped by the social relations of gender and race (Game and Pringle, 1983; Knights and Willmott, 1989). An important outcome of these refinements, has been a diminution of the deterministic flavour which tended to permeate Braverman's work. Within industrial sociology, the labour process debates continue today and as a consequence the explanatory capacity of labour process theory is being sharpened.

The Rise and Fall of Labour Process Theory in Education

By the early 1980s, a number of education scholars (e.g. Ozga and Lawn, 1981; Harris, 1982; White, 1983; Apple, 1986) began applying a labour process perspective to the work of state teachers. These early theorists argued that teachers were becoming proletarianized, by which they meant that teachers were becoming more like industrial workers than professionals as their work was deskilled and intensified by contemporary education policy and practice. This scholarship produced some significant insights, and made an important contribution to the emerging field of teachers' work. However, it became entangled in the 1980s backlash against social reproduction theory, and it was critiqued on the basis of its determinism. In addition, some scholars contested it on empirical grounds, arguing that teachers, far from becoming proletarianized, were developing more skills and experiencing greater autonomy than ever before (e.g. Lauder and Yee, 1987).

Since that time, scholars have continued to selectively employ labour process theory, but the ferocity of the attacks seems to have induced a kind of atheoreticism. That is, labour process concepts such as 'deskilling' or 'intensification' continue to be employed, but usually as descriptors of observed phenomena, rather than as being located within any sort of theoretical framework. Even the term 'labour process' itself is often used as a synonym for work, without any reference to its specific meaning. This lack of a theoretical base has left labour process theory exposed, and has served to dilute its insights. Why has this happened?

With the considerable benefit of hindsight, it is possible to discern the genesis of some of the problems with the ways in which labour process theory has been constructed in education. First, there appears to have been an unproblematic transfer of the ideas and concepts developed by Braverman and other mainstream labour process theorists in relation to skilled and semi-skilled workers in the private sector, across to state workers in the education sector. That is, it seems to have been assumed that the same process of work structuring and organization applies to all workers. Second, and allied with this point, the focus of the scholarship lay squarely upon the effects of the contemporary organization of teachers' work such as proletarianization, deskilling and intensification, rather than on the ways in which work is organized. This tended to produce both a determinism and historicism, which implied an inexorable degradation of teachers' work, presumably from a position and a time when teachers had greater autonomy and were better paid. Third, it set teachers up as pawns in a structural game about which they could do very little. Finally, and perhaps this lay at the heart of the problem, there was little or no reference to the ongoing labour process debates in the mainstream industrial sociology literature. For education, it appears that labour process theory stopped with Braverman. Small wonder that labour process theory in education is now an historical artefact.

In our view, labour process theory in education offers a potentially powerful lens through which to understand what is happening to the work of educators today. But the rejuvenation of labour process theory demands the resolution of a number of theoretical and methodological issues and the systematic development of a theoretical framework. This chapter aims to be a tentative start to that important task.

What Lies at the Heart of Labour Process Theory?

Control is a core concept in labour process theory, and it is this vital point which was missed in the education labour process literature. By staying with the original Braverman analysis, the scholarship tended to assume the inexorable growth of forms of work organization which split conception and execution, thus deskilling teachers and intensifying their work. Because Braverman had assumed that scientific management was the sole form of control, the issue of control itself was hidden in his work. If education scholars had followed the labour process debates, they would have been alerted to this. Instead, they tended to focus on the effects of control, rather than its purposes and forms. As a result, their work took on a Braverman-like determinism. Putting control at the heart of labour process theory provides an escape from the structuralist strait-jacket which constrained the early labour process theorists in education.

So, why is control so central to an understanding of the labour process? This can be best explained by reference to factory workers in the private sector. In that sphere, the production process requires labour to work purposively on raw materials using instruments of production, such as plant and equipment, in order to make goods or services. In a capitalist system, the capitalist owns all three of these factors of production, and the purpose of commodity production is profit making. As one of those factors, the story begins for labour in the labour market.

When the worker enters the labour market, he or she must find an employer willing to pay a wage or salary in return for the disposal of his/her skill, knowledge or physical capacities. Thus, labour power has the status of a commodity, and like all market relationships, the interests of buyers and sellers are antagonistic. In the labour market, the employee will seek to obtain the best possible wages and conditions, while the employer looks upon labour power as a cost to be minimized. Once purchased, the capitalist organizes the labour process itself, wherein the labour power is brought into a relationship with the instruments of production and the raw materials, in order to produce useful products or services. At the end of this process the products of labour are sold, and the capitalist reconverts his or her property back into money. If capital gets back more than was invested initially, then the capitalist has made a profit.

Thus, the labour process should be understood as one aspect of this cycle of capital. It clearly shapes and is shaped by other aspects, but if examined independently, what lies at its heart? Like the labour market, in the labour process the interests of employers and employees are antagonistic. When employers hire workers there is no agreement about the exact quantity of labour that will be expended, not least because capital cannot predict with certainty their day-to-day requirements. The employer's contract reflects the employer's interest by imposing on the employee an open-ended commitment. Rather than agreeing to expend a given amount of effort, the employee surrenders his or her capacity to work (labour power). There is no guarantee that workers will fulfil management's production goals, since they obtain employment to receive wages and may provide only the minimum amount of effort necessary to ensure their continued employment. This renders the employer dependent, to a greater or lesser degree, on the motivation, acquiescence, or cooperation of the worker if the potential contained in the labour power is to be realized to their satisfaction. Labour process theory understands this 'labour problem' as one of the central concerns of management in capitalism. It is the function of management, through its hierarchy of control, to turn the worker's capacity to work into actual productive activity, and so facilitate the extraction of surplus value. The central question of labour process analysis is how management transforms the potential for work (labour power) into work effort (labour). There is thus a control imperative in capitalist employment relations (e.g. Wright, 1996, p. 707).

Control in this context differs from coordination which is required in all social production. That is, coordination is a characteristic inherent in even the most simple of production processes. It means organizing the various elements of production so they mesh efficiently with each other. In small-scale production it can be achieved through discussion between the various producers in order to harmonize effort. However, as the scale of production and work become more specialized, it may be necessary to designate the task of coordination to a single person or a group. But there is nothing in this role that automatically places the coordinator in a position of authority. Indeed, so long as that person remains accountable to the producers themselves, then the role is one of coordination or administration.

In capitalist production systems, the role of coordination has been given to a group of workers called management, who normally receive more pay and greater privileges than direct producers. But management does not just have a coordinating role. It also acts on behalf of capital to maximize accumulation by extracting labour from the labour power owned by the company. That is, management and workers are placed in a hierarchy, with the former seeking to control the latter in order to extract the maximum surplus value from them. Edwards uses this understanding to define control as 'the ability of capitalists and/or managers to obtain desired work behaviour from workers' (1979, p. 17). This ability may wax and wane depending upon the relative strength of workers and employers, but it will always be present. The question is not whether control exists in capitalist production, but how it is exercised, and with what effect. Does this apply to workers who sell their labour power to the state, such as teachers in the public education system?

The Labour Process of State Teachers

Since workers in the public sector are not employed by capitalists, it is not immediately clear whether they are exploited in the sense that private sector workers are exploited. Efforts to answer this question have centred around issues of productive and unproductive labour (e.g. Harris, 1982, 1994). From a labour process perspective the crucial issue is whether or not workers perform surplus labour, and produce commodities that generate use value. Gough (1979) has argued persuasively that, with the exception of high officials, state workers do perform surplus labour. Although such workers are not directly exploited by capital, their experience of such factors as unemployment, wage pressures, and deskilling, is very much the result of their insertion in a capitalist economy and the exigencies of capitalist accumulation. In this sense, public and private sector workers are in a similar relationship to the capitalist.

The concept of the collective labourer offers another way of thinking about this issue. Through their part in skilling future labour power, teachers are indirectly contributing to the generation of surplus value as a part of a total production process. Freeland puts it this way:

> Schooling is essentially linked with the capitalist labour market through the credentialling processes and more directly through developing skills and knowledge which increase labour productivity. In this sense schooling is indirectly productive of surplus value and hence of considerable importance to capital.
>
> (1986, p. 214)

Thus, although the labour process of state teachers is defined by the state rather than by competition in the market, the end result is the same.

All this points to the need to control teachers. Like private sector workers, teachers sell their labour power and are therefore subsumed under the authority of the employer. When they sell their labour power, they are also surrendering the creative capacity of their labour. The fundamental management problem for the state is how to convert labour power into labour. That is, control is as central to the labour process of state teachers as it is to private sector workers. But the indirectness of the relationship between state teachers and capital means that a study of the labour process of teachers must involve a close examination of the role of education in a capitalist society. So how can the labour process of state teachers be described?

It is here, at the very first hurdle, that a number of education labour process theorists have fallen. Despite the fact that an identification of the object of teachers' work is central to an understanding of how and why teachers are controlled, very few scholars have attempted it. This is understandable given the fact that some of the terms and concepts are more at home in an industrial than an educational setting. And yet unless some attempt is made to do this, it makes little sense to claim to be using labour process theory. Thus, the first step is to outline the object of the labour process of teaching.

There are three factors of production – the instruments of production, the raw materials and labour power. In an education setting, the instruments of production include the education resources that exist in any school, such as plant, equipment and teaching resources. These are owned by the state and provided from state taxes. The raw materials are the students who are 'owned' by their parents or caregivers, and by the state in the sense that they are present and future citizens. The raw materials also include the knowledge or cultural capital that the education system seeks to impart. The state owns the labour power of its teachers through purchasing it in the labour market. The state, as employer, organizes these factors into a particular set of relationships of production. It is this organization that constitutes the labour process of teaching. The purpose of the production process is to fuse the raw materials, that is students and knowledge, in order to produce skilled labour power and encultured citizens. Thus formal education is a process of 'value adding' to students, the products of which become citizens and potential workers.

One question that suggests itself from the sparse outline above is what sort of 'value' is being added to students. Connell argues that the object of the teachers' work is the development of the 'capacity for social practice' (1995, p. 97). By this he means processes that help students to acquire learning strategies both for themselves as individuals, and to maintain these as a collective property of the society. The capacity for social practice has economic, ideological and political dimensions. It includes the capacity to labour; capacities for social interaction, involving culture, identity formation and communication; and the 'capacity for power', by which he means the capacity to engage responsibly in political life (Connell, 1995, p. 100). Thus for Connell, the labour process of education is a 'strategic component of any large-scale process of social change' (1995, p. 98). Before turning to this crucial point, it is necessary to round-off the description of the circuit of education. What happens to this education 'product' and who are the buyers and sellers?

If the newly skilled worker moves into the labour market, then the vendor is clearly the student selling his or her labour power to the purchaser which may be capital or the state. But there is another sense in which there is a product for sale. In a system of private and state schooling where a choice is provided to potential purchasers, and indeed of state schooling operating in quasi-market settings, education systems and schools are in the business of marketing the processes they use to skill labour power and enculturate future citizens. The purchasers comprise two broad groups. Capital collectively 'buys' the education commodity through its contribution to taxation, because state education offers a cheap and efficient way to ensure that the labour market is replete with skilled labour power. Citizens collectively 'buy' the education commodity through their taxation contributions, because it offers a process that contributes not only to economic development (i.e. skilling future labour power), but also to the civic and cultural life of the community through the enculturation of citizens. This latter group includes parents, who may have specific expectations of the commodity being purchased, such as enhancing the life opportunities of their children, helping them to develop leisure time pursuits, or inculcating a particular set of values and beliefs. This stark outline reveals a very important fact: that there are some groups involved in the process who have specific expectations of what schools should 'deliver'. Since these expectations do not necessarily coincide, the determination of the nature of the educational 'product' is a political process. This is a point which will be elaborated in the next section. We have enough information now to be able to answer the question: What is the labour process of teaching?

The labour process of state teachers has two aspects. The first is a relational aspect which involves the set of social relations which exist between teachers and others in the education community including managers, bureaucrats, non-teaching staff, parents and students. The second is a practical aspect which involves the employer, that is, the state, bringing the three factors of production into a productive relationship. In broad terms this means ensuring that teachers use their skills and the educational resources available to them, to try to develop the capacity for social practice of their students. Teachers engage in dozens of activities – teaching and assessing, administration, counselling students, extra-curricular activities, meeting and planning, to name just a few – to achieve this end. But as disparate and as numerous as these tasks are, there is a pattern. Teachers' work has been organized in such a way as to facilitate the kind of outcome that is required by the state. Common contemporary features of this organizational pattern include dividing students according to age, providing individual classroom spaces for groups of students to work with an individual teacher, carving up knowledge into discrete bundles called subjects or curriculum areas, and segmenting teachers on the basis of detailed subject expertise (secondary schools) or more general expertise (primary schools).

The key element – the glue that hangs all of these activities together – is the curriculum. The formal curriculum – which can include in varying degrees of specificity such aspects as aims, content, sequence, method and assessment – is not just a description of what students should learn. It builds on and confirms the 'hidden curriculum' – the organizational arrangements and practices which establish the 'right way' to function in classrooms, schools and educational systems. Together, the formal and hidden curricula describe the nature of the 'capacities for social practice' that are being developed. In short, they define the task of teaching. The curriculum is, therefore, the main specification of the labour process of teaching.

So far in this theory building we have established that control lies at the heart of labour process theory; that state teachers have a labour process; and that this labour process is defined by the curriculum. The next task is to determine the motivation for controlling teachers.

Why are State Teachers Controlled?

Why should the state, which presumably does not provide public schools for financial profit, need to control the work of teachers? There are three main reasons, the first two of which are common to all workers. Once the state has purchased the labour power of a teacher, it is faced with the challenge of extracting labour from that commodity. This will partly involve the need to control in order to make sure that the teacher actually does some work, such as turning up to work, completing designated tasks, taking allocated classes and so on. That is, there is an established range of work activities which need to be undertaken if the school is to function at all. There are control mechanisms that operate to ensure that these things happen, although many people turn up to and participate in work simply because they want to. In addition, in common with other 'professions', teachers have often been sufficiently socialized through their schooling and pre-service training as to have such a well-developed work ethic that there rarely appears to be a control dimension at work at all for this purpose.

A second motivation for control, relates to reducing the costs of 'production'. In the private sector, the capitalist will seek to reduce production costs in order to increase profits. For the state as an employer there is a different motivation. It will be argued that one of the state's main functions in a capitalist society is to support capital accumulation. In the case of a state activity like education, this occurs by 'skilling' future labour power. However, state activities are funded from taxation and have the potential to be a drain on surplus value and thus a threat to capital accumulation. This means that the state is constantly under pressure to reduce the cost of public sector activities, while still being expected to meet the needs of capital and the community (Harris, 1994). One option for achieving this is for the state to try to lower its labour costs by devaluing the work of teaching. This might be achieved through a process of deskilling teachers' work, or by employing a large number of para-professionals to support a small number of core teachers who are well paid (Ashenden, 1989). Another option is for the state to ask its workers to do more with the same or fewer resources. This may be achieved through reorganizing work practices, and/or simply wringing out more effort from teachers. For example, teachers may be expected to take more students per class, or to increase their student contact time. Now, given that teachers care deeply about the quality of the education they provide, they may try to challenge or work around the new structures, or resist the intensification of their work. Thus, efforts to reduce the state's expenditure on education will often be accompanied by control strategies.

However, there is a third crucial reason to control teachers that is different from other workers. We referred earlier to the intensely political nature of the whole education enterprise. If the capacity for social practice is the object of education production, it is an object that is very different from the production of physical things like cars or pieces of steel. There is a continuing and intense struggle over the relative importance and meaning of each of the capacities for practice, not to mention the purposes to which they should be put (e.g. Ginsburg, 1988; Bigelow, 1990). Cornbleth, writing about the American experience, puts it this way:

> public schooling in the USA has long been an arena in which battles are fought over American values and priorities as a nation and what vision of the nation will or should be passed on to the next generation. Since the school curriculum is seen as a major vehicle of cultural definition and transmission, a goal of these battles has been control of curriculum knowledge.
>
> (1995, p. 168)

That is, there are powerful groups interested in the nature of the capacities developed. For example, employers have a considerable vested interest in ensuring that the school system produces workers who have an appropriate work ethic and skills. They continue to argue for a work-oriented curriculum, often against teachers who may want to promote a broader curriculum designed to foster the development of the whole child. Universities and the professions may have a vested interest in maintaining the competitive academic curriculum in schools, against the demands of minority groups for a more inclusive curriculum. Curriculum decisions about what is taught, to whom, when and how, result from these struggles (Apple, 1993a).

The state does not play a neutral role in all of this. It helps to broker agreements between the contending parties, and it is then faced with the task of ensuring that its employees, the teachers, implement the preferred curriculum. Since the state cannot be certain that teachers will do this, control strategies have to be devised. Thus, an understanding of the forms of control imposed on state teachers must start with an explication of the relationship that exists between the state, capital and education in society.

Our analysis begins with a neo-Gramscian understanding of the state (Dale, 1989). Gramsci saw the state as a series of loosely connected governmental sites within which the struggle for the leadership of dominant groups is fought. Thus, for Gramsci there was not a unified ruling class, but a ruling alliance of social movements made up of different fractions loosely stitched together to exercise and maintain leadership through the generation of consent. To this neo-Gramscian view we add the work of scholars like Offe (1984, 1985) and O'Connor (1973, 1984) who argue that the capitalist state has three core functions to perform. These are described by Ball as involving three 'fields' of problems:

(a) The problem of capital accumulation and economic efficiency; (b) the problem of social order, social authority and stability; and (c) the technical and managerial problems of the state itself – governance and control (legal and administrative procedures), costs (public spending) and planning.

(Ball, 1994, p. 5)

These problems can simultaneously produce contradictory demands, the resolution of which is never a straightforward matter (Dale, 1989; Torres, 1989; Ginsburg et al., 1990). The state is thus an arena for battles within and between dominant and less powerful groups, all of whom are fighting to assert their own particular set of interests. How does the state resolve these competing pressures?

Gramsci (1971) used the notion of hegemony to explain how the will of dominant groups within society and culture is achieved and maintained through the creation and recreation of a 'common-sense' view of the world. This common-sense view happens to coincide with the interests of the powerful groups. For example, state policy is constructed as serving the public interest, rather than just the interests of dominant groups. Thus, although power is dispersed between different governmental tiers and agencies, such as education systems, the pervasiveness of the common-sense discourse establishes cohesiveness across sites. However, Gramsci argued that hegemony is never complete. Indeed, it is partial and incomplete because 'counter-hegemonic' alliances engage in a 'war of manoeuvre' for leadership of the state. According to Gramsci, hegemonic power blocs try to prevent these counter-hegemonic forces from mobilizing, by organizing compromises which take account of some of the interests of those groups over whom hegemony is exercised. These compromises have been referred to as 'settlements' (Hall, 1990) or 'accords' (Apple, 1988).

Provisional social settlements establish an agreed framework which sets the parameters for social practice and beliefs, and for ongoing conflict and debate (Freeland, 1991, p. 66) for a particular period of time. That is, there is agreement about the range of issues over which there might be disagreement, and about the structures for the resolution of conflict. It is through settlements that minority and marginalized groups can exert some influence on state policy despite not being a part of the power bloc. At the same time, settlements incorporate discontent within parameters that do not threaten the privilege of dominant groups. Carlson observes that 'this means that settlements embody contradictions that generate contradictory outcomes' (1995, p. 410). Such contradictions, combined with changes in the social and political contexts, eventually lead to an unsettling of settlements. These periods have been described by Habermas (1976) as 'crisis tendencies' of capitalism, and the concept of settlement helps to explain how the state deals with these crises. Following the breakdown of a settlement, there is a period when social forces struggle to redefine the social order. This is often a conflictual process as familiar social arrangements are questioned and debated, but eventually new settlements are forged, and these may either advance or diminish any gains made by marginalized groups.

At any one time there are a number of provisional settlements relating to specific arenas and contexts of social activity, and these are relatively autonomous. However, as Freeland observes:

> certain arenas of social practice are more crucial for the maintenance of overall social structures and processes, and settlements in those areas will tend to have a certain dominance over other arenas of practice or regions. Provisional settlements in debates about pivotal arenas such as economic and political practice can establish not only the agendas and parameters for debate and practice in their own region, but also very broad parameters for the debates and practice in other regions.
>
> (1991, p. 68)

Education is one example of an arena of social practice that has a certain relative autonomy, but which is strongly influenced by the prevailing provisional settlements within the economic, political and cultural arenas. This means that state schools, as apparatuses of the state, are under intense pressure to act in particular ways. This is not to say that education policy is determined in any mechanistic way. Indeed, since education plays a key role in the state's often contradictory roles of establishing the conditions for capital accumulation and for democratic practice (Carnoy and Levin, 1985), the production and maintenance of provisional educational settlements are characterized by contestation and struggle. Sometimes this process will produce genuinely progressive education policy that represents at least partial victories for less powerful groups (Apple, 1993b). But usually the balance of an educational settlement is tilted in favour of dominant groups.

An educational settlement incorporates the dominant discourse, legitimates particular sets of social relations and the ways in which these are organized – including the sanctioned forms of educational governance – and establishes a hegemonic view of the purposes of education. All these components are embedded in the curriculum, which is the centre-piece of any education settlement. Carlson describes it thus:

> The public school curriculum...may be appreciated as a negotiated compromise or settlement between dominant and marginalised power blocs and social movements over what 'truths' will be taught in the schools, whose knowledge will be privileged, what voices will be heard and silenced, and how knowledge of 'truth' is to be arrived at.
>
> (1995, p. 408)

Now, since the curriculum is the specification of the labour process of teaching, then it follows that teachers are crucial to the successful implementation of any educational settlement. And yet it is clear that many of them cannot necessarily be trusted to implement its spirit faithfully. This may be for any number of reasons. For example, it may be because their class and gender interests clash with the nature of the settlement itself; it may be that teachers have political beliefs and associations which make them untrustworthy; or it may be because teachers are tied to established practices and beliefs which are dissonant with the settlement. Whatever the reason, the state cannot afford to leave the implementation of an education settlement to its teachers. Thus, if the broad imperatives of the settlement are to be followed, the state must find strategies to ensure that teachers work in particular ways and for specific ends. In short, teachers must be controlled. Thus, the secret to the purpose of controlling teachers can be revealed through an analysis of the prevailing educational settlement, and the broad social, political, economic, and cultural factors which have shaped it.

And so embedded in each educational settlement are systems and strategies of control – we will call them control regimes – that seek to ensure that teachers will faithfully implement the prevailing policy imperatives. But, since forms of control are clearly linked to the nature of the work, and to the people doing the work, there needs to be an examination of the social relations of the school as a workplace before any consideration of systems of control can occur. It is to that question that we now turn.

Who is Being Controlled and Who are the Controllers?

Much of the literature on teachers' work makes reference to categories of education workers such as 'teachers', 'principals' or 'bureaucrats'. Often such categories are used unproblematically, as though those within each group have similar sets of interests, or that relations between these groups are fixed. Such an approach fails to offer a way into understanding how the categories are constituted, or how the relationship between them, and the men and women in the teaching force, are shaped and reshaped. The question about who is being controlled and who is doing the controlling, can only be answered by going beyond descriptive categories to an understanding of social relations. In this section we want to explore the dynamics of two of these social relations – class and gender – and how they operate deep in the labour process itself.

When the state purchases the labour power of educators, it has purchased people who possess certain characteristics and interests. These have been structured by a range of factors, which determine both how the employer will seek to turn labour power into labour, and how employees will respond. One of these factors is clearly economic, but there are disputes within the labour process literature about how this factor should be understood. State teachers sell their labour power to the state, and to this extent they are members of the working class. But this does not take us far because even the most cursory examination shows that the experience of teachers at work is very different from the experience of factory workers who also sell their labour power. Teachers get paid more, they require higher status credentials, their work is more varied and complex, and they appear to have a greater level of autonomy and freedom to make choices in work. In addition, teachers have been historically reluctant to identify with working-class movements. But if they are not working class, neither are they members of the bourgeoisie. Their work *is* controlled and they cannot claim to own or control the means of production. How can we understand the class relations into which teachers enter?

One approach is grounded in the tradition of Marxist structuralism. For example, some education writers interested in the labour process of teachers have used Erik Olin Wright's thesis on contradictory class locations as the backdrop to their work (Apple, 1986; Watkins, 1992). Wright (1985) argues that some class positions are contradictory in that they not only reflect the basic antagonistic class relations of capitalist society, but are also objectively torn between the antagonistic classes of that society. These positions do not have a class identity in their own right: their class character is determined strictly by their location between classes. Apple maintains that teachers fall into this category:

> I am not implying that they are by definition within the middle classes or that they are in an ambiguous position somehow 'between classes'.

> Instead, along with Wright, I am saying that it is wise to think of them as located simultaneously in two classes. They thus share the interests of both the petty bourgeoisie and the working class.
>
> (1986, p. 32)

Why are teachers in this contradictory class situation? This is because teachers share interests with both capital and workers. For example, they perform the 'global function of capital' (Carchedi, 1977) by preparing workers for the labour market, and disseminating, and thus reproducing, the capitalist ideology. For this role they are granted certain privileges not available to the working class, including a degree of control over their work, and a marginally better economic return. To this extent they are closer to the interests of the bourgeoisie. On the other hand, they sell their labour power, do not determine the goals and purposes of their work, and are subjected to control by management. To this extent they are closer to the interests of the working class.

The strength of this analysis is that it does give some clues as to the contradictory interests, tensions, and expectations that construct the labour process of teaching. For example, if the state wants to reduce the financial costs of the education system, it can begin to 'proletarianize' teachers through division of labour, deskilling to reduce labour costs, and introducing overt forms of control. The problem is that this may cause teachers to identify more closely with other workers, and become more militant. On the other hand, although granting teachers a fair degree of autonomy may result in a closer identification with the 'professional classes', this option means that the state has less capacity to ensure that teachers will follow curriculum specifications. This is a delicate balancing act, the fulcrum of which is the importance of teachers to the successful handling of the accumulation and legitimation roles of the state.

What of the principals and bureaucrats who are expected to control teachers? Except for those top bureaucrats who are unequivocally in the bourgeoisie, principals and bureaucrats sell their labour power, and are also expected to exploit the labour power of teachers. From Wright's perspective, this places them in a contradictory position between the bourgeoisie and the working class. The more power they are given, or expected to exercise in relation to the surveillance and control of teachers, the closer they will move towards the bourgeoisie. The more they fulfil a coordination role, and are themselves subjected to control from above, the closer they will move to the proletariat, and to the interests of the teachers they are required to control. This stark outline already suggests the motivation behind current attempts by the state to position principals as the Department's presence in the school.

However, despite these advantages, the structuralist approach has some significant limitations. In particular, it has been attacked because of the primacy it gives to class structures. Through identifying the structure itself, Marxist structuralists claim to be able to unmask the 'real' interests of the individuals located within it. This is consistent with Marx's drawing of a distinction between 'a class in itself' and a 'class for itself', sometimes under-stood as the distinction between a set of objective conditions which define class, and the subjective consciousness which this class possesses. Critics argue that this is a spurious and obfuscating distinction that focuses attention on abstract mathematical-like formulae, at the expense of under-standing class struggle and worker resistance. For example, Connell observes that:

> understanding class relations is essential in understanding teachers. But I do not think an analysis which centres on the trigonometrical exercise of calculating a 'location' on an a priori set of theoretical axes, and reading off the political consequences, is the right way to do it. The collapse of this exercise into conceptual absurdities such as 'contradic-tory class locations' (in all seriousness, a location cannot contradict) is one clear sign that there is something seriously wrong with the proce-dure.
>
> (1985, pp. 191–2)

In terms of the labour process it is claimed, the artificial separation has the effect of neglecting the process of struggle which defines class interests; inhibiting an understanding of the day-to-day impact of particular forms of control; and precluding an explanation of the historical tendencies and vari-ations in the labour process. It produces an over-deterministic functionalism that can portray workers as pawns of management, helpless in the face of strategies to control and degrade their labour.

The response to these concerns has been to look for an approach which offers a more nuanced way of understanding the complex and varying patterns of social conflict that occur within educational institutions, and how these shape the class consciousness of teachers and administrators. One approach has been to focus on *class as a relationship*, rather than as a description of the functions undertaken by different occupations. This perspective replaces an analysis of the boundaries between class places, with an exploration of the dynamics through which places are constituted. This approach to class analysis is based on the work of the famous British Marxist historian E.P. Thompson who defines class as:

> a historical phenomenon, unifying a number of disparate and seemingly unconnected events...I emphasise that it is a historical phenomenon. I do not see class as a 'structure', nor even as a 'category', but as some-thing which in fact happens.
>
> (Thompson, 1963, p. 9)

Thus although classes are embedded in relations of production, they cannot be discussed or identified independently of class consciousness. When applied to education, this approach implies a different focus of study:

> Rather than asking what teachers' class location is, we should be asking what class relations teachers enter. Better still, we should ask through what practices, their own and others, teachers participate in class relations; what their views, purposes and conflicts are; and what are the consequences for the making and remaking of class structure.
>
> (Connell, 1985, pp. 191–2)

In the educational literature on the labour process of teachers, Ozga and Lawn (1981), and Lawn and Ozga (1988), argue for Thompson's historicalist approach to understanding class. They dismiss structuralist class analysis on the grounds that it views class as a static entity; takes on an unacceptable degree of abstraction from concrete work situations; and ignores the dynamic role which people have in society by resisting and creating alternatives. In particular, they are critical of the view of teachers as state functionaries who act for the state's ideological, cultural and economic reproduction and domination. They argue:

> All education does not serve the purposes of the state all the time. The blanket use of the term 'state functionaries' hides too many historical, local and particular possibilities and, importantly ignores teachers' attempts at working class alliances on education and their varied interpretation of their role as perceived by the state and their resistance to it.
>
> (Ozga and Lawn, 1981, p. 84)

Thus, Ozga and Lawn suggest that teachers are workers by virtue of their economic position as employees, they resist the notion that the capitalist or the state can simply dominate the worker and they argue for an understanding of conflict and resistance in the class struggle. They assert that class is not just an economic relationship – it is a relational concept involving several factors, economic, cultural and ideological; and a process, not static condition, taking place over time. This leads them to adopt the E.P. Thompson position on class, and they quote a famous passage from him:

> Class is not, as some sociologists would have it, a static category – so many people standing in this or that relation to the means of production. Class in the Marxist tradition is (or ought to be) an historical category, describing people in relation over time, and the ways in which they become conscious of their relationship, separate, unite, enter into struggle.... Hence class is an 'economic' and it is also a 'cultural' formation: it is impossible to give any theoretical priority to one aspect over

the other...what changes, as the mode of production and productive relation changes, is the experience of living men and women....

(Thompson, 1979, quoted in Lawn and Ozga, 1988, p. 85)

In our view the historicalist approach offers the more fruitful option for the development of a labour process theory which is relational rather than categorical. However, it must be employed with a strong sense of the structural constraints on human action, and a recognition of the fundamental contradictions inherent in the labour process of teaching.

But teachers are not only classed, they are also gendered actors. There is a sexual division of labour which is predicated on a power relationship which is about the subordination of women by men. Thus gender oppression is central to an understanding of the ways in which the labour process of teachers is structured and controlled. It operates in a number of ways and at a variety of levels. One example is that it determines who comes into teaching. In the external labour market in Western capitalist countries, women have been horizontally segregated into female occupations. Teaching has been one of the professional occupations into which many women have moved, and the concept of the 'feminization' of teaching looms large in the literature. However, it is not possible to make generalizations across time and place. A number of studies have demonstrated that feminization has occurred for different reasons, at different times, and in different ways in various national and provincial settings (Prentice, 1975; Danylewycz and Prentice, 1986; Apple, 1986; Bergen, 1988; Theobald, 1996). Clearly there have been demographic, economic, cultural and political forces at work. But common to these has been manipulation of labour market conditions and rules of employment that have been devised by a patriarchal state to the disadvantage of women. As needs have changed it has historically been women whose labour has been seen to be expendable.

Another example relates to the conditions of teachers' work which have been largely gender based. In most education systems, salary benefits, professional development opportunities, promotion procedures, and redundancy provisions have historically had a gendered dimension to them. Women have had to endure and fight a range of male devised rules and regulations which have disadvantaged them, and directly or indirectly advantaged men. An important aspect has been the division between women as teachers and men as administrators, which has characterized most education systems in the Western world. Not only has this limited the access of women to power, and the material benefits associated with leadership positions, but it has also established a situation where it is largely men who structure and control the labour process of women.

Central to understanding the gendered dimension of the labour process of teaching is a ubiquitous patriarchal ideology. This works in a number of subtle ways. For example, it has constructed notions of masculinity and femininity which undergird the external and internal education labour markets, as well as material practices in education systems. Teaching has been constructed as 'women's work' because it involves the caring and nurturing of children which is the activity in which women are engaged in the private sphere. This has naturalized the sexual division of labour (male administrators and female teachers), since 'motherly' qualities are not appropriate to the more rational, scientific practice of management which is constructed as a male domain. 'Hegemonic masculinity' (Blackmore, 1993) can also be seen at work in the division between women as teachers of the very young (e.g. junior primary, primary teachers), and men as teachers of older children (e.g. secondary teachers).

It is important to issue warnings here about the dangers of essentializing. Clearly patriarchy plays a crucial role in the organization of the teaching labour process. But it should not be seen as being embodied in a group of conspiring males closeted away in smoke-filled rooms in state education departments. Rather it is more useful to conceive of patriarchy as being embedded in procedure and discourse (Franzway et al., 1989). Connell puts it colourfully when he suggests that this approach:

> allows us to acknowledge the patriarchal character of the state without falling into a conspiracy theory or making futile searches for Patriarch Headquarters. It locates sexual policies in the realm of social action, where it belongs, avoiding the speculative reductionism that would explain state action as an emanation of the inner nature of males.
>
> (1990, p. 517)

Such an approach also allows for the recognition that female teachers have not been passive in the face of overt interventions into their labour process. They have resisted in a number of subtle and direct ways, and have made significant gains especially in relation to the conditions of their work. But resistance should not be romanticized. Patriarchy is a powerful ideology, and apparent gender neutrality in state policy and educational practice, can disguise gender bias (Blackmore, 1993).

We have argued that control of the labour process is both a classed and a gendered phenomenon. Teachers and administrators have particular sets of interests which strongly influence – not determine – how they act. If the state wants a specific curriculum to be implemented, then the ways in which it structures the labour process of teachers, and the job it expects its managers to perform, will depend largely on its assessment of whether these interests are likely to help or hinder the successful achievement of its goals. Thus, questions about who is being controlled, and who is doing the controlling must be confronted in any labour process analysis. As Apple argues:

The two dynamics of class and gender (with race, of course) are not reducible to each other, but intertwine, work off, and co-determine the terrain in which each operates. It is at the intersection of these two dynamics that one can begin to unravel some of the reasons why procedures for rationalizing the work of teachers evolved...the ultimate effect of these procedures, with the loss of control that accompanies them, can bear in important ways on how we think about the 'reform' of teaching and curriculum and the state's role in it.

(1986, p. 34)

It is time now to turn to an examination of the forms of control exercised upon teachers.

How are Teachers Controlled?

It has been argued that the curriculum represents the specification of the labour process of teaching, and that the precise nature of this specification is something which is highly political and therefore strongly contested. This contestation occurs within the parameters established by the prevailing education settlement. Given that it is teachers who are expected to implement the curriculum, and that they will not necessarily agree with the outcome of this political process, then in any education system at any moment in time, there will be a range of controls set in place which aim to ensure that teachers will work in ways that will achieve the agreed upon outcomes. We will refer to the patterns established by these specific forms of control, as control regimes.

Upon which aspects of the labour process of teachers will the control regime focus? Since the object of the labour process of teaching is the development of the capacity for social practice, it might be expected that a control regime will place a particular focus on the way in which knowledge is defined and then mediated by schools. Bernstein (1971, 1990) argues that this happens through curriculum message systems which define what is taught, how it is taught, and how outcomes are evaluated. Thus, a control regime will include some specification by the state of each of these three message systems, in a way that is consistent with the prevailing educational settlement. However this alone will not suffice. There is also need for mechanisms that will ensure that the specifications for each message system are actually implemented. This will involve procedures to check the quality of the 'product' (that is whether the right capacities for social practice are being developed); and to reward and punish those teachers who succeed or fail in the process.

We are proposing, therefore, that a control regime will coordinate three elements:

1   *Defining the curriculum*: using methods or mechanisms which direct teachers to impart a defined curriculum, including content, sequence, methodology and assessment;
2   *Supervising and evaluating teachers*: involving procedures which enable teachers to be supervised and evaluated in such a way as to identify those individuals who are not performing adequately, according to criteria consistent with achieving the defined curriculum;
3   *Engineering compliance and consent*: establishing ways to discipline and reward workers in order to elicit consent and/or enforce compliance with the defined curriculum.

The important point here is that the form of each of these elements is not natural, even though often it will be made to appear that way. Each element is socially constructed through a political process where certain interests fight to establish and maintain dominance. It is in the interests of those who control the agenda to normalize certain practices and beliefs, and even make it appear that they have been established 'objectively' and 'scientifically'. In fact, the content of the curriculum, the criteria established to evaluate teacher performance, and the split between managers and managed, are socially constructed ways to control teachers for particular ends. It is only when this is fully apprehended that it is possible to conceive of alternative ways to organize the labour process of teachers.

How are all these elements of control addressed coherently? We will argue that there are a number of broad systems of control which rarely operate in isolation, although each is constituted by a specific internal logic. Each system is a way of coordinating one or more of the three elements. In combination at any one time, these systems constitute the control regime of an education system, which in turn contributes to the construction of negotiated order within specific schools. The control regime can be located somewhere along a control continuum which runs from relative to limited autonomy, through to quite direct and coercive forms of control. In this section we will explain some of the self-contained control systems that operate, and/or have operated, in education. First, however, it is necessary to outline the contours of two aspects of control that are better conceptualized as pervading all control systems, rather than constituting stand-alone systems.

First, since the inner logic of capitalism is patriarchal, then it follows that control of the capitalist labour process is also patriarchal. It makes no sense to conceive of it as one possible weapon in the control arsenal. Patriarchal control is constitutive of all that happens in the labour process, and manifests itself in a number of ways. It is a material practice which operates through the systems of control described in this section. It is also an ideology which shapes the ways in which 'reality' is constructed and language is used in education sites.

The second all pervasive aspect of control is the practice and ideology of aspects of scientific management. The post-Braverman debates about the extent to which scientific management constituted *the* form of control in late monopoly capitalism generated a consensus which granted scientific management a significant ideological influence, but denied that it had a widespread practical effect. This consensus is certainly consistent with the experience in education, where there has never been a whole-scale application of scientific management in the organization of work. However, many of its concepts can be found embedded in the control systems outlined below, and certainly it has exercised a powerful ideological influence. In education, there has been an increasing separation of management from teaching, the effects of which have been to confirm the separation of conception from execution. This has been accompanied by a division of labour, where teachers' work has become increasingly specialized (e.g. subject specializations), partly in the quest for greater efficiency and curriculum control. However, the outcomes have been contradictory, and certainly there has been no inexorable trend. Some control regimes have served to partially deskill teachers' work, while at other times control has operated more subtly and allowed teachers a greater measure of control over their work. Thus scientific management has never functioned as a coherent system of control in education, but fragments of its strategies and ideology occupy a ubiquitous presence.

With these two pervasive aspects of control in mind, we will turn now to describing the various systems of control. We have drawn these together from the education literature mainly relating to Australia, Great Britain, the United States and Canada. It is important to recognize that, although there is always a dominant control system, no one system operates in isolation. At any historical moment, a control regime is made up of a hybrid of control systems and strategies. The ways in which these form and change will be the subject of investigation in the case study chapters of this book.

Regulated market control

In order to understand how this control system functions, it is necessary to appreciate how a free market in education would operate. Marginson (1995) suggests that if education operated in a fully developed capitalist market it would have four main features: a commodity is produced which has a use value for the consumer (student, parent, employer) and exchange value for the producer (teacher), there are relations of exchange between producer and consumer, there are relations of competition between individual producers, and there are particular role behaviours expected from producers (e.g. competitiveness) and consumers (e.g. the drive to maximize utility). The key to market success is consumer demand and satisfaction, and this can only be achieved if the 'commodity' meets the needs and expectations of consumers. In education terms this would involve teaching an appropriate curriculum, and 'value adding' to students in a way that the market demands. Not to do this, so the theory goes, is to risk market failure. Thus it is the invisible hand of the market that exercises control over the producers. Success, and profits, will go to those who best meet the requirements of consumers (Gewirtz et al., 1995; Kenway, 1995).

Now the fact is that state education never functions in a pure free market. Capital and society generally have particular expectations of education, and the state will intervene if these expectations are not being met. The degree of the intervention will be determined by the extent to which the education market is meeting consumer expectations, and by the requirements of the prevailing settlement. Thus the market may be regulated through such means as making curriculum specifications explicit, devising ways to monitor and evaluate teacher performance, and implementing systems of motivating teachers, such as rewards and punishment. But if the state is committed to the market as the primary form of control, then its regulatory activities will simply supplement market control. Ball describes the contemporary combination of the free market and intervention by the state in the following way:

> The market is a disciplinary system and within it education is reconstructed as a consumption good. Children and their 'performances' are traded and exchanged as commodities. In relations between schools, the key element of the market is competition. 'The competitive process provides incentives and so provokes effort.... The essence of the whole process is choice by the consumer; emulation, rivalry and substitution by the producer' (Reekie 1984: 37). Teachers' work is thus increasingly viewed and evaluated solely in terms of output measures (test scores and examination performance) set against cost (subject time, class size, resource requirements).
>
> (1994, p. 51)

Technical control

There are a number of control systems which are embodied in structures rather than people. Technical control is one of these. Apple (1982, 1986) points to the integration of 'management systems, reductive behaviourally based curricula, pre-specified teaching "competencies" and procedures and student responses, and pre and post testing' (1986, p. 32), as examples of control being embedded in the education instruments of production. Instead of control appearing to flow from management to teacher, it is built into the more impersonal form of a textbook or teaching materials. And since texts are the 'dominant definition of curriculum in the school' (Apple and Oliver, 1996, p. 424), technical control is encoded into the very basis of the curricular form itself. Thus the 'teacher-proof' materials determine what is taught and how, sequence lessons, decide the form and timing of assessment, and establish the pace of teaching. Apple argues that these materials are often developed through expensive curriculum 'innovation' projects which are often designed to reinstitute academic disciplinary knowledge as the most 'legitimate' content for schools. In this form, technical control is also patriarchal: 'It is the history of the state, in concert with capital and a largely male academic body of consultants and developers, intervening at the level of practice into the work of a largely female workforce' (Apple, 1986, p. 37).

Of course, teachers can ignore or alter some or all of the materials, but often this choice is constrained by accompanying strategies such as standardized testing regimes. To ignore the materials is to run the risk of students failing, the blame for which is easily laid with the teacher. There are many other examples of technical control that have been described, although not necessarily named, by education scholars. These include the architecture of schools which construct teaching methodology in particular ways (Densmore, 1987); and computer technology which can effectively replace teachers or significantly rationalize their work (Harris, 1982; Apple and Jungck, 1992).

Bureaucratic control

Perhaps the dominant system of control in the twentieth century has been bureaucratic control. Like technical control, it grows out of the structure of the education system, rather than from the personal relationships between management and worker. But unlike technical control, rather than being built into the teaching materials and resources, it is embedded in the social and organizational structure of educational institutions. It operates through job categories, work rules, promotion procedures, discipline, wage differentials, definitions of responsibilities and so on. That is, bureaucratic control institutionalizes hierarchical power. It encompasses and makes routine the three elements of control through a set of comprehensive system rules and regulations. Social or organizational arrangements become the basis for promotion and achievement. The education system promises the teacher a career.

The basis of bureaucratic control lies in a highly stratified workforce. Over time, teachers are divided through subject specialisms, experience and length of service, responsibility and perceived skill. A management hierarchy is established including such positions as principal, deputy principal, assistant principal, and curriculum area coordinator. Each job is then positioned within an elaborate salary structure, within which types of jobs are divided into groups and further divided through steps on a salary scale. The whole structure creates differences in salaries, job autonomy, power over other workers, working conditions, and chances for promotion. It facilitates work direction, supervision and evaluation, and compliance and consent through 'rule of law' rather than through rule by the personal dictates of a supervisor. This is not to say that supervisors are no longer required – far from it. An increasing number of them are needed. But now their jobs and authority are legitimated through a panoply of rules and regulations rather than personal authority. And now, they too, are the subject of scrutiny and supervision.

Clearly bureaucratic control shares some common characteristics with scientific management. These include the attempt to establish management control over the specialist knowledge of teaching by separating conception from execution; the need to carefully define each worker's job for the purposes of evaluation and monitoring; and the need to subject management itself to management control. And like scientific management, bureaucratic control is both a structure for institutional practice, and a way of thinking about the world. Its rule laden and routine structures and rituals embed themselves in the culture as well as the everyday practices of schools. Technical rationality becomes something that the school community lives with and comes to accept as natural (Popkewitz and Lind, 1989).

Corporate control

Bureaucratic control has been the dominant management control system this century, but over the past decade it has metamorphized into a different system of corporate managerial control. Inspired by the globalization of the economy, the state has moved to: 'reorient the business of the public sector so that it no longer services a welfare state, but, instead, services a state which defines its primary objective as one of fostering a competitive economy' (Yeatman, 1990, p. 3).

This focus on economic rather than social goods has spelt the end of the welfare state, and resulted in some significant administrative and ideological change in the public sector. It has turned public servants into economic managers with an eye on 'doing more with less' in the context of a competitive quasi-market setting. The organizational culture of the public service has been restructured in terms of managerial prerogative. Collegial culture has been replaced by a lean line-management system where managers are expected to meet goals determined for them by an elite executive management team, within the parameters of a devolved budgetary management system (Considine, 1988).

In terms of schools, corporate managerial control has resulted in the principal moving from being a first among professional equals to being a line manager who is expected to ensure the implementation of centrally determined curriculum policy and administrative guidelines. This administrative arrangement is mirrored within the school by a hierarchical line-management system. In its contemporary manifestation, corporate management forms of control sit uneasily beside a commitment to consumer choice and a regulated education market. Schools are expected to compete for additional resources, and to meet the needs of 'consumers'. Thus corporate managerial control involves a complex mix of control through the invisible hand of the market, centralized prescriptive curriculum control, an ideology informed by such values as enterprise, competition and choice, and the immediate authority of the principal delegated from above.

Ideological control

The control systems described above involve some overt intervention by management into the labour process of teachers. But, control can assume a more subtle, ideological form. Rather than being located in a person or a structure, ideological control is present in ideas, language, and beliefs. Its primary purpose is to organize teacher consent to the values embedded in the prevailing educational settlement, and to the organizational structures and practices which support it. In this sense, it can be linked to Gramsci's (1971) concept of hegemony which explains how dominant groups maintain their dominance in institutions like schools, without having to be coercive. Hegemonic control occurs through moral and intellectual persuasion, and it is maintained through the engineering of broad consent and acquiescence to a particular set of beliefs and values. If teachers are committed to these by working in ways that both support and reproduce them, then there is little need for more direct control. But ideological control systems contain contradictions that can turn them into weapons of teacher resistance. When this happens, management will turn to alternative and more coercive forms of control.

Ideological control can be thought of in two interconnected ways. One relates to the establishment of the hegemonic beliefs, ideas and values which underpin the prevailing educational settlement. This occurs through such means as the construction of officially legitimated versions of the 'good teacher', the privileging of scientific rationality and the concept of efficiency, the promotion of a particular set of values, such as business values, and the dissemination of a patriarchal ideology. The other relates to the strategies and structures which are used to produce and reproduce these ideas and values. This occurs through such means as pre-service teacher education, in-service training and development, the masculinization of administrative structures, the privileging of certain discourses, the use of particular language, and the ideology of professionalism (Blackmore, 1993; Barton et al., 1994; Elliott and Maclennan, 1994).

There are any number of ways in which these two aspects can combine to contribute to a control regime at any point in time. For example, the education system may formally articulate the qualities of a 'good teacher' (Lawn, 1991), and then work to incorporate this view into courses which prepare new teachers, selection and promotion criteria, disciplinary procedures, and policy discourse. In this way it is naturalized, and alternate constructions can be depicted as strange or deviant. To use Gitlin's phrase: 'The hegemonic sense of the world seeps into popular "common sense" and gets reproduced there; it may even appear to be generated by that common sense' (1980, p. 254).

Another example is the way in which a particular dominant discourse sets the terms within which the education debate is conducted, and so shepherds teachers away from alternate constructions (e.g. Corson, 1995). The dominant discourse is often associated with the ideology that pervades a specific control system, such as bureaucratic control being accompanied by the discourse of bureaucratic rationality. The language imbues official department memorandums and policy, as well as the content and process of training and development programmes for teachers. After a time its use, and thus the view of the world upon which it is based, become naturalized. Carr and Hartnett (1996) use the example of the shift from the 1960s education discourse of child-centred education and equality of opportunity, to the market-based business discourse of the late 1980s and 1990s of standards, parental choice, consumers, accountability and school effectiveness. Smyth (1992, 1995a) outlines another version when he shows how the language and the ideology of collegiality and collaboration is being used to sell to teachers the contradictory notion of increasingly centralized authority, alongside a divesting of central responsibility to schools.

Ideological control only works by actually giving, or at least creating the illusion of giving, a degree of work autonomy and control to teachers. When it works, teachers become their own self-regulators and even willing contributors to the reproduction of control which establishes their own self-domination. However, this relative autonomy also creates the space for contestation, and for resistance to the dominant managerial perspective. Sometimes this resistance can bring about the need for modifications to the control regimes, at other times it may serve only to confirm ideological hegemony. This contradictory set of relations can be demonstrated by reference to the ideology of professionalism. The functionalist view of professionalism that dominated the study of teaching in the 1950s and 1960s, measured teachers against the established professions using such criteria as salary, status and knowledge base. Pronouncements were then made as to whether teaching was a 'real' profession, or a semi-profession. Critical analyses of professionalism (Larson, 1977; Ozga and Lawn, 1981; Grace, 1985; Densmore, 1987; Lawn and Ozga, 1988) have focused on the ideological component of professionalism, and its link with the concept of control.

Historical studies in the British context show that professionalism as an ideology was developed by the state as a form of control of teachers, following concerns about continuing industrial unrest, and the growing working-class alliances of teachers (Lawn, 1996). Much of this unrest was the result of the coercive controls that were imposed on teachers at the time. In its place, professional autonomy was promoted by the state as an antidote to militant teacher unionism. Grace calls this 'legitimated professionalism' (1985, p. 11) because it is sanctioned by the state and is exercised within defined parameters. This is seen to involve responsible and non-political behaviour (Lawn, 1987), and a 'professional' work ethic. Since that time the ideology of professionalism has been used to create a sense of separation of teachers from other workers and indeed from each other, to reaffirm a scientific rationality through the notion of 'expert', and an acceptance of an increasing work load (Densmore, 1987; Popkewitz and Lind, 1989; Carlson, 1992). Feminist scholars have also viewed 'professionalism' as a social and historical construct, but they stress the ways in which it privileges a masculinized discourse of scientific measurement and control, at the expense of the nurturant and expressive work that women do (Freedman, 1990; Weiler, 1995).

But the concept of 'professionalism' has not only been used by management as a means to control teachers. It has also been used by teachers as a weapon to maintain and/or regain some control over their work, including resistance to externally imposed curriculum prescriptions, and to argue for improved wages and conditions. As Grace points out:

> ideologies of professionalism can be made to serve the interests of the state for control and containment of teachers or they can be effectively deployed by teachers to improve their terms and conditions of service and their enjoyment of social status and occupational autonomy.
>
> (1987, p. 195)

Thus professionalism is not an objective concept. It is a social construction (Helsby and McCulloch, 1996) that has been used at different times as a form of ideological control, and as a weapon of teacher resistance.

Control through 'disciplinary power'

Foucault's (1977) concept of 'disciplinary power' in many ways combines structural and ideological control. He argues that discursive practices within a society give permission for certain subjects to be talked and written about in certain ways, and establishes who has permission to speak and with what authority. They create a power/knowledge nexus which sets standards and norms of behaviour, which become embodied in a specific set of institutional practices. These practices operate as a disciplinary power on individuals, and rely on the penalty of the norm. That is, a set of expectations (norms) are imprinted on to the 'humble modalities' and 'minor procedures' of school life. Any departure from these norms results in disgrace and punishment.

Technologies of power – hierarchical observation, normalizing judgement, and examination – operate to bind individuals into certain patterns of behaviour. Like Bentham's panopticon they work on and through individuals to impart a sense of ever present surveillance through tightly prescribed curricula, testing regimes, appraisal and record keeping (Hall and Millard, 1994; Goodwin, 1996; Gore, 1998). Hall and Millard point out that: 'As the power becomes more anonymous and more functional within the school setting, those on whom and by whom it is exercised tend to be more strongly individualized' (1994, p.159).

They show how current government changes to initial teacher training in Britain is an attempt to maintain 'disciplinary power' through 'correct training'. The emphasis on practical school-based experience, as an alternative to grappling with educational theory in the academy, consolidates disciplinary power in schools. Teachers are increasingly drawn into learning about the detail of institutional life, including what functions as acceptable and unacceptable practice. This triumph of technique over questions of purpose, produces compliance with government policy. It also constructs as deviant those who question established patterns of institutional life.

In this section we have drawn together and described a number of the control systems that have been mentioned in the literature on teachers' work. For analytical purposes, we have deliberately treated them as self-contained systems in order to come to grips with the essence of each. In practice, however, they do not operate in isolation. Every control regime is a hybrid of systems and strategies which combine in particular formations, although invariably one is dominant and sets the parameters within which the others function. How this actually works in practice can only be understood by studying an education system at particular historical moments. Similarly, an understanding of how control regimes are modified, and eventually breakdown and change, can only be realized through historical study.

What are the Effects of Control on Teachers?

It is this question that has had most attention paid to it in the labour process literature generally, and in the literature on teachers' work more specifically. Scholars have identified a number of material, ideological and political effects of control on the labour process of teachers. The purpose of this section is to draw these together in an effort to round-out the tentative theory that has been developed through this chapter.

The material and ideological effects

From a labour process perspective, the concept that is most used to describe what is happening to teachers' work is that of *deskilling*. It is argued that as key decisions about curriculum are taken increasingly by management – usually outside the school – so teachers lose the capacity to theorize about their work, and instead focus on the more technical task of implementation of other people's ideas. In this way their work becomes deskilled. Some scholars (Apple, 1982; Apple and Teitelbaum, 1986; Densmore, 1987) use the example of the prepackaged curricula that are so ubiquitous across the Western world. They argue that the form of this curriculum artefact both controls and deskills teachers. By separating conception from execution, skills that teachers used to need and that were deemed essential to the craft of working with children – such as curriculum deliberation and planning, designing teaching and curricula strategies for specific groups and individuals based on an intimate knowledge of these people – are no longer necessary. Teachers simply put into operation the goals and designs of outside experts and, as a result, their skills atrophy.

We have some concerns about the unproblematic application of Braverman's concept of deskilling to the work of teachers, and its lack of appreciation of the social and gendered construction of skill. Braverman argued that deskilling is not an incidental outcome for workers. It results from a quite conscious strategy to deskill through the fragmentation and division of work. In this way workers are more controlled, labour power is less expensive, and workers produce more. Now it is far from clear that it is the intention of education management to systematically deskill teachers in this way. Certainly during fiscal crises the state is often constrained to reduce the drain on surplus value by making education as cost effective as possible. This may involve deliberate attempts to lower the labour market value of teachers' labour power through deskilling. But, as we have argued in this chapter so far, the legitimation function of the state implies control of teachers for the purpose of ensuring the implementation of a particular curriculum focus. This is as likely to require reskilling teachers, as it is deskilling them. It can be argued that when deskilling occurs, it is often as much an unintended outcome, as it is an aim, of control strategies.

Thus, decisions by the state to impose a certain curriculum emphasis through, say, a common curriculum, may prevent teachers from theorizing about the goals and purposes of their work, and so dull their capacities in this area. But this is because the state wants to ensure compliance to a particular curriculum emphasis, not because it wants to deskill teachers. In addition such a policy may contribute to a teacher's technical curriculum skills in a positive way. That is, teachers may be the subjects of a partial deskilling process, much in the way of Derber's (1982) distinction between the ideological and technical proletarianization of professionals. For example, the increasing division of labour within teaching (e.g. subject specializations, junior primary, primary and secondary teachers, the creation of jobs with specific tasks such as student counselling) may actually deepen technical skill and expertise in particular areas, even though the ends of these activities may be increasingly determined by the state.

Another concern about the deskilling thesis is that it implies there was a golden age of teaching where teachers were not subjected to deskilling trends. In fact, the historical evidence (e.g. Reid, 1997) indicates that such was not the case, but this does not deny the importance of the concept of deskilling to an understanding of teachers' work. There were times in the late nineteenth century and for the first part of the twentieth century, when teachers' work was less highly divided and stratified than it is now (this does not apply to the sexual division of labour which has always existed in teaching), but teachers were just as tightly controlled. There have been other times, for example during the school-based curriculum development era of the 1970s, when control was less apparent. That is, there is no long-term inexorable process of proletarianization at work. Rather, teachers have always been controlled for reasons outlined earlier, an important effect of which is deskilling in different ways at different times.

An effect of control associated with deskilling is that of *reskilling*. Apple (1982, 1986) uses this concept in two ways. First, as many teachers are deskilled, so too are they reskilled, but in skills that enable teachers to efficiently deal with the changing managerially determined context of their work. For example, technologically prepackaged curriculum materials often require a particular set of new skills to enable their operation. Thus, as teachers are being technically reskilled, so they are being ideologically deskilled. Second, there is often a small group of teachers whose skills are enhanced by an imposed curriculum 'innovation' which may have a tendency to deskill their colleagues. These may be teachers who have been chosen to be part of the curriculum development process of a centrally determined initiative, or who have been appointed as advisors to other teachers in the implementation process.

Another effect of control is the *intensification* of work, which some scholars maintain is one of the most tangible ways in which the work privileges of educational workers are eroded (Apple, 1986; Ball, 1988). In the search for efficiency, and as an outcome of various control measures, teachers are expected to do more with the same, or in many cases diminishing, resources. Intensification of work has a range of effects which includes preventing teachers from keeping up with their field, thus forcing them to rely even more heavily on ideas and processes provided by experts, and destroying the sociability of school staff: 'Leisure and self-direction tend to be lost. Community tends to be redefined around the needs of the labour process. And, since both time and interaction are at a premium, the risk of isolation grows' (Apple, 1986, p. 43).

Intensification of work does not necessarily reduce teachers' skills. Indeed when it is associated with cost cutting it may mean picking up skills in order to do work that was previously undertaken by teachers who, for example, have accepted early retirement and have not been replaced. However, these additional skills are bought at a cost. It can result in a form of intellectual deskilling which cuts off teachers from their own fields, simply because they haven't got the time to keep up (Apple and Teitelbaum, 1986). All of this can reduce the quality, not the quantity, of the service provided. Apple (1986) uses the results of ethnographic studies on teachers to show that the influx of behavioural, objectives-driven curricular packages quite visibly intensifies teachers' work. The associated administrative arrangements, such as constant grading and record keeping, forces teachers to work through their lunch hours, and adds many hours of extra night-time work.

Apple (1986) also points to the gendered nature of intensification. Women teachers often work in two sites – the school and home. When their work is intensified at school, what happens to their domestic labour at home? It could mean that other family members start to bear a greater burden, and this might result in a redefinition of the sexual division of labour in the domestic sphere. On the other hand, and the evidence suggests that this is the case, women might be expected to cope with the increased workload at school without any recasting of their role at home. Whatever happens, the result will be tensions, conflicts and disruptions at home. Thus what happens in the labour process in one site needs to be understood in relation to the other sites in the lifeworld.

A further effect of control is the impact on teacher morale. This includes a diminishing sense of autonomy or control over the direction of their work. A recent Australian Teaching Council Report which sought the views of teachers found a sense of frustration about the contradictions between talk of teachers as professionals, and the interventions into their work:

> Increasingly in all systems, but especially in the state system, teachers feel as though they have to do what they are told (new national curriculum, changing methods of assessment etc.) and that this is in conflict with the image of a professional body.
>
> (ATC, 1995, p. 12)

And, in a British study of about 100 teachers, Buswell (1980) found that work controls alienated teachers and that this led to low morale and a lack of commitment to the organization, which resulted in management attempting to exert more control – a response which simply exacerbated the problem.

In addition to the material effects on teachers there are a number of ideological effects. When control systems work – that is when teachers do what is expected of them either because they want to or because they have to – then they have the effect of reaffirming, and so reproducing, the structures and hegemonic ideologies that shaped them in the first place. An example of this is the way in which technical control can serve to reaffirm a particular construction of professionalism. Many of the so-called 'teacher-proof' packages are not only based on a very individualistic notion of student learning, they also presume individual teachers working in isolated classrooms with a group of students. Thus technical control of the curriculum and the intensification that often accompanies its use, combine to reaffirm the 'privatism of teaching' (e.g. McTaggart, 1989), or to entrap teachers 'within the culture of individualism' (Hargreaves and Dawe, 1989, p. 5). Since everything is spelt out before execution, there need only be minimal contact among teachers. Once again, the philosophy of individualism is privileged over any notion of collaboration, so reproducing an ideology of professionalism constructed as autonomous individuals operating independently of one another. In so doing it strikes at the heart of collectivity which is the basis of successful unionism. Densmore describes it in this way:

> the ideology of professionalism prevents teachers from recognising that their problems are shared by many other teachers and other workers; consequently they tend to view failures and problems in personal terms and do not seek social or institutional structural change.
>
> (1987, p. 155)

The political effects

While it is important to ensure that teachers are not constructed as being helpless in the face of overwhelming control systems, the antidote to this should not be to propose a simple control-resistance dichotomy. The reality is far more complex than this. Teachers do resist controls, both individually and collectively and in a variety of ways. A detailed understanding of resistance can only occur when the study is situated in a specific time and place. But some general patterns can be discerned from the literature. These relate to informal individual resistances in single school settings, and to more formal collective union action across an education system.

A number of scholars (e.g. Wolcott, 1977; Apple, 1982, 1986; Broadfoot et al., 1988; Woods, 1995) use ethnographic studies to show that when teachers are uneasy about or are opposed to, the form and substance of externally imposed 'reforms', they subvert them passively and/or actively in a range of ways. These include ignoring them, recasting them to more closely fit the philosophy of the teacher, just using those aspects considered to be useful, or simply refusing to comply. Perrenoud summarizes these disparate responses nicely when he writes:

> Like soldiers in armies the world over…teachers make the best of a bad job, ride out the storm, laugh things off in self-defence, complain behind the scenes, wait for the minister of education to change or 'calm-down', for the authorities to forget their own decisions or for the experts to repudiate their idols; they are cunning, they conceal what they are doing by working alone behind closed doors, and those supposed to

inspect their work may turn a blind eye. They do not ask to be entirely independent; it is enough to be able to bend the rules.

(1996, p. 516)

Given that what makes up the formal curriculum (e.g. content, assessment and method) is a site of contest and is ultimately determined at the level of classroom practice, it comes as no surprise that the results of so many of the evaluations of externally developed curriculum 'innovations' should indicate a lack of take-up. Teachers have always used the contradictions and spaces that exist in the controls that confront them, to pursue a course that they believe is in the long-term best interests of the students in their care. There is a complex interplay between the beliefs and practices of teachers, and the material and ideological structures of control that seek to shape these beliefs and actual practices in ways that match the ethos of the prevailing educational settlement. The state is not always successful.

At the same time, such resistances should not be romanticized. The resources of the state, its position as an employer, and the ambivalent class position of teachers, mean that resistance at the individual and local level can also have contradictory results. While there may be local victories, individual resistance is often short term because it focuses on the products of control regimes rather than the structures that create them. Thus, classroom-based teacher resistance may reduce the 'effectiveness' of a specific innovation, but in the end this is only tinkering with the detail. What it leaves untouched is the management power and prerogative that structured and imposed the innovation in the first place.

But resistance to control also occurs in a collective across-system sense through teacher unions, and in terms of the labour process this has been a neglected field of study. Once again it is dangerous to generalize, because the extent of teacher involvement, the nature of union activity, and whether union action results in accommodation or challenge to the system, depends so much on the political, social and historical context. Grace (1978) argues from his British study that teachers cannot be treated as a homogeneous whole. Some teachers construct a politicized view of their role as teacher, as one of challenging the dominant order. The vast majority of teachers hold a depoliticized view and look to the union only to protect their job autonomy and conditions, and to fight for higher wages. Clearly, the impact of control on the labour process is crucial here. Ideological control for example, can have a powerful effect on whether or not teachers identify with unionism: the ideology of professionalism has served in the past to distance teachers from union involvement, and from the broader trade union or working-class political movement.

Finally, control regimes also serve to shape the identities of educators and this, in turn, has political effects. For example, the interaction of market forces, corporate managerialism, and the decentralization/recentralization phenomenon of the 'self-managing' school which characterizes contemporary education policy, has at least two major outcomes: by establishing different sets of interests, it separates teachers from principals, and it divides educators against one another. Thus, the role of principal *vis-à-vis* teacher is changing from that of educational leader, professional colleague, curriculum leader and fellow unionist, to that of employer, entrepreneur, business manager and line manager. This has a number of political effects, not the least of which is to hamper the possibility of principals and teachers coexisting in the same union, let alone acting collectively in the industrial arena (Reid, 1998). And current policy approaches are also creating divisions *within* these groups. Thus, in a marketized education system, principals are divided against each other as they seek to grab a share of the same education market. Similarly, as teachers compete for the increasing number of tenured promotion positions, as contract and casual teacher numbers increase, and as it becomes evermore likely that in a devolved system schools will scramble for the 'best' teachers, so are teachers being set up against one another through the creation of different sets of interests.

Signposts for a Labour Process Theory of Teaching

So far we have resisted tackling the issue for which the labour process literature in education has been most renowned: that of the proletarianization of teachers. But it can be delayed no longer. The process of review and theory building in this chapter has suggested an approach to the issue, and addressing it now will also serve to summarize the major points of this chapter. Ozga and Lawn define proletarianization as: 'the process whereby the worker is forced into a closer relationship with capital, which removes the skill (the conception and execution of work) and therefore the relative autonomy of the worker' (1981, p. 124).

Within the literature on the labour processes of teaching, although most scholars are sympathetic to the concept, there are divisions of opinion about the extent to which it is an inevitable process. Some scholars insist that it does not occur at all (Lauder and Yee, 1987); some argue that proletarianization of teaching is already well advanced (Harris, 1990b); some suggest that teachers may become partially but not fully proletarianized (Densmore, 1987); some maintain that there is a very strong tendency for teachers' work to be proletarianized (Apple, 1986, 1993a); and some aver that the process is not inevitable but contested (Lawn and Ozga, 1988).

It should be clear by now from the review and analysis in this chapter, that we believe that there are problems with each of these positions, although if pressed we would side with the last. However, in our view the focus on proletarianization has, in relation to labour process theory, set the hounds off hunting to the wrong scent. It has caused scholars to look for evidence of outcomes of work organization and control in the contemporary educational setting. The implicit assumption has been that if proletarianization is an inexorable trend, then its impact should be showing up now in the work of contemporary teachers. By contrast, we have argued that a study of the labour process of teachers should start with an assumption about control, rather than about proletarianization. This starting point suggests a different set of questions. It leads us back to the purpose for which control is exercised, thus revealing that it is the curriculum that lies at the heart of the labour process of teaching. From this simple truth flow a number of significant insights. One of the most important is that the object of teachers' labour process is the result of a political process which involves a lot of groups both inside and outside schools.

The curriculum is not a static object: it is a social construction over which there is fierce contestation. It should be expected that those who are successful in shaping the nature of the curriculum will not want to stop at defining what it should look like. They will want to ensure that it is implemented, and implemented well. They will expect that the state, as the employer of those who will do the implementing, will ensure that this happens. This is the genesis of control of teachers. Clearly the forms of control will depend upon such factors as the nature of the educational settlement, the degree of likely support or opposition from teachers for the curriculum, and previous experiences with control strategies. Sometimes control will be direct, at other times it will emphasize consent. It involves both material and discursive practices. Control will always have an effect, but the effect will be variable. The point is that these things will be specific to a historical moment. There is no inexorable trend to proletarianize teachers' work. Teachers are, and always have been, controlled. Instead of asking the question: Are teachers being proletarianized? we should be asking: How are teachers being controlled currently, and what effect are the controls having on their work?

This returns us to the start of the chapter where we argued that labour process theory offered a powerful lens into the nature of the problems besetting teachers in many countries. What we have tried to do in this chapter is to demonstrate that how teachers experience their work is determined largely by the way in which that work is organized. This makes the labour process a key to understanding the difficulties in teaching outlined in the first chapter of this book. In a capitalist society, there are certain imperatives in relation to the role of education, and the state must supervise the implementation of these. The organization of the labour process of teachers is the major way by which this occurs.

In this chapter we have developed a labour process theory of teaching which addresses the arguments that have been used to dismiss the labour process as a serious area of study. This theory acknowledges that the experience of work is shaped by both material and discursive practices, and that the forms of control, and its effects, are different depending upon the educational sites in which they occur. That is, labour process theory does not have to become a theoretical strait-jacket. It is eminently suited to picking up on the nuances of educational practice. Indeed, it can only really be understood through detailed ethnographic analyses, at the level of individual school sites, which seek to trace how control is played out at the local level at specific historical moments. That is why in this book we focus on studies in two schools. However, the detail of each of these studies is not treated as though it occupies an independent trajectory. We have argued that there are imperatives for control built into the very fabric of the structures and practices of our education systems. Labour process theory helps us to make sense of what is happening to teachers' work and why.

A labour process analysis of teachers' work is not just an academic exercise. It has a political purpose because it can inform the sorts of political strategies that teachers might adopt in order to resist control of their work. Political action to give teachers greater control of the curriculum must be informed by a deep understanding of why, how, and with what effects controls are imposed. Labour process theory has always been central to such understanding, and never more so than now.

3   The Critical Case Study Method

Introduction to the Nature of Critical Research

The way in which we seek to understand the crisis in teachers' work in this book is through Lather's (1986) notion of 'dialectical theory building', drawing on the approaches of critical ethnography that are given expression here in 'critical storied accounts' of teachers' work. We believe that the idea of dialectical theory building can best be pursued through a stereoscopic view of the relationship between labour process theory and the ideas of critical ethnography. The analysis of teaching needs to start out with the question of how teachers are being controlled (technically, bureaucratically and ideologically), as alluded to in Chapter 2. To fully understand the nature of the educational practices arrived at in different educational sites, requires a research methodology capable of providing depth as well as solidity. The idea of pursuing how the work of teaching is being reshaped, in a context of acknowledging the importance of accessing wider sets of social and political forces, has a good deal of methodological appeal to us.

As we indicated in the previous chapter, we have chosen to do this using labour process theory as the arch between the broader structural issues of what is happening in the global economy, and how we can make sense of the crisis in teachers' work from within the two case studies to be presented in Chapters 4 and 5.

It is important, however, that the style of research employed in the critical storied accounts used in this book are clearly spelt out at the beginning.

There are frequently misconceptions as to what constitutes critical research; for example, that its emphasis is negative or carping, or that it is somehow committed to fault-finding. Readings like this reveal that those making them have not read themselves into the meaning of 'critical' as expressed in the sociological literature.

One of the more concise straightforward explanations of what it means to operate critically, has been provided by Robert Cox (1980), when he said: '[To be critical is to] stand apart from the prevailing order of the world and ask how that order came about' (p. 129). Cox argues that the place of theory is neither incidental nor unimportant in this, and that theory can be regarded as serving two possible purposes. The first view of theory is that it is a guide to help solve problems posed within a particular perspective. This view of theory 'takes the world as it finds it...with the prevailing social and power relations and institutions into which they are organised, as the given framework for action' (p. 128). The second set of views about theory, is that its purpose is to 'open up the possibility of choosing a different valid perspective from which the problematic becomes one of creating an alternative world' (p. 128). Depending upon which purpose we opt for, theory will have quite a different meaning. While for both approaches the starting point is some aspect or instance of human activity, the orientation to the relationship between the parts and the whole is quite different in each case. From a problem-solving perspective, the approach is one that 'leads to a further analytical sub-division and limitation of the issues to be dealt with...' (p. 129). In the case of critical theory, the approach is one which 'leads towards the construction of a larger picture of the whole of which the initially contemplated part is just one component, and seeks to understand the processes of change in which both parts and whole are involved' (Cox, 1980, p. 129). This is a distinction which is fundamental to the case studies contained in the next section of this book.

'Dialectical theory-building' (Lather, 1986) is a heuristic through which data constructed in context are used to clarify and reconstruct existing theory. At the same time, the efficacy of existing theories are challenged as they are subjected to the interrogatory probes of generative themes unearthed from the everyday experiences of those whose lives are being investigated. What is being attempted is the continual modification of existing theoretical constructs to reveal 'counter interpretations' (Lather, 1986, p. 267) through a more intimate understanding of the views of participants. At the same time, sedimented layers of meaning and understanding are being uncovered about the complexities of the lives contained in the interview conversations. In the case of teachers, this means theoretical vantage points are used to sculpt interpretations out of complex verbal accounts given by teachers as to what is happening to their work. The following extended quote from Shacklock and Smyth (1998, pp. 3–4) gives further insights into the complexity of what is being attempted:

> Another way of speaking about this is in terms of the dialectical relationship between particular instances, concrete empirical relations, abstract core concepts, and structure and history. Harvey (1990) speaks about critical research as cutting through 'surface appearances' (p. 19) by locating the issues being investigated in their historical and structural contexts. Critical research, as Harvey argues, continually engages in an ongoing conversation, analysis and critique of these elements, starting from the position that the object of study is not ' "objective" social appearances' (p. 19). Phenomena, from a critical vantage point, are not

considered to stand on their own but are implicated, embedded and located in wider contexts that are not entirely innocent. Furthermore, such structures are 'maintained through the exercise of political and economic power' which is 'legitimated through ideology' (Harvey, 1990, p. 19). Research of this kind raises serious questions about 'who can speak?'

(Roof and Wiegman, 1995)

Critical research then, is centrally concerned with the simultaneous process of 'deconstruction' and 'reconstruction'. It works something like this. Within a piece of research, some core abstract concepts are located which are considered to be central; they are used repeatedly to interrogate situations of concrete lived reality in order to develop a new synthesis. In this sense, theory is not, therefore, simply 'abstract analysis' nor is it something merely to be tacked on to data at the end of some process of analysis; rather, what occurs is a theory-building process involving:

a constant shuttling backwards and forwards between abstract concept and concrete data; between social totalities and particular phenomena; between current structures and historical development; between surface appearance and essence; between reflection and practice.

(Harvey, 1990, p. 29)

The intent is to engage in a constant questioning and building up of theory and interpretations through repeated ongoing analysis until a coherent alternative reconstruction of the account is created. As Harvey (1990) notes, the selection of a 'core' concept is not a final or a single instance; 'it only emerges in the course of the analysis...and it is only "correct" in the sense that it provides...the best focus [at that time]' (p. 30). In many respects, this genre of research is conversational in that there is constant dialogue between core concepts and data about fieldwork situations. It amounts to a kind of 'negotiating the question' (Roof and Wiegman, 1995, p. x) in that what is worthwhile saying or pursuing can never be stated definitively, but only as a consequence of having commenced some enquiry, discussion or conversation. It is very much a case of 'conversation begins in response, not in a speaker's singular assertion' (Roof and Wiegman, 1995, p. x).

Some of the more specific issues to be addressed about this methodology in relation to the two case studies are:

1   What is critical ethnography as a research method?
2   How does it fit with critical, narrative, portrayal, work-storied approaches?
3   Why is critical ethnography appropriate in these settings?
4   Whose voices are heard?

Figure 3.1   Dialectical theory building

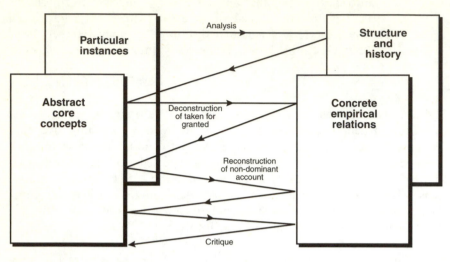

Source: Based on Harvey (1990)

The research process we have developed for ourselves in this book is one that starts out with 'broad structural issues' that focus on globalization and the effect this is having on the nature of work considered from the vantage point of labour process theory. We then narrow the analysis down to two particular instances, and finally revisit the case studies with a view to:

1   explaining what is happening to teachers' work in light of the case studies;
2   commenting on how globalization appears to be operating;
3   examining the nature of the relationship between globalization and the labour process; and finally,
4   exploring the nature of a more democratic imagining of a socially just school operating within a state controlled education system.

In simplified terms, there is a kind of 'hourglass' structure: starting out broadly, narrowing the focus through two case studies, and then extrapolating the understandings to broader settings to which our analysis might be related.

In terms of the actual study: the 'abstract core concepts' being interrogated, constructed and reconstructed are those of labour process theory along with the history, structure and relationship of work to the state (described in Chapter 2); the 'concrete empirical relations' are embodied in the contemporary work experiences of the forces operating to produce the crisis in teachers' work (described in Chapter 1); the 'particular instances' are the cases of Gallipoli High School (Chapter 4) and Appleton College

Figure 3.2   Dialectical theory building – making sense of teachers' work

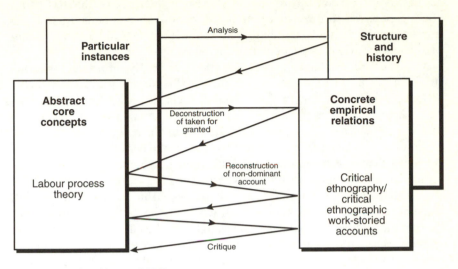

Source: Based on Harvey (1990)

(Chapter 5); both of which are described in terms of the critical ethnography and critical ethnographic work-storied design (described in this chapter).

Our thesis is that we can only begin to make sense of the ideas of globalization by focusing on the way structure, agency and history operate within teaching, and that in turn, these operate on and work to shape and resuscitate the core concepts of labour process theory, in a context of informing and explaining how schools and teachers accommodate to and resist the crisis in their work.

We describe the case studies in Chapters 4 and 5 with each case study being captured by slightly different means, so that we need to give something of the distinctiveness of each. It is worth noting that both employed critical ethnographic approaches, so while we deal with the general features of this kind of research in the case of Gallipoli High School we will not repeat ourselves but refer to some of the more idiosyncratic aspects when dealing with Appleton College.

Critical Ethnography

The case of Gallipoli High School was a critical ethnography, and its features included: the location of the researcher in the setting, and the collection of data through various forms of observation while recording the perceptions of the informants. Critical ethnographies usually, but not always, focus on the lives of ordinary people, and seek 'emancipatory knowledge' (Lather, 1986) while disavowing 'value neutral' orientations of science. Apple (1996b) says: 'For some current interpreters, this has had a chilling effect on those sociologists of education whose major interest was not a generalizable understanding of all schools but instead the development of thick descriptions of particularities' (p. 126).

Critical theories claim that people's lives are deeply influenced by structural forces outside the research setting, with life situations often being influenced by perceptions which entrench them in positions of powerlessness. Critical researchers acknowledge that their existing theories will have an overt influence on the course and outcome of the research, but that these are not likely to be uniform or static throughout the period of the research.

The critical researcher, therefore, looks beyond an analysis of the setting – founded purely on observation and records of the localized perceptions of the participants – to a perspective that is founded in an (avowedly partial) discussion of the historical forces at work in the setting. Analysis thus becomes a creative act, with the researcher and their theoretical constructs being the primary research tool. Critical ethnographers do not attempt to eliminate the effect of their own presence on the data or on the research setting, but are clear that they are part of the social world under study. They also acknowledge that outside 'macro-structural' forces have an influence on shaping the research setting even through the most commonplace and common-sense acts. The researcher and the informants work together, through a process of dialogue, towards an awareness of the contradictions hidden or distorted by everyday or common-sense understandings. Not surprisingly, critical ethnography is vulnerable to criticism for generating theories distorted by the a priori political biases of the researcher, theories that provide no basis for empirical accountability or validity.

This element of theory generation in critical ethnography has been caricatured by critics as a process of pouring the data into a theoretical mould shaped by the researcher's biases. A research programme founded on such an overt value base must, it is argued, be overtly subjective and non-scientific. Overtly partial research, it is argued, leads to circular and internally reinforcing logic where data collection and analysis conforms to a preordinate theoretical position. While these reservations may, in part, be based on a positivist notion of value-free science, the critical researcher needs to take steps to ensure that he or she does not only find what he or she is looking for. The need for reinterpretation and questioning of existing theory is sharpened further by the likelihood that the theoretical constructs of the researcher are in themselves partially a consequence of the researcher's *own* false consciousness. The challenge for the critical ethnographer, then, is to reveal the influences and patterns impacting on and constraining the perceptions and intentions of the actors in the setting, while simultaneously avoiding imposition of his or her own theoretical constructs, and engaging with the participants in open-ended theory building and renovation. This is a condition known as reflexivity.

The term 'reflexivity' (Lather, 1986; Anderson, 1989; Denscombe, 1995) is used by interpretivist ethnographers to describe the researcher's reflection on the relationship between the theory and the data, the effects of the researcher's presence on the data collected, and the nature of the organizational structures and cultures that provide explicit or implicit ground rules for determining what information and ideas are relevant (Whyte et al., 1991). For the critical ethnographer, reflexivity also extends to reflection on their own biases, and an examination of the 'dialectal relationship between structural/historical forces and human agency' (Anderson, 1989, p. 254). Theory building neither precedes nor follows data collection, and the process is steeped with inbuilt tensions between the need to respect the theories of the actors in the setting, and the critical awareness of the influence of the societal structures which help shape those theories.

There are no recipes or checklists for being reflexive. However, reflexivity is central to establishing the validity and trustworthiness of critical ethnography as a research method. The act of reflexively generating open-ended, valid and useful theory is a dialogic and dialectic process, encouraging open and reciprocal dialogue between actors and researcher. The process must ensure that participants in the research are able to challenge the assumptions and biases of the researcher. This reciprocity is more likely where:

1   interviews occur more than once, and in the context of other opportunities to build a relationship with the participant (Oakley, 1981);
2   the researcher shares his/her views, theories and opinions, and encourages the individuals and groups participating in the interview to ask questions and challenge the assumptions of the researcher as well as providing information;
3   the informants are provided with transcripts of discussion, and work with the researcher in the generation of empirically grounded theory.

The principle of reflexivity extends to the generation of theory. While the process of dialogue and dialectic negotiation of meaning is central to the theory-creation process, the theory generated by the process, if it is to achieve its emancipatory (Habermas, 1971) purpose, must evoke recognition and response. This has be described as a 'Yes, of course' response, where people 'click' with the sense of the contradiction in their lives (Lather, 1986). Readers should be able to recognize in the analysis of the data similarity with their own situation, and feel kinship with the emergent theory.

Valid theory will be built on: (1) a recognizable understanding of the world of the participants; (2) descriptions of the daily reality of the setting and the reciprocal perceptions of that reality of the researcher and the people in the setting; and, (3) the outcomes of dialectic discussions about the researcher's and participants' view of the forces constraining people in the setting.

An avowedly partial (Levinson, 1993) ethnographic approach such as critical ethnography does not lend itself to value-free validation, assuming that such a thing were possible. 'Triangulation' (meaning here the development of data and theory with a number of participants in the setting), 'member checks' (participant responses to the emerging theory in an environment which encourages dissent), and the generation of 'contrast data', are employed to encourage the emergence of perspectives which are both supportive of and counter to the emerging theory.

The researcher needs to be able to demonstrate validity by establishing the ways in which the theory is based in the data, and to chart the progress of the change and development of the perspectives of the researcher and the participants through the dialogic processes. The considered perceptions of the participants themselves, called by Lather (1986) 'face validity', where the participants experience a 'yes, of course' rather than a 'yes, but' response to the analysis, is also a test of validity. Donmoyer's (1990) argument makes sense of the commonplace visceral 'Yes, of course' response that many people have while reading about other people's experiences, and he provides a useful perspective on one of the key claims of single setting ethnographies, that they provide a vehicle whereby readers can meaningfully integrate the experiences of others. However, only to interpret the research narrative or report in terms of the psychological schema of the individual parallels the central inadequacy of the interpretivist research paradigm where perception and meaning are explained in terms purely of their setting, and the influences of wider social structures are ignored. For the interpretation of the report to be grounded in criteria for judgement about its validity, the vicarious experience of the reader needs also to be informed by an understanding of the broader dialectal relationships between structural forces and human agency at work in the setting.

At the same time, the adoption of the designation 'critical ethnography' is no guarantee in itself of the appropriateness of the method to the particular setting. Lather (1986) has pointed out the danger of the imposition by researchers of theory-driven and abstract frameworks being imposed on the research participants. Anderson (1989) has warned of critical analysis becoming overly negative, with analysis of the influence of structural forces leading to the view that nothing can be done at the local level until the structures change.

It is clear that the researcher's and participants' approaches to the collection of data and the development of theory are the points at which issues of validity are most sharply focused. While the researcher enters the setting with explanations of the social world and of the influence of social forces, they recognize that they do not have a monopoly to generate the 'correct' interpretations. In fact, the familiarity of the workers with the setting (based on intimate association with the organization over time), is likely to be considerably more advanced than that of the researcher. Empowering data collection and democratic theory building processes have much to offer this ethnography, particularly the emphasis on the learning of all the participants through dialogic interaction, the sharing of power and responsibility between researcher and researched, and the creation of new possibilities for emancipatory action.

The critical perspective of the outside researcher is central to the process, in order that there be sufficient explicit understanding of the conditions in which teachers and researchers work, and that collaborative reform efforts do not simply reproduce the inequalities which currently prohibit serious educational change (Ladwig, 1991). If the perspectives of the people in the setting alone were sufficient, notes Grossi (1981, p. 46): 'we would not need either adult education, nor activists…(and we would deny) the very existence and efficiency of the whole ideological apparatus set up by the hegemonic sectors'.

In both the cases described in this volume, the research projects were founded on the involvement of the people in the setting in theory building, rather than their passive participation within a framework composed by the researcher.

In the case of Gallipoli, a fairly well-defined research process was followed (described below) and while a preordained, staged schedule for research might appear to be in conflict with that principle, it was modified as the research proceeded.

In pursuing critical ethnography Carspecken and Apple (1992) suggest a number of stages:

Stage one. Weak-interactive data collection (observation and 'shallow' interviewing).

This stage of the research, the 'monological' data collection phase involved collection of data from the participants with minimal interference on the part of the researcher, employing 'shallow' interviews with the participants, observation, and establishment of low-inference observation notes. 'Shallow' interviews focused mainly on basic descriptive information about the participants and their routines, and observation of the social life of the group and the school. Observation notes avoided inference or supposition about the subjective states of the participants, intersubjective states of group members, or cultural or group norms. Interviews were recorded and supplemented by hand-written notes.

Carspecken (Carspecken and Apple, 1992) argues that premature analytical dialogue with participants could 'change the routine behaviours of interest to the ethnographer' (p. 1). This caveat was moderated in the interests of the overarching need to establish the high levels of equality, empathy, trust and understanding needed for researchers and participants to navigate the potentially conflictual and uncertain stages three and beyond.

Dialogic analysis of norms, intersubjective and subjective states required high levels of self-exploration and revelation on the part of the participants, and concomitance on the part of the researcher was necessary for the process to be more than superficial. In a practical sense, this meant that inchoate and impressionistic analyses were not conveyed to participants during stage one.

Stage two. Preliminary reconstructive analysis.

Following transcription of the stage one interview and observation notes and audio-tapes, initial analysis took the form of:

1   provisional coding of participant theories and behaviour illustrated in the transcriptions that occur repeatedly throughout the set of field data compiled in the study thus far;
2   notes of possible meanings, writing them within the field notes as they occur;
3   reconstructions of normative factors which make these meanings possible; and,
4   speculations about the subjective states of the individuals under study.

This step involved the writing of speculative comments in the field notes. As Carspecken and Apple (1992) put it:

> Social acts carry meaning only because they referenced unstated, background sets of rules…and assumptions. These implicitly referenced rules and assumptions make it possible for the actor, the people acted toward, and all people observing the interaction to interpret or 'read' various meanings from the act. Understanding meaning, then, involves taking first-, second-, and third-person positions with respect to an act, and this can be done only with reference to certain norms assumed to be in play.
>
> (p. 519)

This meant an interpretation of events and speech acts in terms of norms of the 'normative *realm*'. Elements of the normative realm might be 'authority relationship', 'identity', 'setting'. Validity of the normative reconstruction was assessed by later member checks, and the process lead to dialogue which informed further reconstructive analysis.

Stage three. Strong interactive data collection.

This stage took the form of indepth interview and group discussion, after sharing with participants written copies of the analysis developed in stage two. During this stage the dialogic proceedings were recorded which informed both the preliminary reconstructive analyses stage and prefigured the exploration and explanation of system relationships in stages four and five.

Carspecken and Apple (1992) posit that stage three is definitional to the research process as 'critical' ethnography, as 'it allows the people under study some control over the research process, yielding a more democratic form of knowledge production'. They point out that:

> (d)ialogical methods are empowering to the groups being studied. Since articulating formerly tacit conditions helps one distance one's identity from the structures within which it is frequently embedded, this method can be empowering to the subjects of study, and it can change the ways in which they routinely act.
>
> (p. 531)

This stage facilitated the practical requirements to complete the normative reconstructions of the previous stage of developing 'contrast data' and discovering 'normative structure' (sets of norms that operate in any social act). The researcher and participants created a new normative order during which participants could enact changed identities and develop new norms. These new identities and norms created the conditions within which groups and individuals might express themselves in ways which contrast to those of other situations where they felt constrained. Both the significance of the new data and the nature of the normative order that emerged within the indepth interview or group discussion provided contrasts which helped to understand the norms at work in the daily working environment.

Stage four. Empirical exploration of system relationships.

Whereas the first three stages of the research were primarily concerned with the immediate working world of the teachers involved in the research, stages four and five were concerned with the distinction between 'lifeworld' and 'reason' (Habermas, 1976) or social and system integration. 'Social integration refers to the coordination of action in face-to-face settings, whereas system integration refers to the investigation of relationships between social sites and social groups' (Carspecken and Apple, 1992, p. 535). Giddens (1979) describes a 'homeostatic system' as one which emerges from the behaviour and action of the social actors, which result in a number of unintended effects. System relationships can be mediated through broader cultural forces, such as the official culture and the electronic media. The key distinction between social and system integration is a recognition and an understanding of themes operating across sites.

Stage five. Explanatory use of system relationships.

Recognizing that workplace phenomena are embedded in and given meaning by social relations, stage five has two main analytical purposes. The first is to identify and describe the broader 'interests' (discussed further below) that impact on the work of the teachers at Gallipoli High School, and in particular the ways in which the workplace culture intersects with external forces. Carspecken and Apple (1992) assert that:

> (w)hat (is significant) is the relationship between social constructions and the ability of some groups to enhance their own authority, to regulate others, and to control the social space for their own benefit. Culture and power, then, are not part of different language games but, rather, form an indissoluble couplet in daily life.

> (p. 508)

In this sense interests are defined here as 'the socially constructed means through which (subjective) needs and desires are pursued or secured' (Carspecken and Apple, 1992), and tend towards the satisfaction of objective requirements for survival, whereas workplace culture is largely formed as a result of the ways in which group members actually respond to these interests.

Whose voices, therefore, were heard? The central participants in the research were the classroom teachers who attended junior school meetings at Gallipoli High School. A close relationship was developed with this group over the course of the research. Their labour process formed the nucleus of the local data, and they were the main contributors to the development of theory through dialogue. In order to understand the influence of school-level policy making and leadership on the team and on the development of collaboration in the school, interviews were also conducted with the school principal and deputy. Originally all data from interview tapes were transcribed and encoded as described in stage one of the five stage process, using a modification of the process described by Mishler (1986, pp. 36–7). Participants were identified initially by pseudonym, and non-lexical expressions were approximated phonetically. Particular attention was paid to discrepancies and contrasting perspectives as possible indicators of the participant's deeper awareness of the contradictions in their working life. In the third stage, dialogic reflection on the original data took place through roundtable group discussions (Whyte et al., 1991).

Critically Ethnographic Work-Storied Account

In Appleton College a work-story design was used in which teachers were prepared to talk in unstructured conversational style (Burgess, 1988), about the nature of their work and how it has changed. This study was ethnographic because of the acceptance of an ontological position which recognizes that social life in the school is constructed around the actions and interactions of teachers, parents, pupils and administrators whose behaviour can be understood in terms of their intentions, motives, and reasons; and an epistemological position where knowledge of the social world of the school is obtained from investigation of the intersubjective nature of being and acting in that educational site. It is through the description of the events, and the explication of interpretations that are used to make (rational) connective relations between events, which makes this case an ethnographic account.

The research in this instance was conducted in the natural setting of the school (Appleton College) and it can be considered as an 'insider' (Smetherham, 1978) account due to the researcher having been a colleague of all participants, most immediately, in the second semester of the previous year. It was not, however, a case of 'going native' in the sense that the site was not 'anthropologically strange' to the researcher – it had been, and remained, familiar territory – and the researcher was not engaged in any teaching work, as part of the teaching culture of the school, in the year in which the research was undertaken. (In some respects, the desire to portray the 'unexpected and the significant' in a montage of teaching work as 'an ethnographic display' may qualify the final account as 'ethnographically surreal' (Clifford, 1981).

Methodologically, the primary source of data collection was through interview. These were formally scheduled in the sense that they were pre-arranged for a (mutually) suitable time and location, and because participants had been informed of the general flavour of the focus for the interview. Other data was obtained through notes made from informal discussions with participants, and from school documents including newsletters and memorandums to staff.

Interviews had a focus but were unstructured in the sense that there were no set questions and no two interviews covered the exact same ground. Interviews were more like conversations along the lines suggested by Woods (1985), Mishler (1986), Burgess (1988) and Eisner (1991). The interaction between researcher and participant was more like a conversation between peers without any obvious hierarchical relationship, control of agenda, strict interviewer silence, exchange of viewpoint (Oakley, 1981; Platt, 1981) and so is regarded as 'conversations with a purpose' rather than the formalized 'sanitized interviews' (Burgess, 1988, p. 153) of a more structured kind.

In this case there has been no 'grounded theorising' (Glaser and Strauss, 1967) method employed, yet there has been an attempt to get beneath surface behaviours to a deeper structure (Deetz and Kersten, 1983), to capture the essence of what drives the social relationships and the work patterns articulated and described. Interviews were viewed as a source of data for the documentation of aspects of the lives of particular teachers in a specific setting. Theoretical concepts were employed in the interpretations made in the written account produced from the assembled data. It is not seen as being generalizable beyond the limited 'thematic' sense (Eisner, 1991), or the 'aesthetical' sense (Garman, 1994a), which can occur in such cases.

It is storied data because 'it is rich with threads of time, place, character' (Witherell and Noddings, 1991, p. 1) and it is told in the teachers' voice. The interview transcripts are rich in detail about what it is like to be engaged in the work of teaching: the tasks, the demands, the interactions, the feelings, and the complexity. It is told using the words, metaphors, and conceptual frames that teachers like to use when they talk about their work. It is told in 'teacher-speak', the shared language which teachers use to share, and make sense of, the common experiences from the work of teaching (Nias, 1989, p. 58). It is a narration of the experience of being a teacher, of working in a school, of being a professional, and of co-existing in a world of work with pupils, colleagues, and administrators. The stories of work are told in a teacher's voice which has the multi-tonal character of reflection, hope, humour, anger and despair. The 'feel' of working as a teacher comes across strongly in such stories, like it does in the accounts of teaching assembled by Connell (1985), Nias (1989) and Cortazzi (1991).

It is, therefore, an ethnographic work-story account. It is an insider account, told using the teachers' own voices, of what it is like to do the work of teaching at Appleton College. Work-stories are used by teachers to convey to their colleagues something important about the nature of the work of teaching which they wish to share or make public. Kainan (1992) suggests that teachers use work-stories to 'create and present common ideas, values and features' (p. 446) about their occupational culture. In this project it is the common features and values about the work of teaching at Appleton College which are exposed in the work-storied portrayal assembled from the research dialogue.

The account of teaching at Appleton College is presented as a narrative assembled from storied data about the work of teaching at that school. The narrative is the construction of the researcher and is a weave of many individual accounts of teaching at the same school. As such, it has a multi-voiced character (Quantz and O'Connor, 1988; Miller, 1990), with the account presented in the researcher's voice, from a database constituted by the individual voices of many teachers. The production of a single research narrative, from a collective source, required translation, an act of genre sensitive connoisseurship (Eisner, 1991, p. 78) with the many voices of the participants, into that of the single voice of the narrating researcher.

Here Eisner's notions of educational connoisseurship and criticism, where the aim is to render expressed experience into expressive language, so as to bring about the critical disclosure of the significant qualities of educational experience, are used by borrowing his use of the terms 'rendering' and 'portrayal'. An attempt is made in the narrative production to 'render' the educational life experiences as told in the work-stories into a written form, as a compilative narrative, which allows the reader to vicariously participate in the working lives of teachers at Appleton College. By rendering the work-stories of many teachers into a single narrative of teaching work, it is hoped that significant aspects or qualities of what it means to teach at Appleton College can be highlighted, through 'work-genre' sensitive connoisseurship, in a way that may not have otherwise occurred. It is about creating a space (Miller, 1990) in the discourse of teachers' work for the teacher's voice to be heard in a storied form.

The narrative, as a portrayal, is the presentation of a written account of what it is like to work as a teacher at Appleton College as told with the disclosure of storied data provided during interview. As a portrayal, it aims to provide illumination of significant features of teaching, as a form of work, insight into patterns of work behaviour and their understanding, and illustration of specific instances of what constitutes the work of teaching at Appleton College. As a portrayal, it aims to present an account which: rings true, hangs together, has depth in reasoning, has relevance for its audience, has vibrancy in its use of language, enriches when read, has been presented honestly and with care, and is recognizable as human experience. These attributes are the criteria of quality, for qualitative research, which Garman (1994b) has called: verity, integrity, rigour, utility, vitality, aesthetics, ethics and verisimilitude.

The account endeavours to place the events and lives portrayed into a socially contextualized frame where the working lives described can be located in a bigger picture of teachers' work, its organization and control, than that of one school. Such a frame allows the political relations and agencies of power operative in the definition of teachers' work to be identified and linked to the constraints which envelop the work practices of individual teachers as described in work-stories. Dominant political and economic ideologies impact upon the development of educational policy and affect: the organization of schools, thinking about what is appropriate in curriculum content, administrative and decision-making structures, and the validation of pedagogical styles. Unravelling the connections between social structures, ideological forces, and the marginalization of teachers as active agents in the definition and control of the work of teaching requires a socially critical view. A socially critical view in research, not only aims to uncover how forms of organization and dominant practices are oppressive, in restricting human agency, but aims to give some hope of how reified social conditions can be dismantled. The narrative account produced in this project sets out to be socially critical and empowering through its capacity for ideology critique, while enriching in its goal of transformative possibility. It is an example of socially responsible narrative, or 'critical storytelling' (Barone, 1992), where the 'values, and interests undergirding certain discourses, practices, and institutional arrangements found in today's schools' are placed under scrutiny (Barone, 1992, p. 143).

4 Teachers' Work in a Post-Fordist Era

The Case of the Teacher-Managers of Gallipoli High School

The central question for the research project described in this chapter related to the ways in which the work of teachers at Gallipoli High School was being affected by recent reforms. Gallipoli High had established a collaborative 'flatter management structure', intended to distribute responsibility and accountability for a range of leadership and administrative practices across the teaching staff. As well, a shifting coalition of teachers was attempting to promote a range of reforms intended to improve the teaching and learning of junior high school students. The proposed reforms were predicated on high levels of collaboration, integration and joint work.

Located in a working-class suburb, Gallipoli High School was opened in the early 1960s. The school fronted narrowly on to a right angle bend in a suburban street, its neighbours on either side being single-story bungalows of the Australian post-war dream. Opposite there was a small grassy reserve with a few trees. The first impression was of institutional greyness, squareness and disciplined regularity, with the only colour provided by the green lawns, the olive foliage of slender pine trees lining the path to the official entrance foyer, and in the background, the great expanse of washed-out sky. The buildings were utilitarian in appearance, the embodiment of the practical educational requirements of the post-war period, the mass provision of secondary education. A state-wide crisis in cyclic maintenance of schools had left the school with a run-down, tatty look, and this had not helped allay community fears that the school was about to close.

Three of the wings of the central building formed a 'U' shape running approximately east to west, with a fourth wing to the east attached by an overhead walkway. In the quadrangle between the three wings of the building was a barren, exposed expanse of asphalt; oriented so that it provided little shelter from the prevailing winds of either summer or winter, and was usually empty except for a few cycle racks. Attached to the outside wall at the end of the south wing, an unpainted metal emergency staircase led down from what was once a first floor resource centre. In places the lower edges of the outer walls were cracking, the cement falling away, and when it rained the gutters overflowed. Some of the gutters had rusted through entirely, and during a rain storm water would cascade down on to the ground next to the building.

The main buildings seemed largely unaltered from their original configuration. On each level an echoing corridor ran the full length of the wing, with a number of identical rooms leading off the corridor. Each room had a single door with a narrow glass pane. From the corridor, this pane afforded a view of the teacher's desk, which was usually placed at the front of the class next to a large, fixed 'sash' type blackboard. To see further into the room without opening the door one had to stand very close to gain a restricted view of the first few rows of desks. The teacher was visible to casual inspection, but the class was not. In this sense, teachers in the older, unrenovated classrooms were able to be observed through a largely unidirectional observation window.

However, in some parts of the school, particularly the renovated east science and computing wing, the glass pane in the door had been replaced with an opaque sheet. In these rooms both the teachers and the classes were invisible. While one should not overliteralize this point, the recent sealing-up of the observation pane in the teacher's door neatly symbolized a theme that became increasingly prominent during the research period, that is, the changing nature of the supervision of teachers' work from the individualizing panopticism (Foucault, 1977; Fraser, 1989) of direct observation through the door, to new forms of self-managing professionalism, where teachers 'internalise the gaze and in effect surveil themselves' (Fraser, 1989, p. 23) and one another. Except where the teachers had made an effort to brighten the rooms with posters or displays of students' work, the teaching space also appeared largely unchanged from the day that the school was built, and were of the same angular, Spartan severity as the outside of the building.

The daily work rhythm of the entire institution was shaped and maintained by the unchanging, routinizing control of the bell and the timetable. When the bell rang for the end of recess (mid-morning break) or lunchtime, teachers – mid-mouthful or mid-sentence – would begin moving towards the corridors, as if drawn by an invisible string. There were many other buildings on the campus, most of an elderly 'temporary' wooden construction – a relic of the school's once high student numbers. With funding formulae attached to student enrolments, maintenance of many of these buildings had clearly been a low priority.

Despite the run-down condition of the school, it was clear that many of the staff had been working to make the inside of the rooms attractive. Budget limitations constantly drew on the goodwill, ingenuity and resourcefulness of the staff, and despite the run-down, unloved look of many of the buildings, there was a sense of energy, regrowth and enthusiasm in the school that shone through the peeling paint and empty buildings. Certainly an impending refurbishment was partly responsible for the optimism, as was the increasing student enrolment, and the growing realization that the school was likely to survive the threat of closure.

In the staffroom, teachers sat in mixed-gender friendship groups at the same table, with a core of each friendship group almost never moving from their accustomed position, while peripheral members sometimes spent time at other tables. The table groups sometimes engaged in spontaneous fun activities, particularly during festive times or towards the end of a term, when the intensity of the final rounds of marking and reporting had receded a little.

At the same time, it was unusual to see much sustained 'play' in the staffroom. Although it provided sanctuary from the pressures of the class-room, any 'work-time' leisure activities were exposed to the judgement and scrutiny of administrators and peers, in the same way that it revealed the diligence of teacher-managers poring over administrative paper-work an hour before their day's teaching was due to begin. In that sense the staffroom remained an important disciplinary space (Foucault, 1977; Pignatelli, 1993), and an arena where staff members' commitment to a regime of self-managing professionalism was displayed for the review of peers and administrators. The demands of the timetable and high teaching loads, compressed time for refreshment, the toilet and so on, into two bustling breaks. This physical and temporal compression contributed to a sense of community and a 'culture of collaboration' (Nias et al., 1989), although 'yard duty' (supervision of the school yard at recess and lunch) and other work-related pressures colonized much of this time, and contributed to what Larson (1980, pp. 105–6) describes as a 'chronic sense of work overload'.

The Curriculum

Gallipoli High School was a comprehensive high school, offering a range of 'vocational' and 'academic' subjects. There were five year levels, years 8–12, with years 8–10 roughly corresponding to the 'compulsory' years of secondary schooling (students 13–15 years of age), and years 11 and 12 with the 'post-compulsory' years – during which students worked towards South Australian Certificate of Education (SACE) Level One and Level Two subjects. SACE scores were employed by the local universities in the alloca-tion of tertiary admission to students. The tertiary institutions, and in particular the elite universities exercised profound influence over the content of senior secondary curriculum and its assessment procedures (Collins, 1993) through the Senior Secondary Assessment Board of South Australia (SSABSA). In turn, the senior curriculum articulated the junior curriculum through implicit and explicit achievement prerequisites.

All schools were required, as a matter of state government policy, to adopt curriculum Statements and Profiles from Reception to Year 10, and high schools were bound by the requirements of the Department for Education and Children's Services (DECS) 'Action Plan for the Middle Schooling Years' (DECS, 1994) which in turn was based on the recommendations of the DECS-sponsored Junior Secondary Review (JSR) (Eyers, 1992).

Thus, the GHS junior school curriculum was being aligned with the eight subject areas of the Statements and Profiles, while simultaneously accommodating the pedagogical and structural implications of the Junior Secondary Review. In practice, the Statements and Profiles were clearly seen to be the immediate priority, and their implementation contributed substantially to the problems the school experienced as it tried to take on board the implications of the JSR. The school's administrators and some of the year level managers wished to establish some work practices in the junior school which could broadly be described as 'collaborative'. Some form of team work among the teaching staff was recommended in the JSR, and was seen to be a possible engine for the collaborative change. The recommendations of the JSR were adopted by the advocates of 'middle schooling' and collaboration as the policy mandate that would provide the springboard into joint work on pedagogy and the curriculum. It was the attempt by a group of staff to develop collaborative work practices that is at the heart of this study, and in particular, the ways that these attempts interacted with a more firmly established local reform of teachers' work – the flatter management structure or FMS.

The 'Flatter Management Structure'

The 'flatter management structure' (FMS) at GHS was central to the administrative strategies for dealing with the challenges facing the school. The FMS created a number of teacher-manager positions that were open to application from all staff on an annual basis. The positions were determined by the school's Personnel Advisory Committee (PAC) and put to the staff for approval, and then filled using a 'merit' process based on a written application. Whereas middle management positions in most other schools were usually filled by substantive 'seniors' and tenured 'coordinators', at GHS *all* staff members were encouraged to apply for FMS positions. This meant that the substantive seniors relinquished their automatic 'rights' to leadership positions, and rank-and-file staff were permitted to compete with them for FMS roles, including the management of 'curriculum areas' (faculties). Teacher-managers appointed under the FMS worked to achieve the outcomes of their job specifications, ostensibly using the non-teaching time that had been provided.

There were a number of official justifications for the existence of the FMS. In the words of the principal these were:

[W]e have an ageing and experienced workforce who are excluded under the traditional structure from getting any acknowledgment and quite often any opportunity to broaden their skills....

[We have a] need to ensure that all the non-promotion position people (classroom teachers) have an opportunity to get their skills up and keep those skills up in a contemporary management climate....

Other staff saw the FMS as a pragmatic survival strategy for a small school in an era where management responsibilities were proliferating: 'It is a small school...but...as the school gets smaller the jobs don't get less, they get more' (Magnus, 23 August 1995).

The flatter management structure brought changes to teachers' work that could be broadly termed 'post-Fordist' (Jessop, 1989; Ball, 1990). Post-Fordist organizations demand workers who can enact a range of more holistic, flexible and integrated skills:

a different kind of workforce – one which is capable of handling technical complexity in ways that go beyond simple craft specialisms, and which is far more 'multi-skilled' than the operatives of the classical 'Fordist' production line...more skilled, but more responsible (and) capable of exercising high levels of discretion and its relationship with managements will be based more on trust than on surveillance by the classically Fordist figure of the foreman.

(Jones and Hatcher, 1994, pp. 247–8)

In short, this view appears to bring together an unprecedented opportunity to humanize the workplace, and align the humanistic and developmental preoccupations of schooling with the needs of capital for a skilled and responsive workforce.

The flatter management structure provided for the expansion of managerial positions in the school from ten (principal, deputy and eight subject seniors) to eighteen – a substantial increase in the management capacity of the school, and of the school's capacity to meet the competitive challenges of other schools operating in the same educational market. The school principal and many of the staff were aware of the need to actively promote the school in the community. Declining enrolments had led to school closures, and during the period of the research, competition bringing an upsurge in 'impression management', school promotion, niche marketing and diversification. GHS was in direct competition with two other public high schools, nearby private schools, and 'academic' public schools that were *en route* to the city centre, where many of the local residents worked.

Promotion and the management of public relations were increasingly important tasks that precipitated the reskilling (Watkins, 1993) of the principal and the teacher-managers who dealt with the public, and was one of a number of factors reshaping the nature of the work of teachers at GHS. The slow but steady enrolment growth of the school was seen by the staff and administrators as an indicator of the school's improved public image, and the association between 'image', enrolments, and survival was not lost on the staff.

The school was also actively seeking to become a focus school for 'gifted and talented' students. Being a focus school, especially in 'marketable' areas, provided schools with opportunities for improved profile both within DECS and in the wider community. Being a school with a focus in gifted and talented students, in particular, carried with it a potent penumbra of academic excellence. As the principal put it during a staff meeting discussion: 'The school does have competition [from other schools].... [Having a focus] will influence our prospects. We could be here for another 50 years, but all of our neighbour high schools have a focus except us' (Fieldnote, 22 August 1995).

At the same time, 'extras' such as trials and special foci brought new responsibilities, and although they attracted some extra staffing, the net effect was additional workload that needed to be carried by the relatively small staff group. The workload could not be managed by the formal leaders alone, resulting in the internal 'devolution' of responsibilities to staff, bringing about their reskilling, and the intensification of their work. The additional workload was devolved through the development of the flatter management structure, carrying with it significant implications for workload, class teaching, staff relationships, and professional identity.

Out of this complex milieu there were a number of initiatives that became central to the research project, and provide important 'sign posts' for the reader. There were a small number of *key school-level factors* which, when aggregated, motivated much of the theoretical work that appears in the remaining chapters of this study. These were: (1) the school's attempts to operationalize the 'collaborative' recommendations of the Junior School Review (the middle school recommendations or MSRs); (2) the ongoing influence of the flatter management structure; and (3) the position of the school in a competitive educational market.

Post-Fordism, Knowledge and Power

The junior school reform project clearly intended to impact on the work of the teachers at GHS. At the same time, the senior school curriculum, while not apparently undergoing active reform, significantly influenced the reform climate.

Even when, in the late 1980s, GHS had become so small that some of the faculties comprised a sole staff member, the faculty structure persisted. Faculties were led by experienced seniors, who had been appointed for life. As a group, the seniors had been an influential tier of school management, and their opinions were taken seriously by the senior management. For a new teacher, or teacher new to a school, the subject senior embodied the administration of the school. It has been argued (Hargreaves, 1992a; Little, 1992, 1993, 1995) that teacher identification with a faculty is central to the development and maintenance of professional collegiality. Even with the modification of the faculty structure at GHS, teacher identification with *subjects* was still strong, and a degree of nostalgia for the old faculty traditions existed.

After two years of work, a number of staff meetings where teacher collaboration was endorsed, and exhaustive discussion of recommendations relating to interdisciplinary teaching approaches, tangible results were hard to identify. There had been persistent difficulties in translating the rhetoric into reality, difficulties that have plagued reformers in other places: 'The closer one gets to the classroom and to central questions of curriculum and instruction, the fewer are the recorded instances of meaningful, rigorous collaboration' (Little, 1987, pp. 505–6).

The impediments at GHS operated through three interconnected sets of conditions. First, through the objective conditions and structural relationships that framed the work of the teachers at the school (e.g. time, space and formal structures); second, through the teachers' subjective and intersubjective states that were bound up in the structures (e.g. subject/faculty investments, power relations); and, third, through the contradictory influences of external determinants (e.g. 'rational' management cults, curriculum policy, influences of the state, and economic interests). We will now examine each of these in turn.

Problems Intrinsic to the Objective Conditions and Structural Relationships

A variety of possible configurations emerged in discussion, and some limited and informal experimentation occurred (see Table 4.1).

Team teaching configurations involving class combinations were limited physically by the absence of large teaching spaces, the standard classrooms being quite cramped. The 'special purpose' spaces in the school (science laboratories, art rooms, home economics areas) were large enough for only one class, and the need to deploy the specialist teachers vertically through the school reduced their contact with most students to semester (20 weeks) or half semester (10 weeks or one term) periods. Specialist teachers (music, visual art, home economics, technical studies, German, Chinese) were also excluded from ongoing interdisciplinary collaboration involving teachers teaching the same class group, because most specialist classes were 'practical', involving reduced class sizes and the consequent fragmentation of the class groups.

It was widely felt by administrators and staff, however, that the timetable

Table 4.1 Possible configurations for collaboration

	Configurations	Key epistemological implications	Key organization implications	Notes
1	Interdisciplinary co-planning and team teaching of combined classes employing an integrated or thematic curriculum, involving students in the same year level	Interdisciplinary integration of subject matter	Uniform composition of classes across the integrated subjects \Provision of teacher meeting time\Timetable coordination to allow team teaching	In 1994, two informal 'one off' attempts, Human Society/Art; Human Society/German
2	Interdisciplinary co-planning and teaching an integrated or thematic curriculum in separate but parallel classes. Same year level	Interdisciplinary integration of subject matter in themes	Provision of teacher meeting time\Timetable coordination to ensure all teachers involved teach same year level	Not attempted
3	Intradisciplinary (within existing subject boundaries) co-planning and team teaching of combined classes. Same year level	'Tight' coordination of integrated subject matter	Provision of teacher meeting time\Collaborating teachers assigned to same year levels and subject, and placed on same timetable 'line'	Not attempted
4	Intradisciplinary co-planning and teaching within subject boundaries in separate but parallel classes	'Loose' coordination of integrated subject matter	Provision of teacher meeting time	Sharing ideas at curriculum area meetings, and informally
5	Interdisciplinary meetings to discuss student welfare matters	None	Time for interdisciplinary meetings	1995, junior school meetings were held monthly, after staff meeting
6	One teacher teaching the same class more than one subject interdisciplinarily, for instance integrated Mathematics/Science	Individual teacher planning	Timetabling of the teacher to take same class for both subjects	Not attempted
7	One teacher teaching the same class more than one subject, each one discretely, for instance Mathematics, and Science	Individual teacher planning	Timetabling of teacher to take same class for both subjects	1995/6, Year 8 classes had Mathematics and Science taught by the same teacher
8	Pairs of teachers engaging in 'flexible' collaboration about curriculum; for instance, two teachers teaching one class, one teaching Mathematics/Science and the other teaching English/Humanities	Varieties of 'loose' or 'tight' integration, or for 'linking through the kids' (see later sub-section)	Provision of teacher meeting time\Collaborating teachers assigned to same year levels and assigned to appropriate subjects	A favoured model, but not attempted
9	Models 4, 6, 7 and 8 applied to more than one year level	'Vertical' integration of subject matter	'Vertical' as well as 'horizontal' timetable coordination	Not attempted

was the most pervasive structural impediment to teacher collaboration. The timetable placed teachers on 'lines', with the result that interdisciplinary team teaching of classes was dependent on which line the subjects were placed on. The need to deploy all staff to teach the small senior school classes generated dispersed teaching assignments, disrupting the formation of junior school teams. It should be noted, however, that the tendency to place the same subjects on one line actually facilitated *intradisciplinary* team teaching (e.g. all year 8 Mathematics classes were taught at the same time), but despite these apparent opportunities, intradisciplinary teaming was largely absent. The low levels of collaboration despite opportunities *within* the existing schedule would suggest that structural difficulties alone were not a sufficient cause.

Teachers advocating collaboration also argued that the packed after-school meeting schedule was an obstruction to subject integration. Curriculum area meetings were devoted to alignment of curriculum with the Statements and Profiles, and junior school meetings (held after a full teaching day and a general staff meeting) were preoccupied with immediate student welfare issues. The imperatives of externally mandated policy, and pragmatic concerns about the students repeatedly crowded out agenda items about teaming in the junior school, even where there was a degree of interest in collaboration or teaming: '(Meeting) time has been taken up mainly with national Statements and Profiles. The other curriculum issues we have talked about on and off and the teachers are willing but they don't see how they can actually do more team teaching' (Pauline, 4 July 1995).

While the difficulties of advancing the collaboration agenda were deeply frustrating to the junior school managers (who were the main advocates of the collaborative approach), the angst did not appear to be shared by many other members of staff. There was also no indication of any independent caucus of staff working on forms of formal collaboration.

The particular characteristics of the internal labour market of DECS also presented structural impediments to the development of collaborative teams, with the inter-school transfer of individual teachers from one subject-based assignment to the next being the orthodox approach to system-wide deployment of staff. This practice facilitated the 'plugging of subject gaps' in schools – subject specialists generally being infinitely replaceable – but had a persistently corrosive effect on the development of teams at schools. In the two years of the research project, nearly half the teachers involved in teaching junior classes transferred or resigned, and the pool of potential team members was in constant flux.

The Formal Structures and Teachers' Subjective and Intersubjective States

There was unanimity among the teachers and administrators interviewed that their work was being intensified through a combination of changes to existing responsibilities and the aggregation of new responsibilities. Teachers cited as central to the intensification of their work: (1) increases in marking and administrative load brought about by the requirement that students demonstrate competence in multiple objectives (particularly in SACE); (2) cultural changes and increased student expectations of a varied and stimulating curriculum and teaching style; and, (3) the devolution of highly process-dependent responsibilities to the rank-and-file teachers. The intensifying effects of 'process-orientation' were particularly evident to the more experienced teachers, such as Phil: 'Gone are the days when you clipped [recalcitrant students] behind the ear or sent them to the deputy. You have to work through a process and document it and it is very time consuming...' (Phil, 29 May 1995).

The reskilling required by state and federal policy initiatives was also seen to bear part of the responsibility for increased workload and stress. Of these initiatives the National Statements and Profiles had the most persistent and widespread intensifying effects. Teachers' resentment of the increased workload was sharpened by their scepticism of the claimed benefits to teaching and learning. At the same time some felt a degree of professional anxiety about their inability to implement the policy properly: 'Alison said that implementing the Statements and Profiles requires a complete restructure of teachers' work. With 120 kids per week, she can't profile them meaningfully' (Fieldnote, 9 June 1995).

Concerns about the workload brought about by the Statements and Profiles were partly offset by the belief that the policy would eventually finally be integrated into the labour process, or would be abandoned, whereas the devolution of management responsibilities to teachers (through the FMS) was seen to have *permanently* altered the criteria for a 'normal' workload. However, it was not just that the FMS jobs required more work than could be done in the time allotted for them, although this was certainly an issue. As we have mentioned previously, the FMS had a number of post-Fordist characteristics, and some of these, combined with the culture of collaboration that existed in the school, intensified the work of the eighteen managers in particular ways that would not have been experienced by seniors wielding traditional hierarchical authority. The majority of the staff *were* managers, and their job statements invariably included outcomes which required for their achievement the cooperation and goodwill of the other staff, who were also managers on high workloads. The need for strong lateral relationships was thus paramount, and the managers had to rely on interpersonal competencies, and considerable political sensitivity, to ensure that the outcomes were achieved. The sheer volume of managerial interactions was exemplified in the work of one senior school manager, who, over two nine hour school days, had over one hundred task-directed interactions with other teachers related to his portfolio, leaving him with a total of 32 minutes 'discretionary' time – that is, time where he was not either teaching or dealing with other administrative matters. Frequent requests for information, advice and assistance colonized recess (mid-morning break) and lunch breaks, with unpredictable effects. In this environment, plans and priorities of the sort advocated by 'time management' consultants actually heightened the sense of overload.

While these horizontal relationships depended significantly on the collegial culture of the school, the expected outcomes of the managers' work were also articulated *vertically* through state and federal policy mandates, and managers were accountable to the school principal for outcomes achievement. Thus, while the culture of collaboration brought with it a degree of goodwill, the public nature of the list of outcomes expected of each teacher-manager brought with it degrees of peer judgement that had the potential to threaten the collaborative culture itself. The bureaucratic pyramid had been replaced by the panoptic gaze of peer accountability:

> People are very much aware these days of who is supposed to be doing what...[and] peer pressure is definitely a factor.... There is very little tolerance of people who rightly or wrongly are perceived to be non-performers.... It is almost like a club of acceptance and it is better to be in that club, where if you do muck things up or forget to do something you [probably] have enough Brownie points to cover it.
>
> (Magnus, 28 September 1995)

The official leadership support for formal collaboration was frequent, public and quite unequivocal at Gallipoli High School. The principal and deputy 'talked up' teaming; the school's National Schools Network funding proposals were centred on the development of a collaborative middle school; the middle-school recommendations had been enshrined in school policy; seniors and faculties were portrayed as anachronistic, and there was little overt evidence of social or political alliances based on identification with a subject. Faculty groups did not sit together in the staffroom, and social friendships extended across disciplines. However, it would have been a mistake to imagine that the traditional influence of the subjects was no more. The underlying strength of subject investments shaped the ways many of the teachers saw their work and informed the identities that emerged from their practice.

Teachers came out of the universities with 'backgrounds' in Mathematics or English, and their subject orientation had been nurtured in the past by the relevant faculty:

> when I first started out, trying to survive in the class and not let the kids have you [*sic*] too much. That's where [I valued] the support of [subject] senior staff for a beginning teacher, the program they had developed... just being taken under their wing.
>
> (Colin, 30 May 1995)

While a young teacher's impulse to belong and to 'survive' could impel them to the relatively small and supportive faculty community, Martin, one of the main proponents of teacher collaboration, also saw the faculty as his first home:

> I identify strongly with the faculty. I mean if someone asked me what sort of a teacher I was I would say I was a science teacher.... So I do identify with the science faculty.... I would say that I also teach in maths [*sic*].
>
> (Martin, 5 July 1995)

While at GHS nearly all the teachers interviewed placed their interaction with peers and students and 'doing something useful with the students' above subject orientation as a motivation for being a teacher, the epistemological territory for those relationships was usually sharply defined. When asked whether she could see herself as a teacher of any other subject than Art, Alison said firmly:

> no, no. I taught physical education when I first went out teaching and that was take the kids out on the oval and umpire a game of some sort and when ...I was sent to a school where they assumed that I could teach technical drawing...I tried to make it an art exercise. The kids thought it was technical drawing, but it was not really.
>
> (Alison, 20 September 1995)

Even the minority of the teachers interviewed who claimed to be largely indifferent about the subject as a source of professional identity, were uncomfortable about the pedagogical implications of subject integration:

> I have no problems at all with people sharing resources or whatever, but teams where the boundaries between subjects are less defined I have a problem with. It is really I guess to do with the expertise of the people, and whether someone will finish up doing something in a superficial way because they don't have the background expertise knowledge.
>
> (Phil, 14 September 1995)

The thematic approaches of primary schools, and teaching by non-specialist teachers was considered to be 'dangerous' by some staff, even by those who were strong advocates of interdisciplinary interaction between specialist teachers:

> I think in secondary schools...you must have subject specialists the closer you get to the forefront of a subject area. And that requires fragmentation. That requires people to go off and study particular subject areas.... This concept of the teacher being a generalist I think is dangerous.
>
> (Martin, 5 July 1995)

While the evidence of recent research suggests that teachers who 'view their subject as relatively defined, unitary, and sequential' (e.g. Mathematics, languages other than English) are more resistant to interdisciplinarity (Little, 1995) than teachers of English or Social Studies, the increasing sense of personal accountability for student achievement of specific curriculum outcomes, had reduced the leeway in all subjects for teachers to spontaneously follow their own enthusiasms or those of their students. More experienced teachers like Magnus felt the constraint strongly:

> What I am saying is that whereas you may not have a person standing over you and making sure that you are doing these things, the result that you have to deliver at the end is specific enough so that there might as well be someone standing there.
>
> (Magnus, 28 September 1995)

One of the implications of this internal discipline, shaped in part by the discourse of 'outcomes-orientation', is to individualize the teacher's sense of responsibility for the delivery of the curriculum, and to discourage joint work, a point elaborated below.

In the same way that personal knowledge and enthusiasm was the very essence of a 'good' secondary teacher, personal characteristics were seen to be fundamental to teacher collaboration – the right interpersonal 'chemistry' for working in this way with both other adults and the students. Angus, who had been involved with both fledgling experiments in interdisciplinary collaboration, was thought by other staff to possess the right personality for teaming: 'Steffi said that the collaborative teaching worked because Angus had a particular way of relating to kids' (Fieldnote, 8 August 1995). 'He just was wonderful to everybody, and helped everybody. That is something you can't learn, you can't buy. It is just an innate sense that you have or you haven't' (Alison, 20 September 1995).

While interdisciplinary classroom experiments ceased after Angus' appointment to another school, the appeal of forms of interdisciplinary work that did not involve surrender of specialist status was evident by the voluntary attendance of staff at meetings called by the junior school manager to discuss collaborative possibilities.

Contradictory Influences of External Interests

However, just as it is possible to overdraw the significance of subject affiliation as a basis for the professional identity of secondary teachers (Little, 1995), or to see collaborative practice purely as a function of the right interpersonal fusion, it would be equally erroneous to construct the *opposition* to subject integration purely in these terms. The issue went far deeper than that, and was bound up in struggles that were precipitated and intensified by: (1) the contradictory impacts on subject disciplines of the national curriculum; (2) the penetration of public schooling by market ideology; (3) the impact of the discourse of vocationalism in all subject areas; and, (4) the impulse of teachers to 'insulate' (Flinders, 1988) themselves as a response to the combined effects of these pressures.

Subject Disciplines and the National Curriculum

While the imposition of the national curriculum through the Statements and Profiles may have begun the process of shifting the control of the curriculum away from the states, at the school level, the national curriculum actually reinforced subject divisions and status hierarchies. The writing of the Statements left mathematics, science and English largely intact while other areas were the product of 'shotgun marriages', uneasy subject combinations that Collins (1994) has described as 'rough piles' and 'unacceptable bundles'. Penny, like many of the teachers at GHS, shared Collins' view of the appropriateness of the subject divisions:

> Because I am a business trained teacher, I don't fit into a learning area, but I go to the technology [curriculum area] group because keyboarding fits into technology, but when they start talking about home economics, tech studies and computing, the only part that is relevant for me is the keyboarding.
>
> (Penny, 26 June 1995)

The organizing epistemological principles behind the lower status national curriculum areas were partly incompatible with the existing knowledge divisions of the school, and the reauthorization of the high status subject divisions entrenched their separation from other subjects.

Of more long-term significance for the school's collaborative project, was the potential for the outcomes-orientation of the national curriculum to reach into the classroom, and further individualize the pedagogical process for both teachers and students. The ascribing of levels to students based on the individual achievement of preordained learning outcomes encouraged a reductionist view of knowledge. During the period of the research, outcomes checklists became a favoured way of systematizing and stream-lining both the Statements and the Profiles. This process was tacitly and overtly encouraged during training sessions outside the school, as can be seen in the following extracts taken from notes of a cluster professional development meeting:

We should be writing programs from the Statements book. (Displays chart with Statements 'dot points' arranged as a checklist.) Check your programs against this [chart] and make sure all the dot points are covered in a year.

(Cluster Arts coordinator, 5 July 1995)

People at the conference said [about a checklist based on the Statements], 'At last, that's what we want'.

(Alison, 5 July 1995)

Teachers of English and Humanities argued that the articulation of their subjects to externally determined curriculum objectives resulted in less 'room to move' than they had experienced in past years. Magnus, an English teacher, asserted that:

we are also having other constraints put on us like the Statements and Profiles as one more level of complexity about assessment, and in the end I think that is having [a constricting] effect on pluralism within the classroom in terms of what we do. It is cutting out so many things that might have been valuable but unless they can be directly tied to the objectives and the assessment plans we haven't got time for them and we don't [do them].

(Magnus, 28 September 1995)

It was posited by one teacher that an objectives-driven curriculum eroded collaboration, because the behavioural outcomes reduced the skill demands on teachers to the point where it actually reduced the *need* for collegial inter-dependence. This planned, deliberate, mastery-oriented learning milieu would appear to be hostile to the growth of the 'spontaneous', 'develop-ment-oriented', and 'unpredictable' relationships that Nias et al. (1989) and Hargreaves (1990) assert are at the heart of authentic teacher collaboration. More fundamentally, the relationships described by Nias and Hargreaves may have become anachronistic, even 'unprofessional' in a post-Fordist workplace. Staff involvement in the FMS was predicated on a degree of identification with the perspective of management. This was achieved in part through a recasting of the moral commitments of teachers in line with the objectives of the school and the system. Through the ideological co-optation (Derber, 1982) of the moral and ethical consciousness of the teachers, the sense of shared commitment to the students, industrial solidarity and peer collegiality that made up the culture of collaboration at GHS was superimposed by a powerful sense of obligation to the wider system, further facilitating the penetration of the morally and politically 'neutral' ideology of management. This in turn paved the way for the intensification of the teachers' administrative load, and contributed to the mixed emotions that many of the staff felt about taking on teacher-manager roles. Some, like Melody, noted the potential for the workload associated with management roles to bring about neglect of students:

> There are a few pluses [about the FMS] but the minuses are mainly related to juggling time. Also it is playing really heavily on my conscience that the special ed. [teaching] side of my job is being neglected, a lot, and I have to do something about that. I can't let that go on like it is.
>
> (Melody, 29 June 1995)

The ideology carried in the lateral discipline and accountability of FMS was essentially managerialist, characterized by a performance-orientation and adherence to school and systemic plans, emphasizing unity of purpose and the efficient and timely completion of administrative tasks. As was penetratingly observed by Magnus, when this was combined with very high levels of task interdependence and peer scrutiny, the nature of professionalism itself was altered:

> Whatever people say or do is more visible than it used to be, but I think for a lot of the time that I was a school teacher there was a much more pluralistic view of what kind of people could be teachers, even a view that people who were a bit slack in some ways were actually good for the school because they put the work ethic into perspective, and they gave kids a different view of the world than some of the others. Maybe their teaching was a bit more lateral in its approach.... Sometimes they were remembered by kids as the only teachers they really got on with, or the only one that really taught them very much. I think the tolerance for such people is strained.
>
> (Magnus, 28 September 1995)

In this changed environment, the spontaneous forms of collegiality described by Hargreaves were bounded by interests and investments that had their sources outside the school. One staff member who was an articulate and outspoken critic of the Statements and Profiles said that she would implement them even though she objected to them because:

in this school...we work as a team, and it would be letting [the principal and deputy] down...if we didn't do it. And I think that we are a fairly professional team, and so we try and do what is expected of us.

(Marg, 29 August 1995)

Thus, the external discipline of the outcomes-oriented curriculum interacted reflexively with the lateral discipline of the flatter management structures to produce new forms of self-managing professionalism. Overt control by the principal was rendered largely unnecessary, and he was able to remain on 'professionally friendly' terms with all the staff:

So what I am saying is that you don't need inspectors. You can afford to have a friendly principal. He knows also that what he has got – a staff that is overwhelmingly on the competent, capable and productive side – and he is able to use his positive reinforcement technique.

(Magnus, 28 September 1995)

The prerogatives of management were legitimized by the participation of teachers in management functions, normalizing their subordination to school and system goals, replacing formal hierarchy with informal relations, and ensuring that both administrative control and teacher resistance were restrained by the moral obligations of collegiality. Furthermore, the potential for the influence of the reskilled teacher-managers to expand beyond the confines of their classroom extended their realm of influence (Sewell and Wilkinson, 1992). In this sense, the FMS was productive of teacher power, but at the same time, their new influence required adherence to the new forms of discipline.

Thus, just as panopticism relies on the awareness of subjects that they were being watched, peer scrutiny, combined with the possibility of public failure, invoked a powerful disciplinary force. 'The controlling function of middle management...[was] simply...incorporated into the consciousness of the [teachers] themselves. In Foucault's terms, the [teachers became] bound up in a power situation of which they themselves [were] the bearers' (Sewell and Wilkinson, 1992, p. 284).

Survival in the Market

Although the school's leadership and staff marched in loose formation towards common policy objectives, the school was not without conflict, especially when subject survival was threatened. These internecine struggles were both sublimated to and intensified by the broader goal of the survival and growth of the school itself. Staff said that the school had been in 'low ebb' in the early 1990s, and had barely escaped closure. School closures meant the dispersal of staff to other schools, and the possibility of years of itinerancy on short teaching assignments, a fate that most teachers tried strenuously to avoid. It was also clear that most teachers were happy at GHS, and had invested considerable emotional and professional energy in the students and their peers. The principal was seen to be a 'good boss', and the small, intimate nature of the school increased the sense of individual responsibility for its survival. This moral commitment was integral to the conviction of most of the staff that the role of the school was to help students to develop identity, a sense of self-worth, learning strategies for living, and control of their own education so that they might be prepared for 'the twin goals of a life of work and a life in society' (Soucek, 1993, p. 164). This 'humanistic existentialist' (Cross, 1995, p. 2) perspective was associated with a sense that the school had a role to play in providing disadvantaged students with wider life choices than their socio-economic status would normally allow them. While the language of accountability, individualism and instrumentalism was beginning to become evident in staffroom discourse, education was still seen by most staff to be a 'public' good. Nevertheless, the trajectory of the 'measurable curriculum outcomes' logic was paralleled in the ideology of 'corporate' management in which processes of public agencies were reconceived as product-like entities (Considine, 1988). In other words, the constructivist, process-orientation of education was being challenged by apparent demand for a product format which would allow 'consumer choice'. Putting it simply, schools' product priorities would provide consumers with a basis on which to choose a school. Simultaneously, the profound influence of big business in shaping the national agenda through reports such as the Finn and Mayer Reports (Brian Finn, IBM; Eric Mayer, The National Bank) placed public education under tremendous pressure to produce students who possessed the vocational competencies needed by business. Kenway et al. (1994a) crystallize the issues neatly: 'The master discourse is economics, and to put it crudely, financial anorexia. Education is to cost the state less, hence the devolutionary impera- tive. It is also to serve the economy more, hence the vocationalising imperative' (p. 1).

The 'relative autonomy' of schooling to the economy is also related to the transformation of education into a product-like entity. Fritzell (1987) argues that, in periods of fiscal crisis, both the form and the content of schooling are more strongly articulated to the economy through the commodity form, brought about in part by a view that the emphases of humanist education on social education, personal development and self-realization are inade- quate, and that both the forms (the way schools are configured as organizations) and the products (the technical and interpersonal competen- cies of the students) of schooling need to be brought more closely into line with those demanded by capital (Ball, 1990).

In the micro-ecology of the school, the commodification, vocationaliza- tion and marketization of education could be seen in two overarching effects; first, in the school's attempts to position itself strategically in the local education market by exploiting its perceived advantages (such as its small size), and, second, by developing and profiling marketable properties, such as a focus on 'gifted' students. Considerable effort was put in to promoting the school's qualities through activities such as the annual Open Day, by courting students and parents at local primary schools, and through the production of promotional literature. The school principal, senior and junior school managers and the student counsellor were all involved in the enrolment of students, and in politely but persistently 'selling' the school to perspective parents. The school's still precarious position, smallness and lateral accountability demands ensured that all staff were conscious of the need to contribute to its public profile:

> [On Open Day] everybody did their bit.... In this school with a smaller staff people feel more connected and staff [usually don't stay] in their own little areas doing their own thing. I think the size of the organisation maybe has a lot to do with it. In a bigger organisation it is maybe easier to get away with not coming to Open Day, the school BBQ, the school social and stuff like that.
>
> (Penny, 26 June 1995)

Second, the unifying effect brought about by the pressure to market the school against an external threat was in part negated by the market's tendency to enhance the privilege of some subjects over others, and, within subject boundaries, the technical elements over those elements which are seen to have the least employment potential. High status subjects sharpened their boundaries to ensure they continued to be a distinct epistemological entity, and low status subjects became more 'theoretical' and more 'vocational' in an attempt to be seen as a credible option, a logic that can be seen in Colin's pragmatic reasoning:

> Now physical education, I see as becoming more important, because there is increased leisure time available...you can have recreational... outdoor education type things...for the...non-academic [students].... And you can also pursue the skill development so that they become good at some specific type of sport. They learn about movement and they may get some job working in a gym. The theory behind setting up weight circuits and that sort of thing. So you can make it academic and you can make it recreational.
>
> (Colin, 30 May 1995)

Individualism or Insulation?

As has been pointed out, teacher collaboration on classroom teaching at Gallipoli High School was both rare and fragile, and that this was at least in part due to a combination of structural, political and organizational factors conspiring to keep the teachers apart. At the same time, these elements do not explain why teachers of the same subjects, on the same timetable line chose not to work together. The moral imperative to collaborate was predicated on a view, to put it plainly, that isolation was bad, and that collaboration was good – a view that has considerable support in the literature. In general teachers paid lip service to this view, and acclaimed the culture of collaboration that existed in the school, but their classroom practice indicated a powerful predisposition to working alone. Some commentators (Lortie, 1975; Hargreaves, 1992a) have explained this 'conservatism' in terms of the culture and traditions of the teachers themselves, and indeed, some teachers at the school explained the privatism *of their colleagues* in terms of their fear of exposure to the scrutiny of their peers:

> The threat lies primarily in a sense of insecurity that what you do may not be as good as what somebody else does. That you are more likely to be worse off, that somehow or other your weaknesses will be exposed rather than your strengths recognised.
>
> (Magnus, 5 June 1995)

At the same time, they tended to explain *their own* privatism in terms of structural obstacles, or significantly, that they were able to teach their subject quite adequately without direct help from a peer or peers. A number spoke of the professional satisfaction from being in front of a class and imparting knowledge. When asked what she liked most about being a teacher, Ntina said:

> The students there are there because they have chosen *your* subject, and you try to give them the best obviously, and just knowing that they are coming to your classroom and you are the one that is teaching them…. I love being in front of a class, and having students and just teaching them.
>
> (Ntina, 30 May 1995)

Phil agreed that the 'up-front' teaching was central to his choice to become a teacher, and to his choice to continue teaching after more than two decades: 'The [curriculum] delivery from the person who was usually up-front…was the bit that I wanted to do…and I guess there is still a bit of that left in me, and when that goes I will take a [separation] package' (Phil, 29 May 1995).

The soundness of the concept of interdisciplinarity itself was also questioned by a number of staff, perhaps not surprising in light of the nebulous language that had been used to describe it at GHS.

When these perspectives are placed within an organizational context of very high workloads, limited time to plan, uncertain interdisciplinary alternatives, reified subject divisions and unrelenting pressure to interact with colleagues and students outside the classroom, the relative structure and predictability of class teaching also provided a degree of seclusion from the intensity of the out-of-class administrative turmoil. While this is not to underplay the demands of the classroom, we would argue that teachers at GHS were not convinced of the 'cost-benefits' of collaboration.

A number of trends were emerging in the school during the period of the research. First, the administrative load, brought about by devolutionary and competitive pressures on the school, was being spread across the school staff through the adoption of aspects of post-Fordist management ideology, most clearly evident in the flatter management structure. Second, another organizational element characteristic of the post-Fordist workplace – establishment of collaborative teams of workers – was being interrupted by lack of time and space, high workloads, and the lateral accountability pressures that were an outgrowth of the public expectations of the teacher-managers' performance. Third, the tendency to conflate 'interdisciplinarity', 'teaming' and 'collaboration', each one a notoriously slippery concept, blurred the purposes and potentialities of the collaboration project beyond any recognisable form. Fourth, the tension and anxieties embedded in a subject status hierarchy; the role of the universities in authorizing the separateness of the high status subjects; and, the influence of the national curriculum in further crystallizing the paradigmatic integrity of high status subjects (while making rough piles of others), opened up further divisions between subjects and subject teachers.

The Flatter Management Structure and Gendered Management at GHS

The increase in the range and type of tenured 'coordinator' positions increased women's access to promotion positions in all schooling sectors, although it is significant that these provisions seem to be most effective in expanding the labour market at the bottom of the promotion hierarchy. The establishment of coordinators in high schools altered the prevailing gender-identity of leadership. Unlike the traditional 'senior' classification, the nature of the coordinator roles reduced the need for a teacher to establish proven ability in a particular subject area; a requirement that had advantaged (usually male) teachers with unbroken, full-time records of employment (Acker, 1992). The generic nature of the coordinator positions provided promotion opportunities in non-faculty leadership, and the shorter tenures have allowed women to take on leadership positions as their domestic circumstances allowed. Class teachers' increasing participation in management functions blurred the lines between administration and class teaching, and, as we argue later, the increased participation of women in management positions has changed the nature of management itself. At GHS the FMS provided another avenue for women teachers to participate in management. Moreover, FMS positions also shared many of the character-istics of formal tenured coordinator positions – the only clear differences being that they did not carry a higher salary, and were generally tenured for a shorter time. We assert, for the analytical purposes of this chapter, that the GHS flatter management positions were virtually identical to formal, paid coordinator positions. In fact, anecdotal evidence from within the DECS bureaucracy indicated that the model provided by the FMS teacher-manager positions was seen to be a desirable advance on the official coordinator posi-tions, being closer to the flexible, self-managing ideal advocated in some sections of DECS.

As we have argued repeatedly, the newly formed management positions at Gallipoli High School were post-Fordist in nature, running in an uneasy and contradictory alliance with the traditional discourses of bureaucratic management. Court (1994) asserts that within orthodox management discourse:

> there exists an awareness of the significance of team-building in educa-tional leadership, in the processes of decision making, of motivation and in job satisfaction. [Such] team work requires the skills of affilia-tion, and the ability to build and maintain relationships and a sense of belonging. These are the very skills that have traditionally been learned by girls and women within socializing processes.
>
> (p. 46)

While post-Fordist work reforms at GHS can be seen to be having both affil-iative and (largely unanticipated) competitive outcomes, the *intentions* of the reforms (as espoused by their proponents at GHS) were collaborative, and oriented to improved teaching and learning. The positions were also clearly attractive to the women staff members at the school, with half the teacher-managers being women. Women were equally represented as school section managers, held four curriculum area management portfolios (Arts, Health and Physical Education, languages other than English, and Mathematics) and were equally represented in the other teacher-manager roles.

The majority of the staff were teacher-managers, and their job statements invariably included outcomes which required for their achievement the coop-eration and goodwill of the other staff, who were also managers on high workloads. Like formal coordinators, and unlike traditional seniors, the teacher-managers were not part of a line-management hierarchy, and they wielded no formal authority. The fact that the teacher-manager positions, unlike the formal coordinator position, were not officially recognized on the 'organizational map' exaggerated for teacher-managers the dilemma also faced by official coordinators who were 'in some sense located above teachers in the educational system hierarchy, but without the formal organisational authority to manage or control teachers' (Ginsburg, 1987, p. 90). As their roles invariably required the cooperation and active support of their peers, their effectiveness was based largely on the exercise of interpersonal competencies, tact, and political sensitivity, exactly the sort of characteristics that women are generally thought to embody (Ginsburg, 1987; Redclift and Sinclair, 1991; Apple and Jungck, 1992; Court, 1994).

Even though some women staff felt that the substantive male seniors were still wielding considerable informal influence despite their absence from the formal hierarchy, women legitimized the flatter management structure through the application of gendered skills necessary to make it work, and reskilling – implicit in teacher-manager participation in administration – involved the productive application of skills that women developed in the domestic sphere. Nevertheless, the intensification associated with the new roles created 'conditions that foster(ed) continued difficulties in their own labor' (Apple and Jungck, 1992, p. 27). The FMS challenged teacher-managers' ability to maintain quality relationships with their students and increased teacher vulnerability to deskilling through their need to accept the 'help' of externally designed curriculum frameworks. 'Feminine' skills carried the flatter management structure, but at the cost of an increased workload that impinged on teaching and learning and curriculum autonomy. In short, they occupied a position of subjugated centrality.

While the flatter management positions were gendered by being (intentionally or otherwise) configured to fit skills traditionally enacted by women, their promise of a holistic blend of teaching and management could be a double-edged sword. On the one hand, the positions appealed to women who wished to stay in the classroom while gaining some management experience, but on the other they carried burdens of intensification and accountability that had the potential to upset the balance of domestic and working life. Melody, following a meeting that was about the implementation of the middle-school recommendations, said that:

> she felt very frustrated at the end of the meeting, but had gone home and talked it over with her husband. She had decided that she was now going to concentrate her energies on her students and her family. I joked that, with her track record, that resolution would probably last for about two days.
>
> (Fieldnote, 9 August 1995)

On another occasion, Marg, teacher-manager of the problematic Health and Physical Education curriculum area, observed that: 'when I come home angry on a Monday, my husband always says, "Had another HPE meeting have you?"' (Fieldnote, 18 August 1995).

It can be seen that the teacher-manager positions enabled women to take on duties that had previously been the province of the seniors. At the same time, the fact that these positions had no 'line' authority and depended largely for their effectiveness on peer collaboration and cooperation calls into question the degree to which they could be regarded as leadership positions in the traditional hierarchical sense. It could be argued that by replacing the original Taylorist pyramid with a participatory structure that devolved administrative responsibilities to a new cohort of teacher-managers, the nature of leadership itself was changed – with a bureaucratic model giving way to a more democratic, collaborative, approach. Evidence that this had in fact occurred would suggest that rationalizing discourses of management and curriculum were under threat. Why, then, was femininity entering masculine administration at this point in history? How does one resolve the apparent contradiction between the cohesive, holistic, non-aggressive, affiliatory approach that is the preferred leadership style of many women (Ozga, 1993; Court, 1994) and the reductive and competitive discourses of management, the market and standardizing curriculum? How is progressive management practice (which clearly 'fits' with women's management practice) reconciled with a policy environment which privileges competition, entrepreneurialism (Ozga, 1993) and a cult of efficiency? Acknowledging that the answers to these questions are always going to be shaped by contradictions, hegemonic influences, spaces and tensions that exist within schooling at any given moment (Giroux, 1988), we offer the following possibilities.

First, in the 1980s women in schools and in the public service struggled to remove official and unofficial impediments to their access to promotion positions and to democratize the bureaucracy (Yeatman, 1990). While some of these gains have been rolled back in the 1990s (Smyth, 1995b), initiatives in legislation, administrative guidelines and in 'consciousness raising' (Lewis, 1990) have improved the access of women to promotion positions. This is not to suggest that issues of gender equity in schools had ceased to be problematic, but that overt forms of career discrimination against women had been acted against, with the result that, in lower hierarchical positions at least, more women were applying for and 'winning' promotion positions.

Second, both men and women gained promotion positions in part through demonstrating their familiarity with the dominant discourses. Without a degree of fluency in managerialist rhetoric they were unlikely to be able to demonstrate either that they were in tune with the 'organizational culture', or that they understood key themes such as the 'outcomes-orientation'.

In other words, while a holistic, affiliative management style might have been women's preferred approach to management, their subjectivities and ideologies were not immune from patriarchal hegemony. As Lewis and Simon (1986) note, patriarchal power, as a local form of 'government' (Rabinow, 1984), operates through women as well as men:

> Patriarchy is a social form that continues to play on through our subjectivities, affecting conceptually organized knowledge as well as elements that move us, without being consciously expressed. It continues to provide us with vantage points, and positions us differently within relations of power.
>
> (Lewis and Simon, 1986, p. 458)

Third, participation of women teacher-managers in the reproduction of hegemonic discourses should not be taken as evidence that the school was a level playing field. The links between masculinity and authority provide men with a 'natural' aura of authority denied women (Court, 1994). However, the participation of women in the symbolic language of masculinist management discourse provided women with some space and shelter to enact feminine leadership styles. In other words, women learned to speak the language of power, but in doing so did not entirely obliterate other existing discourses, such as 'professional teaching' or holistic leadership (Court, 1994).

Fourth, the sphere of the influence of women's leadership was seen largely to be limited to low-level school administration. While this undoubtedly reduced women's influence in the production of masculinist discourses, their influence in the *reproduction* of the discourses was significant. As women teacher-managers were situated in the worlds of teaching and administration, they represented an important link in the policy sequence, and were able to apply discretion to the interpretation and implementation of policy, in the process infusing 'man-agerial' policies with feminine meanings.

To manage these contradictions, 'women who move into management positions in schools (were) thus...enmeshed in a kind of "schizophrenic" existence' (Court, 1994, p. 40), constantly drawing on their ability to juggle several tasks at once (Court, 1994, p. 41) so that the demands of home, administration and teaching were managed, and core feminine values were protected. Paradoxically, these skills, through their recognition of the complex subjective, historical, interdependent, interpersonal dimensions of management, contributed to the legitimization of the cult of rational management by making it appear to work, but at the risk of silencing the 'illegitimate' (Lewis and Simon, 1986) feminine experience and discursive forms in which the skills were based.

Collaborative Leadership

The accountability of teacher-managers to public job specifications was not a neutral management technique, free of social and micro-political effects. Teachers' work was articulated with a set of jointly constructed expectations, monitored, albeit in a constructive and collaborative way, by the principal; and the job descriptions of the teacher-managers' roles provided an outcomes-oriented performance benchmark for self-assessment, and for the evaluation of the teacher-managers' performance by their peers. In one sense, the monitoring of the job specifications, as a form of top-down externalized control, was more congruent with state Fordism than the internalized discipline of individual professionalism. A narrowing of what was considered professionally acceptable, and reduced tolerance of teachers whose performance, style or priorities fell outside professional standards, suggested also that a process of standardization and normalization (Pignatelli, 1993) was beginning to occur. Evidence of normalization could be seen in an 'increase in the technical elements of teachers' work and a reduction in the professional spaces for professional autonomy and judgement' (Ball, 1992, p. 3). Under these circumstances, processes of teacher *self*-normalizing and 'internal homogenisation' (Simon, 1992, p. 10) also take place, as the discourse of professional teaching is colonized and displaced by a discourse of accountability and management by objectives. Assessment of a teacher's professionalism is then predicated on a limited range of technical state-legitimated or 'common-sense' market-legitimated forms, 'that constitute experience as already filled with essential and unitary meanings' (Britzman, 1991, p. 7) and 'sustain an appearance of the world as given and received, and of reality as existing on its own' (Britzman, 1991, p. 55). Uninterrupted, the process becomes cyclic and reproductive as teachers' self-managing reflections, and their expectations of the management practices of peers, subordinates and superiors, are increasingly conditioned in terms of these 'truths'. Ability to 'speak the truth' then conveys power on the speaker 'the capacity to control their social environment or the behaviour, feelings, and thoughts of others by being able either to produce a particular event or to prevent its occurrence' (Fay, 1977, p. 202), whereas the unenlightened, or those unwilling to adopt the discourse, find it increasingly difficult to convey their meanings. In this way, the fluency in the discourse becomes potentially productive and desirable for people at all hierarchical levels. Ball (1994) describes how the discourse of management, emanating originally from ideological caches outside the organization, constructs, at the level of the local organization and the individual, the disciplinary practices of self-management.

At Gallipoli High School, the flatter management structure (FMS) provided a conduit through which the discourses of professional management flowed. As we have pointed out earlier, the FMS both empowered and disempowered the teacher-managers. They were able to take on management-style administrative responsibilities and exercise some leadership and influence with their peers. Their expertise in their management portfolio was enhanced, but at the same time, their performance was subject to the panoptic gaze (Foucault, 1977; Fraser, 1989) and normalizing judgement of their peers. The FMS, designed to encourage teacher discretion and initiative in the delivery of outcomes, engaged worker desires for autonomy and self-management, appealed to the status symbolism attached to 'management' in a professional context (Derber, 1982), while avoiding the resistance that would be generated by overtly coercive or bureaucratic attempts to interfere in the professional discretion of the teachers. The management logic of the FMS created a level of ideological consensus among the staff (as could be seen in the relative uniformity of the teachers' views about the FMS), the main objections relating to the impact on teaching and learning (concerns that had their roots in the older discourse of professional teaching). Thus an open, low-profile, efficient, personable, non-hierarchical, unspectacular leadership style, what Fraser (1989) calls 'modern leadership', made considerable sense in this milieu.

What, then, were the consequences for teacher collaboration of this discursive interplay? It has been argued that some forms of teacher collaboration have been thoroughly integrated into the new managerialism. Smyth (1991) notes the coincidence of:

> this reincarnation of an educational concept that has been around for a long time is…enjoying its new found popularity precisely at a time of massive international reform and restructuring of schools aimed at ensuring that schools more efficiently and effectively satisfy national economic priorities.
>
> (p. 324)

and suggests that collaboration is a means of harnessing the creativity of teachers in a way that is 'embedded in the very hierarchies and social relationships of the way in which people live their school lives' (Smyth, 1991, p. 336). Others have attempted to characterize the types of interpersonal relationships (Wallace and Louden, 1991) or organizational conditions (Hargreaves and Wignall, 1989; Hargreaves, 1990) that are likely to foster joint work among teachers, however, confusion over the range of meanings attached to words like collaboration, collegiality and cooperation, and difficulties associated with defining and evaluating empowering and emancipatory forms of collaboration (as opposed to administratively contrived forms) continue to pose theoretical and practical challenges.

At GHS, the competing demands of autonomous collaboration and organizational accountability merged in the implementation, by collaborative teams of teachers, of the Statements and Profiles. The school council had approved regular early school closures to allow teachers to engage in the

Statements and Profiles exercise. When asked whether he was monitoring how the time was being used, Don said:

> I [have] not conducted an audit of what is actually being done during that weekly half an hour.... I do not intend to conduct such an audit. Statements and Profiles work is being done but not necessarily at this time. I know that the English faculty has not yet met to do any Statements and Profiles work in the time made available rather choosing to do other work.... It doesn't worry me. They have met at other times. Individuals and teachers have...considerable freedom with the what and when, and I am not being defensive in my answer here. The aim of the timetable changes was to create some work time for staff...and my view is that you have to provide a balance by giving some work time if you are expecting staff to give private time.... [T]he only way that the school council would agree to give teachers time was for work with Statements and Profiles. We will use some of the time [for organizational priori-ties]...once we start picking up the assessment and reporting task the school has committed itself to as a trial school...but as much time as possible should be available to people to do the things that are of priority to them, wherever possible as small groups to collaborate. There was no hidden agenda. The [motivation] was to create some quality work time. I needed to have a credible, honest and pressing reason for the provision of that time.... [T]o have the school community support us in providing some of this, and for the staff to see [the] value of giving up some instruction time. The original proposal...was [to close the school an hour early] one day a week.... [T]he staff [wanted] to reduce the instruction time half an hour and I [accepted their decision].
>
> (Don, 1 June 1995)

This account reveals the judicious application of a number of leadership approaches: (1) an authoritarian determination (based on accountability to external policy mandates) that Statements and Profiles would be the focus of teacher work; (2) facilitative skill in framing the need for extra time in terms of interests of both the staff and the parents, and in recognizing the partic-ular needs of the English faculty; and (3) a future intention to allow the time to be used for democratic/empowering, collaborative work of teachers. Pessimistically, one could speculate that the democratic/empowering moment would always be on a constantly receding horizon, repeatedly displaced by accountability to other, more immediately pressing, organiza-tional requirements. In such a scenario, an open 'human relations' style of leadership and autonomous collaborative teacher work might still be employed to facilitate and legitimate desired organizational outcomes, as an 'open' (Blase and Anderson, 1995) style is likely to more effectively deliver 'closed' outcomes than a 'closed' style.

Thus, the management dilemma is clear. On the one hand, too much interference in collaborative work stultifies the teachers' creativity and motivation, and on the other, complete autonomy and unpredictable outcomes are inappropriate in an environment where: (1) schools, principals and teachers are increasingly accountable to state-policy and market disciplines; (2) resources are declining; and, (3) teachers' work is intensified to the point where time cannot be risked on projects that have uncertain outcomes.

The issues surrounding the practice of an 'empowering' approach to leadership can, in part, be understood in light of, (1) the challenge to comprehensiveness posed by a market increasingly constructing education as a commodity for personal investment; (2) an organizational milieu where power was largely directed through a combination of ('subordinating') formal-vertical and ('empowering') informal-lateral accountability requirements; and, (3) the heterogeneous impacts of a leadership style that combined high-level interpersonal skills with a low profile.

Can Collaborators be part of the Resistance? Towards a Productive Practice of Collaboration

At the point of our disengagement from the school it was easy to look back and find evidence of the expenditure of a great deal of effort on the part of a number of teachers but more difficult to find evidence of a paradigmatic shift towards joint classroom work. Nevertheless, the determination of the principal to establish a middle school in the spirit of the middle-school recommendations remained undimmed, and key change agents such as Martin were still advancing collaborative reform through the school's decision-making process. Teachers were under pressure to be more collaborative, but they also wanted to be so.

During the period of the research over 50 examples were recorded of apparently spontaneous, unplanned collaboration between staff. During interviews teachers gave many other examples of how staff had helped one another and worked together. These were *indicative* of the culture, rather than being the culture itself, which was a less tangible but powerful aura that surrounded the school, colouring and strengthening the relationships between the staff. The praxis of institutional collaboration formed at points where individual impulses to collaboration coalesced.

While there was clear evidence of collaborative reciprocation between teachers – through sharing classroom tips, trading materials, 'linking through the kids' (Little, 1995), lending a sympathetic ear, jokes and games – it became clear that the culture of collaboration had its limits, and that, with a few exceptions, collaboration ended at the classroom door. As far as the act of teaching was concerned, a culture of isolation prevailed. Nevertheless, like Flinders (1988) teachers at GHS did not regard isolation as *automatically* pathological. Flinders (1988) argues that:

isolation may...be understood not as a problem in need of redress, but rather as part of the teacher's solution to the practical dilemmas of providing classroom instruction on a day-to-day basis. This 'solution' stems from a highly professional motive: to provide the best instruction possible. For those teachers working with scarce resources and heavy instructional demands at least, isolation from colleagues may be essential to maintaining some reasonable level of instructional quality.

(p. 25)

It is also conceivable that approaching teaching work as individual 'bricolage' (Hatton, 1988, p. 338) was, for some teachers (like Magnus), relatively efficient, satisfying and productive within the current historical conditions of schooling. Bricoleurs:

review the tools, materials etc. they have to hand and consider how they might be used to complete, or approximately complete the project.... It is the possible uses of the materials presently to hand which determines the degree to which the project is completed...(and) the bricoleur's means are largely determined by his [*sic*] past experiences and are heterogeneous and finite.

(Hatton, 1988, p. 338)

Certainly Magnus' description of himself as a 'Jack of all trades' with a heterogeneous and 'eclectic' approach to his work is suggestive of elements of Hatton's analysis. Nevertheless, we would argue that the historical circumstances of teachers' work – intensification, shortage of uncommitted time, increasing management responsibilities, rigid spatial and temporal structures, escalating accountability and scrutiny – are strongly implicated in the bounded creativity, pragmatism and opportunistic use of pedagogic theory that Hatton asserts are associated with bricolage in teaching. Its persistence may also be suggestive of (rarely stated) scepticism about the pedagogical benefits of teachers collaborating on the curriculum. Despite its limitations, bricolage is a strategy that allows teachers to retain a degree of intellectual autonomy, and it appeals to a teacher's right to be an individual, and to the freedom of individualism. As Fullan and Hargreaves (1991) have pointed out, individual teachers have the potential to be agents of critical analysis in the face of collaborative 'groupthink' (Fullan and Hargreaves, 1991). In the case of women teachers, feminists have warned against strategies which submerge individual identities, arguing that 'it is better to have an understanding of power for the individual which stresses both its dimensions of competence, ability and creativity and does not lose sight of effective action' (Hartsock, 1983, p. 253).

It is also perhaps unsurprising, in light of the conditions of teachers' work, that outcomes of teacher collaboration – such as improved efficiency

(Hargreaves, 1993), productivity (Little, 1987; Austin and Baldwin, 1994) and the development of an ethos of continuous, team-based improvement (Hargreaves, 1990) – are difficult to realize in practice.

As the culture of collaboration is important to teacher morale, engagement and productivity, workplace reforms, both in 'competitive' or 'collaborative' incarnations, need to be examined closely in terms of their potential to (1) damage the collaborative culture and (2) create the conditions for productive and empowering forms of work. The search for empowering moments within systemically authorized labour relations is likely to be found in the cracks between official practices and policies, and in reflection on and resistance to normalizing discourses. Nevertheless, Ball (1994) notes that the (undertheorized) 'secondary adjustments' which characterize teachers' responses to policy may also take advantage of the emancipatory potential of official policy. He argues that:

> we tend to begin by assuming the adjustment of teachers and context to policy but not of policy to context. There is a privileging of the policy maker's reality. The crude and over-used term 'resistance' is a poor substitute here, which allows for both rampant over-claims and dismissive under-claims to be made about the way policy problems are solved in context. I also want to avoid the notion that policy is always negatively responded to, or that all policies are coercive or regressive.
>
> (Ball, 1994, pp. 19–20)

Like Ball, I would caution against 'overclaims' about the benefits of individual teacher empowerment and autonomy, as if such a condition was automatically and benignly guided by an overarching, unitary agenda. Rather than autonomous individualism 'the goal should be a "communal identity" (where) empathy, tolerance for ambiguity, and communicative competence become more valued and important to the successful practice of teacher agency' (Pignatelli, 1993, p. 428). Autonomous individualism also has the potential to revivify and legitimize teachers' freedom from scrutiny of their classroom practice, and absence of feedback and collective responsibility for their performance.

Post-Fordist Collaboration

'New work reform ideas' such as 'innovative pedagogy (and) middle school programs' (National Schools Network, 1996) remained central to the NSN doctrine, and were deeply infused with a belief that post-Fordist concepts such as 'collaborative teacher teams' and 'participative workplace procedures and decision-making' were intrinsic to reforms that would 'meet the learning needs of students more effectively and better equip them to cope with a rapidly changing world'. It is difficult to find any traces of a social critique or even mild scepticism about these truth claims. The central thrust of 'top down support for bottom-up reform' (National Schools Network, 1996) would appear framed within a broader purpose to align schools and students so that they might 'cope with change'.

Such post-Fordist solutions that lie somewhere between Taylorism and workplace democracy (such as team-based management approaches) have contradictory effects that are both collegial and competitive. As this study has pointed out, these solutions are difficult to implement in schooling. Unlike the factory, where quality standards and production goals provide a relatively fixed target for collective endeavour, the nature of teaching as a labour process without a sharply defined product (Reid, 1993), the capacity of teachers for adaption and outright subversion of mandated policy, and the privacy of teaching work creates very high levels of systemic dependence on teachers' individual expertise and collective cooperation. Where the roles of teachers are more clearly defined (through for instance, teacher-manager job specifications), team-based collegiality is replaced by organizational discipline as the *differences* between the roles of the teacher-managers and the distinctive nature of the responsibilities of each teacher-manager exposes their work to the disciplinary gaze of their peers and superiors. While the disciplinary gaze is focused on the degree to which the individual's speech and behaviour is consistent with normalizing discourses, structures such as the FMS have greater potential for building commitment among teachers to implement mandated policy than relatively chaotic and unpredictable (authentically) collaborative structures.

Clearly, the FMS was productive of forms of teacher power, as the potential for the influence of the reskilled teacher-managers to expand beyond the confines of their classroom extended their realm of influence (Sewell and Wilkinson, 1992), and the fact that a majority of teachers continued to support the FMS was indicative of their view that teacher-manager positions had empowering possibilities. The capillary nature of power, allied to the influence of teacher's in job design through the school's personnel advisory committee leads logically to the likelihood of the FMS roles (both their design and implementation) being infused with pragmatic, teacherly interests, so that the role statements would increasingly focus on teaching and learning and job design and would take account of the likely impact on the workload of the teacher-manager and their peers. While the FMS operationalized the vision of the principal and the requirements of the system, it was supported by the fragile scaffolding of teacher participation, which changed the nature of management at the school.

'Teacher power', however, is not an incontestable ontological category, as it is infused with 'institutionally privileged' (Britzman, 1991) normative discourses about what is justifiable and possible. For expressions of teacher power to move outside the 'exhausted predestinations' (Britzman, 1991) of the officially possible and the rationally inevitable, Pignatelli (1993, p. 419) asserts that individuals must reflect on self-normalizing practices as well as engaging in 'an "outer" questioning of the conditions within which the self is constituted'. Apple (1996b) also recognizes the potential for freedom residing in critical analysis of normalizing discourses/texts, arguing that:

> the critical moment in critical discourse analysis is accompanied by a positive or constructive moment as well. Unlike some of the more aggressively postmodern positions that even deny its existence, one of the major aims of such critical research is to 'generate agency'. It wishes to provide tools to students, teachers and others that enable them to see 'texts' as embodying particular 'representations' of the social and natural world and particular interests. It wants to enable people to understand how such 'texts' position them and at the same time produce unequal relations of institutional power that structure classrooms, and educational policies.
>
> (p. 131)

The problems associated with contrived and bounded collaboration are well documented in the literature. Smyth (1991) notes how collaboration has emerged as a mechanism for harnessing teachers to the job of economic reconstruction through manipulation of their subjective impulses to establish collegial forms of professionalism. Hargreaves (1992a) observes how

> collegial energies may be harnessed less for the purpose of giving teachers a say in the development of their own initiatives and the management of their own professional growth than to squeeze out dissentient voices and secure commitment and compliance to changes imposed by others.
>
> (p. 217)

He also asserts that deliberate and planned forms of collegiality fail on the grounds that they are 'not representative of the way that teachers usually learn from one another' (Hargreaves, 1992a, p. 217). Little (1992) also notes the tendency for collaboration to be directed to the fulfilment of agendas that have been established outside the collaborating group. However, objections to 'unauthentic' forms of collaboration should not be coloured by the tendency of grand overarching abstractions (e.g. the market, post-Fordism, rational management) to discount the power of human agency. If these idealizations worked, effective educational management could be reduced to a room full of policy levers within a centralized 'managerial husk' (Seddon, 1995). 'Market forces' could be brought on-line to produce excellence, 'outcomes management' would result in increased accountability, 'collaboration' would produce worker engagement, creativity and efficiency and the application of 'international best practice' benchmarks would raise standards.

Extracting the Problems from Discursive Regimes

Overarching theories, such as those discussed above, spawn policies which Ball asserts are:

> intended to bring about idealised solutions to diagnosed problems. Policies embody claims to speak with authority, they legitimate and initiate practices in the world, and they privilege certain visions and interests. They are power/knowledge configurations *par excellence*.
>
> (Ball, 1990, p. 23)

As power/knowledge configurations, their subjugating potential is therefore likely to be drawn from their power as regimes of truth as much as from their directly coercive, bureaucratic power. Thus, the potential for adjustment, resistance and adaption is a function of autonomous action within and outside the apparent policy intentions, *and* is predicated on the capacity to bring critical consciousness to the normalizing discourse practices that construct human subjectivity.

According to Giroux (1988, p. 103) this sort of 'intellectual' work also:

> points to the way in which (teachers') labor is objectively constructed; that is, it provides an analysis of the conditions under which people work and the political importance of these conditions in either limiting or enabling what educators can do.

Teachers' intellectual work theorizes the problems and possibilities that emerge from the way that teaching is controlled and education is managed.

As Pignatelli (1993, p. 429) observes, 'teachers both generate and are constrained by the official discourse', and as such their 'agency' is maintained by and helps to maintain the overarching 'objective' conditions of their labour process. The possibility that teachers both construct and are constructed by their labour process should not, however, be taken to be a sign of teachers' advocacy of the *status quo*, or of their inevitable compliance with reforms, as the daily 'problems' of teaching work are neither abstract or neutral. Instead, as can be seen throughout this chapter, problems intrude into the working life of all teachers – problems which separately might be named 'intensification' or 'deskilling', or as an ensemble, might be called 'proletarianization'. Pignatelli (1993, p. 425) calls for 'a teacher politics (that) begins as an orientation within the contingencies of a carefully delineated problem that presses upon oneself as an educator'.

At the same time, the 'objective' conditions of the labour process are mediated by teacherly ideologies of professionalism and collegiality that simultaneously ward off and borrow from discourses of the market, post-Fordism and rational management. An outright rejection of these discourses is, according to Jones and Hatcher (1994): 'an enormously difficult step to take, because it seems to carry reformers into an apparent wilderness in which – as purist dissenters, in a political climate unfriendly to radical thought – they have no means of influencing change at all' (p. 259).

Nevertheless, enthusiasm for the potential leverage that might be gained from bounded participation in orthodox economic/educational discourses also needs to be moderated by clear understanding of the weaknesses inherent in the discourses themselves. For example, for post-Fordism to have productive potential, industry's demand for 'universally high levels of technical skill and social understanding' (Jones and Hatcher, 1994, p. 259) must be realized in actuality. If, as is claimed by Jones and Hatcher, post-Fordist reforms are '(in)compatible with the polarised societies of the late twentieth century', pursuit of post-Fordist reforms that involve the partial surrender of school autonomy would appear to be wasteful and sadly misguided, and a more pragmatic course for teachers would be to connect '(public) educational policy to a more general program for economic and social change, so that arguments for enhancing levels of skill and creativity were linked to policies for restructuring the economy and reorganising social provision' (Jones and Hatcher, 1994, p. 258). Jones and Hatcher acknowledge the difficulties of such a course, particularly in a current political environment dominated by economic rationalism and official antagonism to progressive agendas. They go on to argue, however, that:

> these difficulties should be compared, however, with the intellectual and practical consequences of uncritical acquiescence – a political stance from which the educationalists make literally fantastic assumptions about the benefits of change, in compensation for their own inability to intervene against the presently dominant tendencies in economic life.
>
> (Jones and Hatcher, 1994, p. 259)

This is not to suggest that post-Fordist skills, attitudes and competencies are inherently valueless, rather that it is naive to assume that those skills *in themselves* will automatically improve the position of future workers in the employment marketplace or the workplace. However, there seems little reason to doubt that the abilities to collaborate, to think laterally, autonomously and creatively, to analyse and critique, are essential if, as Soucek (1993) puts it: 'the economic and administrative system is to undergo any future incremental modifications with respect to the issues of social justice and equity, and the social and moral maturity of our increasing global community' (p. 165).

Skills that have been learned in the lifeworld – such as cultural understanding and moral maturity – can also be brought to bear on managerialist discourses in schools in ways which enhance team-building, shared educational leadership, participatory decision making, motivation and job satisfaction.

Even if these reforms do result in a tighter fusion between school and the factory/office, surely it is better for students to be prepared for a multi-skilled, creative, team-based working life than a degraded labour process harnessed to the rhythm of a machine? And for teachers, surely a bias towards collaboration, higher skill levels and increased levels of autonomy are more desirable than isolated, hierarchized endeavour?

The answers to the first of these questions is complicated by the idealism on which the whole concept of multi-skilled work is predicated. Jones and Hatcher (1994), drawing on the history of work reform in the UK, argue persuasively that analyses of post-Fordist work trends are often based on sanguine projections of economic progress, and are insufficiently nuanced to deal with the polyvalent effects of workplace reform. Instead, they argue that:

> the evidence suggests that technical change does not amount to unequivocal social progress: the introduction of 'flexible specialisation' in manufacturing industry is reliant on, and in turn reinforces, deep inequalities within the labour force.... Even the opportunities offered by the collective task-sharing and problem-solving approach of group work permit an involvement with decision-making only at low levels of the workplace hierarchy. In spite of post-Fordist rhetoric, the social division of labour remains intact...'multi-skilling' entails little alteration in the traditional prerogatives of management. 'Conception' at the level of company strategy and product design is still very much separated from execution; and job flexibility is better regarded as a matter of the intensification, not the enrichment, of work. At the level of the firm and its sub-contractors, then, the post-Fordist thesis of multi-skilling and a growth in the demand for 'collective intelligence' is not borne out. Indeed, inasmuch as it entails a blunting of trade union organisation in the name of collective workforce responsibility, post-Fordist techniques offer a kind of change which possesses...a strong regressive element.
>
> (p. 253)

Similarly, Apple (1996b) argues that: 'the claims made by neo-liberals about the [productive] connections between schooling and the economy...are at best based on very shaky evidence and at worst are simply incorrect' (p. 136).

Clearly, post-Fordism has both progressive and regressive features. Ball (1990) and Smyth (1991, 1993b) note how the progressive features simultaneously legitimize and mask the regressive aspects.

To return to the second question about teachers' work, Smyth (1991), discussing the re-emergence of collaboration among teachers, asserts that:

> this reincarnation of an educational concept that has been around for a long time is [occurring] precisely at a time of massive international reform and restructuring of schools aimed at ensuring that schools more efficiently and effectively satisfy national economic priorities.
>
> (p. 324)

while Ball (1990) warns that the: 'new progressivism, despite its team work activities, is primarily oriented to individual performance and reward, based on graded assessments, as opposed to the batch examination, mass, class-teaching approach of the liberal-humanist tradition' (p. 136).

Nevertheless, the fact that teachers at Gallipoli High School and else-where in Australia persist, in the face of considerable difficulties, with attempts to establish joint work practices cannot be lightly dismissed.

5 Teachers' Work-storied Accounts of Professionalism and Intensification

The Case of Appleton College

Introducing Teachers' Work at Appleton College

The research reported here is about teachers' work. It arose out of the experience of one of the authors, as a teacher, of doing the *job* of teaching at a time when massive changes in the conceptualizing and the organization of that work were occurring. The motivation came from the desire to understand and contextualize changes to the daily grind of teaching, changes which seemed to originate in the appropriation of educational interests by spheres of influence removed from those concerned with the things that teachers believe matter in teaching, namely, students, learning and colleagues. In this sense, it is research that attempted to locate the role of teaching work, as experienced by teachers in the working world of classrooms and schools, within a bigger framework about work and schooling.

Teachers inhabit classrooms workplaces where they are engaged in the work tasks of teaching and administration. Their working day is highly structured and their work practices are highly organized. Put simply, teachers are workers, teaching is work, and that work is organized and subject to workplace controls (Connell, 1985; Seddon, 1990). The importance of thinking about teaching in this way is that it allows theoretical insights from the labour process discourse to be applied to the work of teaching in order that teacher's occupational lives can be located within a complex of influences that affect the macro and micro aspects of teachers' work (Ozga, 1988). Among the strongest of the influences which impact on teacher's conceptions of their work, and themselves as workers, are ideologies of professionalism (Densmore, 1987). Ideologies of professionalism are important in teaching because they legitimate work practices and strategies for control in teachers' work, delimit possibilities in the workplace, and set boundaries for the disclosure of knowledge about the work of teaching. The research reported here sought to locate ideologies of professionalism within storied accounts of the experiences of the work of teaching in one school. As a portrayal of teachers' work in the 1990s, the research explores a localized occupational culture of teachers for insights into how the ideological base in which schooling is embedded affects how the *job* of teaching is organized as a labour process.

Appleton College

Appleton College is a non-denominational, co-educational independent (non-government) secondary school. It is situated in an Australian provincial city which serves as the urban centre for an intensive and varied agricultural region. A population of over 100 thousand people live within a 50 kilometre radius of the city. Beyond the usual retail, commercial, and public sector employment opportunities for a city of its type and size, the town supports a range of food processing industries and allied light manufacturing and transport industries. The district's economic well-being is closely aligned to the economic health of the rural sector with employment opportunities and local business confidence correlating strongly with the rise and fall of farm commodity prices. At the time of this study, the effects of the recession and depressed prices for farm produce had a noticeable effect on the local community as reflected in the shutting down of some small businesses and the closure of a 100-year-old milk products factory due to the restructure of its larger parent company.

Established in 1982, Appleton College grew rapidly in its first seven years from 92 students in its first year to a maximum enrolment in excess of 350 in 1989. Since then enrolments have declined and in 1993 it had around 300 students, 35 teaching staff, and 13 administrative and support staff. Projections made during the initial years, which set a likely enrolment for 1992 at 460, were not realized. The school is situated on a 17 hectare site on the outskirts of the town and is bounded on three sides by roads and a new residential subdivision on the other. About half of the school site is currently occupied with buildings and sporting fields. Adjacent to the main wing of classrooms is a large grassed and well-shaded space used by students as an eating area and recreation space. On its other side is a lake which separates the school buildings from the main sporting field. Smaller specialist science, music, library and administration facilities cluster around the main wing of classrooms. All classrooms are well appointed and air-conditioned. General purpose classrooms are carpeted and have a pleasant appearance with high ceilings and plenty of natural light. Buildings are mostly surrounded by garden beds and grassed areas and are connected by paved walk-ways. It is an appealing and attractive school campus.

Students attending Appleton College come from the town and surrounding districts. Around 90 per cent, including most town students, arrive and depart the school *en masse* at the same time each day, on shuttle buses. More than half of the students make connections with other buses to get to and from school. In the morning, the school is at one moment virtually devoid of students and in the next, bustling with student activity and then later, in the afternoon, the reverse occurs. Five to ten minutes after the last class of the day, the only students left at the school are the small number having sport or music practice.

The teaching staff at Appleton College appear committed and dedicated to the school. More than half of the teaching staff have taught at the school for five or more years, with at least seven having been at the school for ten or more years. Most of the teaching staff have taught elsewhere and the number of inexperienced teachers, those with two or less years teaching, had always been low, but did increase significantly during 1992 and 1993, the year prior to, and the year of, this study.

Appleton College offers a standard junior secondary curriculum for years 7 to 9 which includes specialist work in LOTE (languages other than English), music, health education, and physical education. Junior classes usually have around 30 students. At year 10 students participate in driver education, work experience and outdoor education programmes and an elective system allows them to choose additional courses in areas of interest. At years 11 and 12 students have a wide range of subjects to choose from in completing a course of study leading to a statewide Certificate of Education. Co-curricular offerings include sport, dramatic arts and music.

When it opened, a little over a decade ago, as a new private school, without links to an established school, or any church affiliation, Appleton College had to forge its own identity, philosophical outlook, and school tradition pretty much as it went. The founding principal and school council launched the school with a philosophy statement which emphasized, at the top of a list of aims, 'the development of individual potential to the greatest possible extent in academic, creative and personal areas'. As the school grew its embryonic outlook developed along those lines in curriculum, pedagogy, policy, administration and staffing. However, since the departure of the foundation principal, eight years after the school began, the articulated school philosophy changed under other principals in the years leading up to the research. Descriptions of the school's aims and objectives now highlight an academic orientation for the school with an emphasis on academic standards and student achievement. This shift has been reflected in changed circumstances in some aspects of school life for the staff and students. Indeed, this has been the case since the late 1980s when enrolments peaked at around 360, but in recent years the school has struggled to keep student numbers above 300, and as a consequence staff numbers have declined. With diminished revenue from tuition fees and per capita funding, Appleton College has experienced a difficult time fiscally in the 1990s with reduced staff numbers and reduced budgets for teaching departments from the tightening of sources for capital and recurrent expenditure. The pressures associated with this contraction, financially, and in terms of the educational programme, have been sharply felt by the teaching staff.

The teachers

The research focused on the working lives of eight secondary school teachers from Appleton College and the account which follows developed from what they had to say about their work to a former teacher at the school, now a researcher, who had some prior knowledge of their workplace. These teachers agreed to spend time during their 1993 school year in conversation about aspects of their work: the values, the pressures, the frustrations and the rewards of teaching at Appleton College. As a group, they made a varied occupational profile, women and men with a broad mix of teaching skills and experience: from a second year teacher, to some with 15-plus years of classroom teaching experience; teachers with important administrative responsibilities; teachers with leadership roles in pastoral care and in subject coordination; teachers of practical subjects and teachers of mainstream academic subjects; and teachers of both senior and junior secondary students. There was no attempt to obtain any representative mix; the eight volunteered their participation after an invitation had been extended to the entire teaching staff of the school.

The identity of the researcher cannot be disconnected from previous work as a teacher at Appleton College. While no longer associated with the school, they did have some of the status and the privileges associated with being an *insider* to the school and its teaching culture, especially through an intimate knowledge of: the history of teaching and learning at the school; the organization of curriculum and administrative structures in the school; and the evolution of the pedagogical ethos of the school. This insider perspective became an important passport for admission into the working lives of the teachers through a methodological environment of teacher-to-teacher conversation. At the same time, it presented difficulties; which are the subject of a reflexive discussion in the full research account (Shacklock, 1995).

Research processes

This research drew upon various methods from the growing repertoire available for qualitative educational research. Given the centrality of *teacher accounts* to the project's purpose, and the desire for workplace authenticity, the collection of empirical material was framed to allow teachers to engage in a dialogue with the researcher about their work using their preferred words, metaphors and conceptual frames. Epistemologically and methodologically, the research focused upon the loud and clear articulation of teachers' voices about teachers' work. Specifically, this meant the collection of biographical and life-story material (focused on the work of teaching) from the teachers. It was a case of researching lived experience, through the teachers *telling it like it is*, in personal and contextualized accounts of what it meant to be a teacher embedded in the labour process of teaching at the school. These accounts were often specific, though not necessarily continuous in a historical sense, interpretations of the struggles, dilemmas, contradictions and ambiguities of teaching. They were told in ways that brought out the complexities of school work in a way only practitioners are capable of expressing within a rich tapestry of experiential knowledge.

The primacy of the teachers' voices in the accounts was integral to the construction of an empirically based portrayal of the work of teaching, one which has at its core the presentation of verisimilar images of these teachers' understandings of: professional identity, purpose in their work, organizational patterns and controls in their work, and relationships to other people co-existing in the workplace of the school. The reliance of this research account upon the articulation of teachers' voices made for an important admission of expressive modes used by teachers in the description of their work into an academic discourse about teachers' work. In this sense, the research contributes to that discourse which aims at editing teachers back into research accounts by deliberately subverting the *silence* of the teachers' voice that often exists in research about teachers and their work. It contributes to an ongoing affirmation of the role which the many *quiet voices* of ordinary teachers can play in the development of an understanding about labour processes in teachers' work.

The methodological use in this research of teachers' voices, in the presentation of an insider-style account of what it is like to do the work of teaching, is conceptually framed as *work-story* research. This research uses narrative accounts, as methodological devices, for the exploration of understandings and the generation of insights about teaching as work, as is the case in teacher-to-teacher talk that aims to explain what happens to teachers in their work. The stories of work are told in voices which have the multitonal character of reflection, hope, humour, anger and despair. The feel of working as a teacher comes across strongly in such stories, like it does in the accounts of teaching assembled by Connell (1985), Nias (1989) and Cortazzi (1991). *Work stories* are used by teachers to convey something important about the nature of the work of teaching which they wish to share or make public. Kainan (1992) suggests that teachers use such stories about work to 'create and present common ideas, values and features' (p. 446) about their occupational culture. In this research it is the common features and values about the work of teaching at Appleton College which are exposed in the *work-storied portrayal* which follows. The portrayal has a multi-voiced character (Quantz and O'Connor, 1988), as an account presented in the researcher's voice assembled from field-data constituted in the individual voices of teachers who work at Appleton College.

Taking a socially critical view

The work-story accounts developed in this research provide an empirical base for a socially critical narrative of teachers' work. The adoption of a socially critical view adds a very important sociological dimension to the storied picture of teaching life at Appleton College, one where accounts are not accepted as given, treated neutrally, or valorized, but are contextually narrated against a critique of the values and interests that influence teachers' work. It is the socially critical stance of this research which offers the possibility for a social analysis of work practices and patterns of power reported or symbolized in the storied accounts about teachers' work at Appleton College to have currency beyond that single site.

Moving beyond functional and apolitical framing of teaching, the adoption of a socially critical view recognizes that teachers' lives and work settings are linked with historical, social, and cultural qualities which influence schools and teaching. A socially critical view problematizes these dimensions in teachers' lives by making them a focus for critically framed research into teachers' work. While it is not possible to nominate everything which might be included under the umbrella of these three dimensions, the following are important. First, the place of teaching in society and the status attached to it as an occupation give a social dimension to the issue of teaching, which is reflected in the linkage of teachers' work to various agenda outside schools. Second, the changing structural conditions of teachers' work and the links with occupational identity forged through public discourse on professionalism are part of the politico-cultural dimension of teaching. Finally, there is the historical location of teaching which grounds the evolving position of educated workers in the labour processes within society at large. In this research it is the threads, between teacher professionalism, the degradation of teachers' work, and the social context which binds them together, that were relevant and worthy of investigation.

The Boundaries of Professionalism

The literature on the sociology of the professions and the evolving nature of professional work is large and diverse making it somewhat arduous to garner theoretical insights useful in making connections between patterns of organization in different forms of work. Larson (1977) argued that a common set of beliefs about professionalism, which have origins in the *work understandings* of the older professions, are generalized and shared by diverse occupational groups aspiring to be professional and that ideological constructions of professionalism have become powerful determinants of what is legitimate and possible in forms of work and in workplaces. Such beliefs permeate occupational cultures becoming accommodated in common-sense understandings and embedded in many different *local* conceptions of professionalism. For example, Densmore's (1987) case study of first-year teachers gives empirical support for this position applied to teaching. She found that 'while the ideals of professionalism bear little relationship to the circumstances of teachers' practices, as an ideological construct, professionalism informs teachers actions' (p. 130) and that this occurs most often through a 'general school ambience of professionalism' (p. 141).

Lawn's (1989) assertion that professionalism is 'a key contested term in the history of teaching' (p. 159) suggests that research into teaching which seeks to elicit an understanding of the place of professionalism in the labour process of teaching must begin with teachers, and their understandings of themselves, as workers. This requires an inside view of the day-to-day complexity of professionalism when accommodating the organizational and relational aspects of teaching as work. When teachers work with their pupils and colleagues, they already hold views and assumptions about the role of professionalism in their work, while at the same time being aware of, and influenced by, the views held by those outside the world of classrooms and staffrooms. To tap into how professionalism is used in this sense, as teachers themselves use and experience it, requires the teacher's voices to be heard. Work-story accounts allow for a narration of powerful and specific images through particular cases of professionalism in action suitable for another person to vicariously encounter the 'feel of being a teacher' (Nias, 1989): the caring and the conflict; the convictions and contradictions; the tensions and contentments; the hopes and fears; and the exhilaration and exhaustion that are embodied in teaching.

Work stories about professionalism

For teachers at Appleton College professionalism was an important definitional element for how they saw themselves in relation to students, colleagues, parents and the general community. While it remained a complex construct, generally they were amenable to labelling their work as professional and were able to provide some justification for this against grounded occupational criteria of their own choice. Most believed it to be a commonly held view within the occupation, but there was some doubt about how much the general populace knew of the *realities* of teaching, like its complexity and intensity as work.

Reflecting on his brief experience as a teacher, Bob – a teacher starting his second year of teaching felt that he had his image of teaching as a profession confirmed.

> I felt I was joining a profession when I became a teacher. My perception is, I think almost universally, the teachers I've come across at this school, that I've had contact with care. I think that's a wide perception, that teachers are professional.

Bob made an association between teachers who care and teachers being professional. Also, he did acknowledge that there are people who hold the contrary view – that teachers are not professional – but was inclined to regard them as being misled in their assessment, probably because it was based on an inadequate knowledge of what teachers actually do in their work.

> I think also the perception of the time involved in teaching is vastly inaccurate. I mean, generally people think that doctors and dentists work long hours and they work hard and study for five or six years. If some teachers study for three years and they work from nine to three-thirty, that wouldn't help because it doesn't look like a very demanding job at all from the outside, does it? I think there probably is, in a lot of people, a perception that teachers aren't professionals. If I had to give a reason for that, I would say the hours issue is probably the most important one, people don't realise the time that is spent.

Naturally, as a novitiate teacher, Bob has a limited set of teaching experiences to draw upon in making comment about teacher professionalism, yet despite this he was articulate in contrasting his own view with those held by others. His colleague Benita, a teacher at the other end of the teaching experience spectrum presented a similar overall position in her remarks. She was strong and quite specific in her acceptance of teachers being called professional.

> I do believe that teachers are professionals, they should be seen as professionals, and that should be part and parcel of the whole thing. Well, I think you're in a very responsible position…and I think that you do need to be professional about that. You need to be treated as a professional, because there are many years of study that have gone into that [becoming a teacher] and you have to keep up to date. I mean you're just as much a professional as anyone else, as a doctor or an accountant, or anyone like that.

Benita expressed a belief that it was lack of awareness, on the part of those outside the occupation, about the time put into their work by teachers which was the most likely reason behind the poorly informed assessments about the professionalism of teachers and their work.

> I think that we would like to think that we are professional, that we are seen as professional, but I think that sometimes the general public don't see us as being professional. I think the majority of parents certainly would see us as professionals…but they're not aware of the number of hours that teachers work, outside of actual class time. I think probably their main expectation is that you try to do your best by the student.

Bob and Benita's comments indicate a belief that teachers generally do, or want to, regard themselves as professional, and that parents are also likely to hold this view. Significantly, both Bob and Benita identified an *invisibility* of the time and effort that goes into the work of teaching as the most likely cause of people (other than teachers) not associating teaching with professional work. For them, it was the invisibility of the time spent, especially outside of class contact, which gave an impression that teaching work is not very demanding and that teachers, therefore, do not work as hard as other professionals.

Ron, another experienced teacher who had taught in several other schools, but only for a short time at Appleton College, argued the same case in arriving at a similar position.

> I see it as a profession. I think they [teachers] have seen it as a profession and as something that they intend to work at for the whole of their lives. It's not something they intend to do for ten years and get out. They usually put a lot of training into it and, particularly in recent years, they are continuing to train and most of them have done it in their own time and at their own expense. Again, to me that's a sign of concern and professional go ahead. I think the majority of teachers do have a real concern for kids and they are teaching because they want to impart something to students to go out and get ahead. It's a dedication to the individual and I think you see it particularly in the pastoral care system here. That, I think is part of professionalism in teaching, that caring concern beyond the norm. They knock teachers, but I don't think a lot of people see the after-hours work which does go on in pastoral care, in areas like that, and in preparing work for students.

For Ron, the necessary ingredients of the professional teacher centre on: care, commitment, training, and ongoing development. He chose to highlight 'care beyond the norm', as if to say, that while a certain (minimum) amount of care in working with students is a usual expectation for teachers, for him a professional teacher is one that does more in this area. While Ron was not specific about how that might happen, the implication was that this may exist in the relationship between teacher and student as manifest in a commitment to principles of pastoral care. Again, like Bob and Benita, he identified a lack of knowledge of the time commitment involved in teaching, due to the invisibility of things like: administrative work, after-hours meeting attendance, time spent counselling students and telephoning parents, preparation and correction done at home during evenings and on weekends as the likely cause of the misunderstanding about teaching from those who 'knock teachers'.

In generating a response based upon her experience as a teacher, Mandy felt that a professional teacher 'goes out of their way to do the best they can' for pupils and colleagues. Furthermore, in her qualification about complacency, there was a sense that, in terms of teacher–student relationships, doing your best may be more than what (usually) might be regarded as enough when something better is possible.

> I suppose the sorts of things that I think make someone seem professional are: going out of their way to always do the best they can for the students and to help other teachers. Yes, and to never just sit back and think: 'oh well this'll do', and be complacent. Yes, and to always do the right thing by the students.

This sounds remarkably similar to the statement about 'caring beyond the norm' and it would seem that Mandy's position on professionalism was also linked with a commitment to care. Like her colleagues, Mandy felt that outside the occupation it was only parents who were likely to consider teaching a professional activity. She had her doubts about whether the general populace does not regard teaching as a professional activity. 'Probably most parents have a pretty good perception of the teachers here and they'd see us as professional, but I have the feeling that in the general community though, people don't feel that way about teachers'.

Josh, an energetic and developing teacher, also had a confident view of the professionalism of his colleagues but, at the same time, in the light of his experience at other schools thought that in the wider community of teachers there were some to whom he would apply the term professional, and some that he would not. He chose to be very specific about things which he felt clearly reflected the professionalism of his current colleagues.

> Here, our professionalism is seen in how we respect the kids and each other, and we respect the knowledge that we've got to offer. It's not often that I can't go up to my co-ordinator and say: 'look, what's this next topic about?' I don't get the big long looks like I should know, I get the answer and a couple of articles thrown in just in case I want to know more, and I think that is very professional. We feel very comfortable to walk into each other's classrooms. I'm often in Sue's class because I'm often wandering through [to his office] and a kid will put up a hand asking for help and we have this relationship where it's fine for me to stop and help the student and I think that is because of the overall professionalism of the [staff] group.

Josh places big emphasis on respect for children and colleagues. The highlighting of 'important values and qualities that present the image of a "good teacher"' (Kainan, 1992, p. 448) in contrast to situations where they do not exist, as Josh does here, is a regular feature of teachers' work stories and plays an important role in the reassertion of common values in the occupational culture (Kainan, 1992). Like his colleagues, Josh is sure that, outside of schools, many people have little regard for the professional status of teaching, as is evident in his telling of this very personal story about wider community perceptions of teachers as professionals.

> No, I'd say that quite emphatically [that teachers are not regarded as professionals in the wider community]. I had a lot of criticism when I first started teaching. A lot of doctors I played sport with said: 'why be a teacher?' I often, nearly weekly, got a comment from someone like: 'why don't you go and earn a living being a systems analyst'. You know, one person even said to me last week: 'earn a real living!' [Laughter] Her ears got burnt with my wife on one side, and me on the other, as she walked down the hall.

Beyond some obvious amusement in the telling of this story, and in relating the remarks made by his friends about him being a teacher, Josh was making a significant point about the widespread lack of credibility (and subsequent) devaluing of teaching as a suitable occupation for an educated professional person, as seen from the perspective of some other professionals. This is not surprising given comments about teachers as 'academically weak' by a university vice-chancellor (Richards, 1994).

If there were stand out features in the comments made by these teachers it was the commitment to care and the invisibility of teachers' work. They believed that much of the work teachers do apart from classroom tuition is not seen by the general community, with the possible exception of some parents, because it is performed behind the scenes. That is, a lot of the hard work of teaching takes place in the relative isolation of teacher offices, staffrooms and homes. These are places where teachers spend long hours engaged in a huge amount of administrative and other activities fundamental to the support of the more exposed, and hence publicly visible, pedagogical aspects of teacher work.

Work stories about invisibility of teachers' work

Significantly, the invisibility of the time and effort that goes into the work of teaching was identified in the work stories as the most likely cause of people other than teachers not acknowledging teaching as professional work. It was thought that the invisibility of the time spent, especially outside of class contact hours, might give the impression that teaching is not very demanding and that teachers do not work as hard as other professionals.

Teaching is often solitary and private work (Dreeben, 1988) and a lot of the hard work of teaching takes place in the relative isolation of teacher offices, staffrooms and homes. It is, as Connell (1985) found in his study of teachers' work, that:

there is something a little mysterious and evasive at the heart of the business of teaching...[and that while] the popular image of school teaching is of talk-and-chalk in front of a class...there is much more...to keep a school humming or bumping along.

(p. 71)

As Connell (1985) described it, the 'bits of work' (p. 71) that teachers do besides the visible work of classroom contact with students 'would take pages' (p. 71) to fully describe.

However, this lack of knowledge about what it is like to work in schools is not confined to those who have no recent contact with teachers. Appleton College teachers described how their work was not even adequately understood by family members. In Bob's case, he was surprised that his spouse, a health professional person working at the local hospital, had doubts about the professional status of his work as a teacher.

I don't think she considers teaching as professional as her own area. I don't know why that is, because she knows a lot about me and my teaching, and she says she under values my skills and knowledge as a teacher. I always thought she would be the last person who would think that.

Jack, too, was disappointed that common perceptions about teachers' work, that teachers get it easy, should gain publicity in the local newspaper, and that his friends and family had little idea of what teachers actually do in their work.

In the local paper our MLA [State Government Parliamentarian] said: 'teachers have had it easy for a long time and that they've been insulated from the changes of the last ten years'. That thinking comes from a lack of knowledge of what a teacher's role is. Perhaps teachers really need to spell out what they do. I know that in talking to friends and brothers, they have no idea of what a teacher does and they are very surprised that we don't get paid anything on a school camp over, you know over a week. They only have to go away overnight and they get paid for it and they get a motel room and meals and the lot. They couldn't understand why we'd go away for a week [on camp] and not get paid [extra] for it.

Ron also spoke about the role played by the media in maintaining a poor public image of teachers and supporting the invisibility of their work. Selectivity and sensationalism in reporting often fed public misinformation about teachers and their work leading to poor conceptions of teachers. He gave a particular insight into how reporting the activities of teachers and schools can be based upon little information and motivated by self-interest.

> I have an older brother who is a journalist [with a capital city daily] and I always find it amusing when he talks critically about teachers. When I say: 'but, I'm one', he says: 'yes, but you're not like that'. He can't even give me people he knows who are like that either. Both his parents have been teachers as well, and he says: 'no, I'm not talking about them, I'm talking about the others'. He holds a senior position as a News Editor, which means he's been responsible for some of the headlines having a shot [at teachers] lately. I think, he thinks he's presenting what the public wants…he admits that it's editorial instruction.

Teaching, as a form of work, by its very existence and organization in schools is hidden from public view. Even teachers often have little opportunity to see the work done by colleagues in classrooms and offices because of their heavy workloads and the spatial isolation and dispersion of teaching worksites (Dreeben, 1988). When teachers themselves have a limited knowledge of the work of other teachers, it is not surprising that the nature of teachers' work is largely invisible to the public. Unfortunately, until there are more accurate representations of the work that teachers do as organized labour like other more recognizable forms of work, the poor public image of teachers' work seems likely to remain.

An Ethic of Care in Teaching

The relationship between teacher and student was central to the way in which teachers from Appleton College sought to ground the role of professionalism in their work. The importance of *care* in the way these teachers defined themselves, in their perceptions of a professional way of working as a teacher, was very strong. Significantly, it came time and again in accounts about themselves and their work and appeared in their statements of belief and intent. If there was a definitional essence for these teachers, about the qualities of their work, in what they elected to cover in their work stories, it was this notion of *care*. This extended concept of care in the work of teachers at Appleton College can be theoretically grounded in Nel Noddings' writing on 'an ethic of care' (1984, 1988, 1992). Noddings (1992) suggests that 'caring is the very bedrock of all successful education' (p. 27) and that all teaching moments can be seen as caring occasions.

There appears to be a strong degree of similitude between 'an ethic of care' and the practical definition of working in 'a professional way' given by these teachers. Soder (1991) gives general support for grounding teacher professionalism in an ethical base by arguing that 'teaching is an ethical activity...if one wishes to talk about teaching as a profession' (p. 295) and that teachers must seek to define themselves through the 'strong sense of self-worth, of importance, or self affirmation which is to be found in the very nature of teaching, in the relationship between the teacher, the student, the parent and the state' (p. 300). This is a persuasive argumentative link for the strong connection between the theoretical framework provided by Noddings' ethic of care and the empirical base found in the views on teacher professionalism offered by the teachers from Appleton College. However, as is the case with any notion of professionalism in teaching, there is potential for contradictory and contested meanings in the development of an ethic of care in teachers' working lives. Indeed, the nature of this contestation will become clearer in the following sections of this account of teachers' work.

Work stories about caring in teaching

In the light of this theoretical perspective, the following work-story accounts illustrate how these teachers exercise an ethic of care in their work. For example, the primacy of the relationship between teacher as carer, and student as cared-for was fundamental.

> Often I think you do something for a student which would be seen to be against the attitudes of the parents and the school. I'm thinking of a former staff member who advised a student to go out and get a job. Now that probably went against their nature as a teacher, but they looked at the capabilities of the student, looked at the emotional unrest for them [in staying on at school]. They were thinking about that student as a person, rather than as a piece of putty...it seems to have been, so far, from what I've seen, the best thing that could have happened for that student. He went to TAFE (Technical and Further Education) and was doing a lot better and now has a job. Twelve months later, leaving at the time he did probably benefited him more than sticking to a year 12 regime and not finishing.

In this case the teacher, in exercising professional judgement in order to do the right thing by the student, eventually recommended a course of action for the student which was different to that advocated by the parents and the school's administration. Another possible course of action out of this dilemma, which might in some ways be considered just as educationally defensible, would have been to try and influence the student to stay on at school and attempt a potentially unsuitable and unhappy year at school. However, in following an ethic of care, to do the best by the student, located in the preservation of the relation between the student and the teacher, influenced the nature of the advice given, and the actual final outcome – the student leaving school. The result for the student, according to the story, was very satisfactory.

In a sense, the professional competence in the technical aspects of teaching, and the adoption of a professional ethic of care in the work of teaching, are not seen as the same thing. Dealing with social problems of various kinds, that are not directly connected with the pedagogical concerns of the classroom teacher, yet play a part in what a teacher must address and cope with in their day's work, was a common problem and source of stress for teachers; and in Benita's case it was a strong incentive in her decision to undertake a part-time course of study.

> Years ago you went in and taught your class, and they had a test and if they passed, well, you thought you were successful. But I think now, there is a lot more; with family breakups and with other things, I think success is measured differently. The pressure is on not only academic things, but also on pastoral care, and as I said, I don't think it's just academic now, it's more rounded, it's much broader and teachers have to be able to cope [with that]. That was why I did the Graduate Diploma in Student Welfare, because I felt that I wasn't coping as well as I could, as I should be, and I felt myself a bit inadequate in being able to help these students who were being faced with separations and divorces and things like that. So to me, it was important to be able to learn a little bit more, so that I was able to help the students in my care.

Caring is all about doing something more, about putting yourself out, in an attempt to do the best by your students and it may involve large sacrifices in time and energy on the part of the teacher. This was especially the case when it comes to co-curricular activities held at lunchtimes, after school and on weekends. Caring can also be about the more mundane aspects of teachers' work (Rogers, 1994): about taking the time to listen to students, about taking an interest in students' lives and problems, about the production of appropriate learning materials, about the promotion of democratic class-room processes, about the prompt return of submitted student work, about welcoming cultural diversity, about developing cooperative learning environments, and about encouraging respect between students.

It is about putting the preservation of an individual relation of care by maintenance of the primacy of the student's interests; it is about addressing social and educational injustice and disadvantage; it is about motivational displacement, or 'putting oneself out', in constantly seeking to create opportunity for students to learn and be creative.

Work stories about caring for colleagues

The nature of the relationship between colleagues was also central to the way in which the teachers at Appleton College chose to talk about professionalism in their work. The way in which teachers worked together within the school was seen as a very positive aspect of school life and specific aspects of collegiate interaction were highlighted as indicative of professionalism in action.

Mandy told about the importance she attached to her concept of 'going out of your way to always do the best' by colleagues. In the first instance, she reflected on how the heavy load of teaching and administrative tasks, for which she had responsibility, meant that some areas of her work, support to teachers in her department, received less attention than they deserved.

> I just feel that my mind has to go in so many different directions at once. Worrying about how people are going in my department, particularly the teachers in the lower levels who are new. That's why I said I worried. That's all I did, I worried! I didn't get any further than worrying about it; other than feeling guilty because I was doing nothing about it. That is poor, and that's probably the thing I've done worst this year and which I'm not happy about at all!

She felt unhappy that she had not been able to, or did not go out of her way to, monitor the progress of the less-experienced teachers in her department and, by her own standards, that was not the professional way in which she would ideally like to work. Indeed, she admitted feeling guilty, for having knowingly let her younger colleagues – for whom she felt some responsibility – down, in some unspecified way. A reaction of this kind is not unexpected given the impact of devolved horizontal management on the work of teachers with coordination and peer-supervision responsibilities (see Chapter 4). In another case, Mandy described how she dreamt of the luxury of being able to escape the burden and frustration of the responsibility attached to the various non-teaching duties she carried by returning to the classroom full time. She thought that her classroom work should be her top priority.

> That's the bit I do best and it's the bit I'm trained for and that I'm comfortable with and I do resent it [the other things that get in the way] and I get very annoyed. I can see that in a small school you have to do it, but I also feel very guilty, constantly, because I'm not doing a lot of it as well as I'd like and that worries me. I still feel fine about teaching [but] I just wish that I could stop taking on roles. I mean, I could by just saying: 'no, I won't do it', but then that's not really a very professional thing to do.

Despite knowing that having said 'no' to additional responsibility would have provided an immediate solution to her current discontent over having too much to do, Mandy articulated why, for her, it really was not the answer:

> Someone has to do it. In a big school you'd probably have people queuing up for the jobs that I do, but here there's no one [who would want them]. [Laughter] I probably sound really negative, [but] I don't feel negative, I just wish that I wasn't as rushed and scattered as I am. It's certainly a challenge though [laughter], but anyway, I suppose I'll get there.

Mandy is to be admired for her good humour, confidence, and resilience in the face of the demands her work places upon her resources. She felt that to carry on doing what she does, despite its less than satisfactory impact on her, and her ethical ideal, was the professional thing to do. She is following her own professional credo, putting herself out to support her colleagues, because she senses that no one else would want to take on those tasks and the burdens they bring. The burdens of her work in the school were viewed as a challenge and something to be done despite there being no solution to the feelings of being pulled in multiple directions. Her ethical ideal-self remained intact, and the obligation to care for her colleagues remained strong in her continued willingness to take on responsibilities and the consequent burdens of workload and time they created. Her desire to follow the professional way and do the right thing by her colleagues seemed to prevent her from taking the solution she had identified for the mitigation of her problems with time and the attendant feelings of guilt. Mandy's ethic of care manifested itself in an obligation to engage in a supportive relation of care with her colleagues by taking on the extra jobs. It could be said that, as a source of contradiction in her work, it plays a role in both the making, and unmaking, of her professional identity.

If the relation between teacher and student(s) lies at the hub of any internalized notion of teaching as professional work then radially beyond and connected to that are collegiate relations. For the Appleton College teachers, doing the right thing by your colleagues was closely linked to the rubric of 'doing the right thing by your students' in the professional ethos central to the teaching culture of the school. In such an ethos, collegiate relations are developed and preserved by caring teachers in ethical relation to the other teachers they work with in the pursuit of common goals.

Work stories about relations with parents

Appleton College teachers had some ideas about what parents might expect and think of the nature of the relationship which should exist between teachers and parents. Each teacher indicated with some confidence that most parents would, consider the school's teachers to be professional and have some expectations of teachers that they might label professional. The basic criterion used by the teachers in defining their own professional status, to do your best for the students in your care, was also thought to be the likely basis for parental judgement about the professional status of a teacher's work. Sometimes the expectations of parents are (predictably) parochial and, at such times, may be unrealistic and even possibly unreasonable, and this may present a possible source of stress and difficulty for teachers. An instance of this, and the pressures generated by it, were evident in Jack's telling of the things teachers sometimes get asked by parents to do.

> I think the parents here expect more of you than perhaps they should. They come and tell me: 'so and so is doing their homework in front of the TV and they shouldn't be and can you have a word to them' [and] 'what are you doing about it'. You know, you don't say anything, you sort of fumble about and try to say something, but really, basically what you want say is: 'well yes, what are you doing about it?'! This school, being a private school, where you've got to keep the customers happy, puts a lot more pressure on you because in a way you can't be as blunt as perhaps you should be.

High expectations for academic success are common among parents, and the articulation of these desires can create pressure on teachers to produce results which, in turn, can be a cause of workplace stress for teachers. As was the case with the teacher, who acted out of an ethic of care, advising a student to leave school, against the wishes of parents and school administration, a focus on outcomes, in this case highest possible grades in academic assessments, can sit in contradiction with a teacher's ethic of care. Ron was worried by the strong focus on results at Appleton College. He saw it as being in tension with, and at the expense of, the needs of individual students and believed that it conflicted with his educational philosophy, that is, it went against his ethic of care and his decision making about students on an individual (relational) basis. He found that his Principal can apply just as much pressure as parents in the pursuit of examination results and high pass-rates is a major goal for the school and its senior students.

> I am scared that the education of the whole student might not be a target in schools. If we're teaching to produce results, we're not teaching the student. Teaching to me isn't just getting 'A+s', it's producing someone who can think for themselves, as an individual, [but] individuals don't rate well in a school that's going for academic performance. It's one of my biggest fights with Peter [the Principal] because he believes that, whilst we are [here] to educate, to survive financially

you've got to be able to say: 'we have 100 per cent this and 100 per cent that'; and to me that's not education.

Ron and his colleagues found themselves in the difficult position of being encouraged by their Principal to accept the very pragmatic assumption that the financial survival of the school, and hence ultimately their own employment security, depended upon the quality of results obtained by the school's students in the external year 12 assessment process. Ron's 'fight' with his Principal was situated in a contradiction between the assertion of his belief about an ethic of care in teaching, and its informant role on relationships with individual students and their learning, as opposed to the primacy of the educational ends like results and pass-rates. The focus on pass-rates, focused the teaching-learning process on predetermined outcomes of schooling, which, effectively undermined the individual relational nature of that process by reducing it to a technical process associated with the pursuit of a final outcome, a 100 per cent pass-rate, divorced from the individuals involved.

However, not all pressures which come from parents, either directly, or indirectly, are focused upon examination pass-rates and the head-long pursuit of academic success. As would be the case in most schools, parental expectations at Appleton College are high in the area of pastoral care. Parents expect to be kept informed about any problems faced by their child(ren), such as lack of progress or misbehaviour, which Fred sees as a direct manifestation of teacher–parent accountability. 'Parents expect communication to go home and to be told before it [the problem with their child] gets too serious and out of hand. It's part of their expectation. I suppose you could call it accountability.'

This sense of responsibility, or accountability, to the parents goes with the territory for teachers in private schools. Accountability was something which is never far away, in the parent–teacher relations, as Fred explained:

> you get the occasional one who says: 'well I'm paying X number of dollars and I expect that [outcome] type of thing'. At the same time the majority of the parents put into the school, they certainly assist and support you [in working with their children], so it's a two way situation. We work as a team and the one who benefits is the child. That's what they expect of teachers and professionalism. If you want, call it accountability.

In raising the spectre of accountability, Fred has given an indication of the awareness that some kind of client relationship exists between teachers and parents. Attacks of this kind can be hurtful for teachers and are difficult to fend off because they are often borne of frustration and disappointment on the part of the parent, and the *who pays* rejoinder is the biggest stick they can wield at such times, when there is not much else they can legitimately say. The interaction between teachers and parents at Appleton College is obviously complex, where a tense professional–client relationship, while cooperative and supportive on many fronts, through mutual engrossment in the interests of the child(ren), remains unpredictable and a source of potential conflict due to an accountability factor associated with the payment of tuition fees. The existence of this factor, while essentially unwritten and informal, is nevertheless present in the background when decision making occurs.

Intensification and Proletarianization of Teachers' Work

Teaching is what teachers do. Teaching takes place in schools with students, other teachers and school administrators. As an enterprise, teaching has been, at different times, variously described as: a calling, a craft, a moral activity, art, professional practice, and a host of other purposeful things. More recently, it has been seen as work (Connell, 1985; Seddon, 1990). The teaching of students in classrooms, and the attendant support activities that go with a teacher's lot in school, like preparation and correction, pastoral care, co-curricula involvement with sport, music, and so on, have been increasingly seen, by those interested in understanding what teachers do, as just another form of work, which in important ways is not dissimilar to the work performed by other workers. In this conceptual development of teaching as work, schools have come to be seen as worksites where the work of teaching is organized and divided (Ozga, 1988) and there is a recognition that 'there is a labour process in teaching [which] is increasingly regulated by managers and employers' (Lawn, 1989, p. 158). A labour process perspective on teaching provides a different window on the organization and history of teaching (see Chapter 2); that is, teaching as production and teachers as workers involved in production politics (Seddon, 1990).

Like all forms of white-collar work teaching is undergoing significant change due to the reorganization of work practices resulting from the application of technologies of control aimed at increased productivity and efficiency in schools. The ideological nature of recent attempts at school reform, based largely in the massaging of the rhetoric of teacher professionalism, makes a discussion of different conceptions of professional work and the fragmentation of white-collar work (as described in the proletarianization thesis within orthodox Marxism) an important playing-field for the discussion of labour processes for teachers as workers (Smyth, 1991).

For example, Harris (1982) argues that proletarianization should be viewed as a process of socialization which stems from the degradation of work skills and value of labour because 'proletarianization is the limiting point of the economic process of devaluation of labour power from skilled to average levels' (Harris, 1990a, p. 195). The processual nature of proletarianization is important in Harris' view and he makes the point that while proletarianization is associated with the work of the proletariat, this does not necessarily mean that white-collar work is being converted into blue-collar work, but that with educated labour like teaching, work tasks and forms of work organization take on patterns found in blue-collar work.

Support for this view is found in work which suggests that features evident in proletarianization in other work locations, namely: deskilling, routinization, and intensification are demonstrable in teaching (Aronowitz, 1973; Ozga and Lawn, 1981; White, 1983; Aronowitz and Giroux, 1985; Densmore, 1985; 1987; Apple, 1988b; Lawn and Ozga, 1988; Hargreaves, 1992b; Ozga, 1993). Yet another recognition of this trend is found in Connell's (1985) assertion that 'teachers' work can be understood as a particular labour process...which can expand almost without limit, and the work could be intensified indefinitely' (p. 86). Likewise, Apple's (1988a) recognition that intensification in teaching 'has many symptoms from the trivial to the more complex' (p. 105) is developed into Hargreaves' (1992b) telling list of ways in which work intensification occurs in teaching.

1   Intensification leads to reduced time for relaxation during the working day, including 'no time at all for lunch'.
2   Intensification leads to lack of time to retool one's skills and keep up with one's field.
3   Intensification creates chronic and persistent overload (as compared with the temporary overload that is sometimes experienced in meeting deadlines), which reduces areas of personal discretion, inhibits involvement in and control over longer-term planning, and fosters dependency on externally produced materials and expertise.
4   Intensification leads to reductions in the *quality* [his emphasis] of service, as corners are cut to save time.
5   Intensification leads to enforced diversification of expertise and responsibility to cover personnel shortages, which can in turn create excessive dependency on outside expertise and further reductions in the quality of service.
6   Intensification creates and reinforces scarcities of preparation time.
7   Intensification is voluntarily supported by many teachers and recognized as professionalism (pp. 88–90).

As a list, it gives a guide to how intensification may occur in the work of teachers and is recognizable in the stories of intensified work at Appleton College.

Work stories about teaching as work

Hargreaves (1992b) is accurate when he says that: 'whatever else might be said about teaching, few would disagree that the nature and demands of the job have changed profoundly over the years. For better or worse, teaching is not what it was' (p. 87). The following storied accounts tell, in very personal terms, about changed working conditions and expectations and the impact on teachers. It is important that stories like these are heard, not because they are unique or special representations of teachers' work, but because they tell something of one of 'the silences of schoolwork' research (Lawn, 1989, p. 147); technologies of control in the labour process of teaching and their impact on day-to-day work in schools. The storied-montage of remarks below encapsulates these trends.

> Fred: I think when I first started teaching it was very teacher centred but there has been a very big swing to student-centred learning where the teacher is the facilitator. I see a difference in what I do in class in that regard.

> Benita: The way we teach and our expectations of students are different. Students are much more outspoken and they want to be part of the learning process.

> Josh: I think technology has scared teachers, but they are now starting to realize that it can help them, and that it will be a significant tool for them in terms of collecting information. Kids will have to be taught how to handle masses of information.

> Jack: We're looking at more interactive classes; much less of the teacher who sits in front and lectures and writes things on the board.

Comments like these reflect different teacher–student relationships and changes about what counts as learning in the classroom. For Jack, it meant coping with more and different ways of learning happening in the class-room.

> I think in the past kids were more willing to accept routine and more willing to run with the crowd, to be the same, whereas now I think kids want to be different and you need to cater more for those differences. So, you end up running less chalk and talk, or group [focused] classes, and you tend to focus more on individual desires and challenges. It was a lot easier to stand up in front of the class, and do something with all of the class and that's it, but now you've got to be willing to let more happen in the class, for the kids to go in various directions.

No longer is it possible to prepare a lesson regarded as suitable for all students; a variety of approaches and materials are needed to cope with individual learning abilities and needs. For Mandy this meant more, and different, preparation in order to cope with the demands of new teaching methods and learning strategies.

> I suppose there is less writing down stuff. You try to get the kids to think more and that means less textbook stuff. You're trying to think of ways to help students develop attitudes, and think about issues. It's less, up front telling them what to do, and more encouraging them in talking about why they react in certain ways. So, that means your preparation is different and it is harder because you have to look around for new and different resources.

The Appleton College teachers also believed that there has been widespread curriculum change in schools and that currently schools must provide learning in many areas in addition to the traditional academic subjects. The pervasive aspect of the remarks below, would indicate that this has caused an expansion in administrative tasks associated with classroom work.

> Fred: At the moment curriculum ideas seem to be on the run. Whether we're giving students a broad education, a vocational education, or just tunnelling them down to meet the university [entry].

> Brian: I think with the Certificate of Education there is a lot more work, record keeping and other work out of that. I think we've accepted that we need to give more information to parents.

> Bob: I think half, or more, of my time is not teaching. It doesn't mean it's waste, but it's not what I'm trained for and you do an awful lot of things [like that].

> Benita: Schools are expected to teach much more now. Before, it just tended to be the disciplines that you taught; now there's all these other things, like: health and sex education, driver training, and outdoor things, which are expected to be taught in the school...a lot of things are not being done in the home, and so more responsibility is falling to schools to teach those things.

Work stories about intensification in teaching

How teachers used the time available to them in their work, and how they coped with the constraints that time places upon their ability to get work done, gained much comment from the Appleton College teachers. There was a lot of talk about the pressure of 'too little time' in meeting the demands of day-to-day work, especially through concern about having too many things to do in the time available. The following montage shows how three of these teachers chose to make *time* a central factor in their descriptions of their work and how they felt about the way in which they *cope* with the demands of their work. The notion of time, as a limited quantity which determines what work can occur, comes through strongly; as does, the defining role time plays in conceptions of teachers' coping skills. In these remarks, lack of time can be seen as generative of problems in coping with the workload of teaching, and the likely cause of stress and other difficulties faced on a daily basis in the working life of a teacher.

Mandy: I never have enough time. I reckon I could do better in the classroom, but I just don't have the energy, or the time. I just feel scattered most of the time. I feel frazzled because there are so many things happening all the time, there are so many demands. Teachers don't know whether kids have handed stuff in because they haven't marked it off simply because they haven't got the time. Professional development gets shelved because people haven't got the time. There's just not the spare hours around.

Fred: Well, the demands on time this year, compared to other years, have been quite extensive with so many things to do. I enjoy my involvement with kids at sport but it was biting into my time for other things. Things come up, and because your time has been stretched, and stretched, and stretched, there's not enough hours in the day at the moment at the school. Everyone's so busy, there's no time for reflection. I haven't really had a chance to sit down and look at my program, and try to keep up to date with what is going on, because I've got a thousand [other] things to do. Looking at two or five years ahead, there is very little of that, and the reason is you haven't got the time. It's been a tough year, it's been stretched, more things going on, and more demands on your time.

Brian: There just seems to be more, and there is pressure to spend more time [with students]. The time you spend doing that is time that you can't relax and unwind, or prepare for lessons. You've got to have some time to yourself. People feel that they just haven't had time to do things properly. I just don't set as much work, I wouldn't have the time to correct it. You have to give nearly all of your time to them [the students], so the other things suffer. You've got to give up your Thursday night, Friday night and Saturday morning [to school activities].

Two things are evident from these remarks. First, the importance of time in the way teachers talk about their work is unmistakable because the allocation, organization, and management of time in teaching is central to how these teachers see and evaluate their work. Second, there is evidence of chronic work overload: less preparation and correction, reduced opportunity for professional development, and the demise in long-term planning. All of these things are indicators of intensification in the work of these teachers and, as such, are contributors to the breakdown of *quality factors* in their workplace lives.

The pressure of time manifests itself in having to cope with more work to do in a finite amount of time and an inability to meet an expectation to get everything done. Mandy encapsulated this in her work story about how she felt that not enough time was made available to her, in her teaching load, to do all that was expected of her. She thought it would take complete breakdown from work overload before her need for time would be recognized.

> At this school, if you seem to be coping you will get something more to do in the next year and I have this feeling that they'll keep doing that until you don't cope anymore. Sad, but true. It's probably typical of anywhere, but I really feel very strongly that if you don't run around having a nervous breakdown they think you're going OK, and that: 'oh well, she handled that no worries, let's pile a bit more on'. I have to fight very hard to get the time allowance that I know I need to be the year 11 coordinator. They want you to do jobs, especially year level coordinator, where I need time at school because I've got to see kids and I've got to see staff. But I have to really fight to get the time I need. Now quite frankly, I'd rather just teach a full load and not to have to worry about doing this other stuff. If they want me to do it, well, they have to give me the time. This year, they gave me some time to do it, but then loaded me up with extras and duties.

Mandy felt she was constantly being pushed to the limit. She was fearful that this would only cease when she failed to meet the expectations of her employer by no longer coping. However, in order to not fail in meeting those expectations, and so cope, Mandy found that she needed to work differently, by cutting corners with preparation and correction, in order to accommodate the demands she faced each day. While this helped her achieve the immediate goal of survival, she was not happy about it as a solution to her problem.

> Oh, she's only on nineteen, we'll load her up. I feel very strongly that that's not the right thing to do and I've told them, if they want me to do this job, then I need this time allowance, otherwise someone else can maybe do it in the time that they're happy to give. So, it's sort of an

ongoing battle. I don't prepare at school, or correct at school, there's no time at all for that, and I accept that I have to do that at home, but sometimes you need to use the photocopier or something else. It's the same with writing reports, that's all done at home unless I'm very lucky. I do find it hard when I've got to do stuff at school where I need contact with other people and I run out of time. That's hard because there's nothing then that I can do, by working more at home, that isn't going to solve the problem. That's what I find most difficult. Duties mean that you can't catch up with staff, or see students, and that sort of thing. I'm never really in a state of control, I'm always thinking, 'oh God, I've got all these things I have to do'. To be quite honest the classroom comes last, it really does. Sometimes it's a pest, you think, 'I've got to go off to class, I can't, it's interrupting what I've got to do'. That's very difficult, especially if you've got kids who are having difficulties and you need to see them. So, I never have enough time [exhausted laughter]...it's constant.

The vibrancy of Mandy' work story about the difficulties caused by lack of time during her year's work allows vicarious participation in her exasperation with her lot and the sense of pain that her working life had to be like that. However, having coped with the pressures of time during the year did not make the circumstances which had produced those pressures any more acceptable. Brian has also felt the strain on his time due to an expectation for spending extra time with students on co-curricular activities. Like Mandy, to fit the extra things in, he had to cut corners in his work.

Well, I've cut corners this year, not so much with my preparation, but with my correction. I just don't set as much work – I wouldn't have the time to correct it. You've got to have some time to yourself. I know I didn't set as much, and part of that was having two year 12s, because it was a lot of work, particularly when the external assessments were around. You have to give nearly all of your time to them, so the other things suffer. And I'm doing it again next year!

Brian admitted cutting corners and felt unhappy about having lost some of the quality feel to his work. As with Mandy and her work, this is a likely indication of the intensification from the burden of an expanding co-curricular load. Also, like Mandy and Brian, Fred felt the burden of time acutely in meeting his non-classroom responsibilities.

I get about five periods for careers [counselling]. At the beginning of the year there's not much involved except preparation and making sure you've got everything ready, but from about mid-year onward it just gets chaotic, and as it gets towards the end of the year it gets worse, and worse, and worse. I found this is where my senior classes suffered. I had to do some of that [careers] work when I'd usually do preparation, then that [preparation] I'd do in correction time. It [correction] was all going home, it wasn't done at school. Careers were also missing periods because of all the other work involvement. I enjoy the sport, but it was just biting into other time. Overall, you're given more things to do and your time has been stretched, and stretched, and stretched and the jam on the sandwich is getting thinner, and thinner, and thinner. There's not enough hours in the day at the moment at school to do things. In the end, you try to take corners, and in the end, you get caught out.

Fred's account of his working life at Appleton College makes a vivid expression of too much school work to do in a given amount of time. Like his colleagues, Fred also felt the pressure of time and experienced difficulty in distributing it, as a finite resource, over the many tasks he dealt with in his day-to-day work. While it might look all right from the outside, in terms of quantity, on the inside the quality is just not there.

Work stories about stress in teaching

The accounts of changes to their work activity presented in the work stories about the intensification of teaching also show the appearance of stress in the lives of these teachers. This occurs as a consequence of their reactions to the many stressors which impact on their working lives. Events and happenings like those described in the work stories: the pressure of time, the burden of an expanding workload, and the loss of important professional development opportunities are all workplace stressors in the lives of these teachers. The appearance of stress is especially evident in comments about: cutting corners, doing things at home outside of normal hours, and making decisions about priorities so as to determine which parts of the normal work routine can be allowed to slide. Such things are indicative of a loss in quality aspects of the work of teaching, and in the failure to meet expectations of satisfaction from work, which arise out of the subjugation of quality to quantity in teaching. As has been argued, this is a consequence of not having enough time to do all that is required, or expected, in your work and, furthermore, it is the expression of feelings like anger, guilt, and anxiety, which can be interpreted as reactive signs to the stressful aspects of teaching (Farber, 1984; Blase, 1986; Applied Psychology Research Group, 1989; Cole and Walker, 1989; Dunham, 1992).

Research into workplace stress indicates that it is a manifestation of a worker's perception of the demands of (their) work which is linked to changes in (their) physical, emotional and intellectual states (Applied Psychology Research Group, 1989). In teaching, stressors generative of a changed perception about the work of teaching include things like: workload pressure, discipline problems, new curriculum, time burdens, and administrative tasks. In addition, personal stressors, especially those connected with relationships (with students and colleagues), may also impact upon a teacher's perception of the quality and demands of their working life (Blase, 1986). Continued stress in work can cause an expansion in the presence of symptoms leading to feelings like: lack of control over the extent of workload and the expectations inherent to it, helplessness in the face of increasing work pressures and problems, powerlessness to exercise any change in the circumstances of the workplace, and confusion over the purpose of the work leading to possible role ambiguity and conflict. This is a dangerous scenario because the continual loss of quality aspects of work and the continual lack of fulfilment of the need for self-esteem eventually lead to feelings of inconsequentiality that end in total disillusionment and burnout (Edelwich and Brodsky, 1980; Farber, 1984).

Harassment of time is one aspect of the stressful nature of teaching which can lead teachers to a sense of failure in not meeting their (own) expectations for their work and a feeling of not living up to their ideal view of themselves. This can prove very confronting for most teachers and, as such, is a likely source of workplace stress generative of emotional reactions like anxiety. Sometimes teachers experience feelings of anxiety when they perceive that they are not coping with the demands of their work which pull them in multiple directions at the same time.

> Mandy: they're not coping very well, I think a lot of teachers blame themselves. It depends how confident you are I suppose, and if you know what you are capable of. I think a lot of people even subconsciously stop doing things to make it easier for themselves.

However, by making it easier for themselves, by being selective about what gets done, and ceasing to do certain things because of insufficient time, teachers can create problems for other people in the school. Blase (1986) found that 'teachers reported that to save time, they gave less homework than was necessary for adequate instruction [and] in addition, homework was either not corrected or corrected mechanically, seldom including the kind of explanatory feedback necessary' (p. 29). Mandy described how this was happening at Appleton College.

> They [stressed teachers] cut back on their preparation, certainly corrections, contact with students whose work isn't getting done, and feedback to students with correction coming back at the right time. That's a problem I have with year 11 teachers quite often. The kids hand their work in and don't know for a very long time if it's OK, or not. It disappears for a while and teachers don't know whether kids have handed stuff in, because they haven't marked it off, because they haven't got the

time. So I don't know, sometimes, until it's too late, that someone's behind in their work, and that makes my job harder.

The source of stress, in this case administrative work, gets moved down the line to another person. As indicated, Mandy was aware that cutting corners can be a coping strategy when the intensifying nature of teaching produces feelings of non-control and helplessness in teachers.

> I think, because there's so much pressure, things that they can get away with go by the wayside. I don't even know if they're aware that they're doing it. They just think: 'oh no I won't do that yet'. I think people tend to wing it a bit more on classes too. They think: 'I've taught this before, I'll just go in and...' which, you know, can't be successful. Forward planning, because it takes a bit of time, it also goes by the wayside. Kids will get assessment tasks on the last day, things that are not reasonable, but you can see why it's happened, because people are very busy and just haven't worked out in advance what they're doing. They suddenly think: 'oh God, I haven't done this particular thing'. It happens and I don't think they are aware of it. They're just surviving!

Teachers often just manage to get by, in completing their work, through ways that are, ultimately, not satisfying. It is, as Mandy has described it, just a matter of survival, of getting through the demands of the day. Unsatisfactory practices and events which may take place are, therefore, a result of the pressure of time and work overload because 'positive attitudes and behaviours essential to good teaching seem to be difficult to maintain over the long run' (Blase, 1986, p. 33) in the face of a persistent presence of stressors. Her witness to the problems faced by her colleagues in this regard, and her insight into their origin, has enabled Mandy to recognize evidence of the same behaviour in herself.

> I reckon I could do a lot better in the classroom, but I just don't have the energy, or the time. I feel as though I'm having to give my attention to so many areas, that I'm not really giving it to any one area properly, it's all just fragmented, that's the hardest thing.

For Fred, the anger which he felt at having too much work to do outside school hours found its expression in an action of self-preservation, an assertion of the self, in easing the burdens of work overload and the accompanying feelings of stress. His frustration and anger are poignantly conveyed in his remarks:

> when they start loading you up with more work. In the end I just say: 'well bugger that [*sic*], I'm not going to do that'. At times I'd go home

and I'd have work, a whole lot of correction and that kind of stuff, and I'd just be fed up, and say: 'stuffit, I'm going to watch TV tonight' and then head to bed around half past nine. Next morning, I find I'm quite happy, you haven't done the correction, but it doesn't really matter. OK, if I go to school the next day and I get into trouble – too bad. I think that works for me a few times during the year.

For experienced teachers, like Fred, refusal to use 'large amounts of personal time to compensate for the scarcity of time to complete work satis-factorily' (Blase, 1986, p. 30) was a common response to the persistent experience of stress from chronic work overload. Another personal cost of intensification and stress in teachers' work was shown in the following comments, where Fred described the negative effects that the continual pres-ence of *work-tired* feelings had on him and his family life.

I've found this year that a lot of time I've been very tired. You go home and you take your work home and you do an hour or so. In the end I decided to sometimes not take work home and [instead] to see my family, or go for a training run, or swim. I think my family has suffered. Betty [his partner] has taken all the load as far as the kids go, running them to ballet, Brownies and that type of thing.

Tiredness in the workplace can lead to the diminishment of many positive outcomes and benefits otherwise expected from a work environment. Importantly, in schools, this can result in an undermining of the commit-ment for interaction, both socially and professionally, with peers through the cumulative effect of everybody being 'very tired' all of the time. Withdrawal from other people at work is another consequence of workplace stress. Brian explained how he noticed a general decrease in interaction between his workmates in recent times and his belief that it was linked to the work-weary state he and his colleagues found themselves in.

I think the staff isn't as cohesive as when I first came here [four years previously] and I think that is a direct result of people being very tired. You know we haven't had a good staff 'do' all year. This staff used to get together regularly, socially.

For him the loss of this valued and positive aspect of his working life at Appleton College was unwelcome because he believed that it would make work less interesting, detract much from the multidimensional nature of his working life, and possibly negatively affect the social dynamics of the staff group.

Socially Critical View of Teaching as Work

Approaches to the study of schools and teachers' work which draw upon the ontological and epistemological assumptions of critical social science seek to place the grounded understandings of teachers into a context where the dominant social, political, and economic forces are regarded problematically. Fundamentally, it is about the 'intersection of history, social structure and biography' (Popkewitz, 1984, p. 47). It seeks a clear (ordinary language) explication of the conditions which work against satisfaction of needs; the expression, through ideology critique, of contradictions present in self-understandings constituting false consciousness; and through the specification of how social change can dismantle the effects of false consciousness. Such a stance can be called 'taking a socially critical view' (Smyth, 1993a) and it requires the questioning of taken-for-granted assumptions about accepted social practices and how they came about. In this approach, questions like: 'what is this phenomenon?', 'why is it happening now?', 'what is it that really lies behind this notion?', and 'what is wrong with it?', (Smyth, 1993a, p. 1) allow seemingly normal and neutral educational practices to be placed under scrutiny.

According to Smyth (1994) critical research should aim to:

* interrupt social practices;
* study oppressed or marginalized groups;
* challenge conventional interpretations;
* locate meaning in broad social, cultural, economic, and political spheres;
* be reflexive of its own biases, limitations, distortions, and agenda;
* be advocacy oriented;
* be concerned with the forces that have brought about a given situation;
* edit the researcher into the text;
* develop categories and themes, but regard them as problematic; and
* aim to impact on producing more equitable and just social relationships (p. 4).

Fundamentally, being clear on the origin of ideological formations about teachers and their work, and the interest such formations serve, is the essence of taking a socially critical view with research of the kind reported here.

A socially critical view of teacher professionalism

It is important to restate that professionalism is a 'key contested term in the history of teaching' (Lawn, 1989, p. 159) and that it has long been associated with attempts to promote, define, reform, restructure, and control the work of teaching (see Chapter 2; Lawn and Ozga, 1986, 1988; Darling-

Hammond, 1988; Shanker, 1989). Current times in Australia are no exception, where recent attempts to solve important social and economic problems have sought to link pupil learning and teachers' work into solutions for poor national economic performance (Bluer, 1991; Marginson, 1992a; 1992b; Carmichael, 1993; Jackson, 1993).

International literature shows that professionalism is a malleable term in teaching which 'has no fixed definition or some universal idea irrespective of time or place, [and] it is a socially constructed word which changes in relationship to the social conditions in which people use it' (Popkewitz, 1994, p. 2). The promotion of teaching as professional work, or of teachers as professionals, at any given time can usually be traced to a motive situated in the social and political imperatives of the time, and inspection of the rhetorical use of the term, at such times, will reveal the interests and values it serves. However, this is not to say that, as far as teaching is concerned, professionalism is necessarily all bad for teachers and that they have no way of turning the construct to their advantage in working against external control of their work. There are always possibilities for resistance, because, as Lawn suggests: 'professionalism is an expression of the struggle over the control and purpose of schooling and involves the possibility of resistance and creation of alternatives [and] it can create a defensible space around teachers' work' (Lawn, 1989, p. 154), which can help teachers attach their own, local and empowering, meanings to *teacher professionalism*.

Given that the Appleton College teachers' work stories are full of confident references about the quality of their work and the supportive relations which appear to be the norm among the teachers at the school, their comments suggest that, if there is any lack of confidence about teachers and teaching, it lies outside the occupational culture, and its domain, the schools. A lack of confidence in teaching is something which has been *talked-up* in the media (Sheridan, 1988; Barnard, 1992; McGuiness, 1993), by the 'right-wing sting' (Maslen, 1994) emanating from New Right think-tanks, politicians (Dawkins, 1990), and government agencies (Schools Council, 1990). Smyth (1993c), in arguing forcefully against economic rationalism in education, provides support for the work-story framed confidence of these teachers in questioning the motivations behind such extensive and pernicious assaults on the credibility of classroom teachers.

> There has been no catastrophic decline in the quality of schooling in this country...it is not so much a struggle over standards and quality, although it is put in those terms, so much as it is over the way knowledge is to be represented, in whose interests, how it shall be taught, who shall have a predominant say in shaping it, and within what kind of educational structures.
>
> (1993c, p. 11)

At Appleton College the teachers developed a practical definition of professionalism through a contextually saturated ethic of care. They were
suspicious of misinformed public views of the teaching which failed to
acknowledge the relational nature of their work. While there was an indication that these teachers were resistive of attempts to externally define
elements of their work, in terms which were not grounded relationally, it is
not possible to know for certain how their ethic of care, as a professional
ethos, would stand up to any significant redefinition of professionalism in
their work. However, the drive towards the specification of teacher professionalism in terms of competencies is about the structuring of *good* teaching
practice in a technically prescribed fashion which would stand in opposition
to the expressive and relational determination of teacher professionalism
preferred by the Appleton College teachers.

A socially critical view of an ethic of care in teaching

The work-story accounts of professionalism in teaching given by the
Appleton College teachers demonstrate the primacy of caring relations in
work with pupils and colleagues. In the stories there is an overwhelming
sense that professionalism in teaching is equated with care, and that the
commitment to respond to the needs of pupils and colleagues through the
development of relations of care is highly valued in the peer group, to an
extent where it is central to judgements about good teaching. Indeed, the
desire to behave in ways which demonstrate care indicates that an ethic of
care is fundamental to the local teaching culture, where it is effectively used
as a lens through which teaching and administrative practices are closely
examined and evaluated as professional, or otherwise.

The strong contextually bound nature of this ideology of professionalism
is evident in the way in which the school presents itself to its community of
students, parents and teachers. Appleton College's mission statement
includes a self-description of itself as: 'a school which provides a caring,
supportive and disciplined environment where the intellectual, artistic, social
and moral development of each individual is fostered'; and the school's
behavioural code states 'all members of the School Community are expected
to show: (1) respect and care for self; (2) concern for the welfare of others;
and (3) care for, and sensible use of, property'. Further, invocations to care
are sometimes made when teachers are expected to give more in their work
through the giving up of spare time for participation in extra activities with
students. Ideas and values about care, which affect the work teachers do,
abound in the social construction of the school and its image.

A message which must be seen as being clearly supportive of the maintenance of the ideology of care in the work of the school's teachers was
communicated to staff through a document which argued, in market rhetoric
terms, the need for teachers to reflect in their work the basic values of the school.

As a teacher what is your job description when it comes to marketing the school? Lots of people in schools think they don't need marketing – the attitude is that it is self evident what we offer – the need is obvious – that we are a school not a business which sells commodities. The reality is we need to aggressively market our service. We are a business – we need customers – if we don't think in terms of the customer we will run out of business. As staff, as employees and stakeholders in a company with a mission and a marketing job to do, we all have a responsibility to be living examples of the image of our institution.

(Appleton College, 1993)

A statement of this kind places teachers, and their work, at the centre of the success, or otherwise, of the school. It is, perhaps, not altogether surprising that this statement was made in a document circulated to teachers at a time when the school was struggling to combat a sustained period of falling enrolments, where its very survival was at stake. It is, however, a strange twist, full of contradictory importance, that praise of the value of care in the work of teachers in the survival of the school – which it must be remembered the teachers chose to articulate in expressive forms and language – has to be conducted by the school administration within a market rhetoric through the use of terms like 'customers' and 'commodities'. Indeed, it is indicative of the colonization of the discourse of education by market language (Baldwin, 1994) where students are customers and education is a product to be sold.

However, the inescapable message for teachers contained in this statement is that the school's predicament is connected to their work as teachers in a very direct way. If the school does not survive, it will be because of their failure, as teachers, in upholding their responsibility to 'be living examples of our institution'. Further, in its most practical sense, this document represents a call for teachers to extend their professional ethic of care, by giving more, through the expansion of what counts as an acceptable workload at Appleton College. This was seen, during the period of this study, through the school administration's attempts to get more work from less expenditure, as evident in: the loss of preparation and correction time, greater demands for co-curricular activities, increased face-to-face teaching loads, greater demand for out-of-hours involvement with school activities, and reduced opportunity for professional development.

In living up to the expectations of their school by striving to do the right thing by the school's students, essentially by doing more, by extending their professional ethic of care, the Appleton College teachers have seen their work processes, the labour process of teaching at the school, undergo substantive change. Their ideology of professionalism, an ethic of care, while strongly affirming and defining of the valued qualities of their work as teachers, has masked the restructure of work practices and expectations that has led to the rapid intensification of teaching work at their school. The effects have been plainly witnessed and described in the work-story accounts given throughout this portrayal of teachers' work at Appleton College.

A socially critical view of intensification in teaching

Those who have written convincingly about the intensification of teaching have drawn heavily on the theorizing of proletarianization available in the work of Larson (1980). Larson describes intensification as:

> one of the most tangible ways in which the work privileges of educated workers are eroded. Its symptoms go from the trivial – 'no time at all' for lunch – to the more serious – no time at all to keep up with one's field, to retool one's skills. The most common source of intensification in mental labour is *chronic work overload* [her emphasis], which takes many forms and has different consequences in different work settings.
>
> (p. 166)

In a work setting where teaching occurs, intensification is present in the form of chronic work overload manifested in: burgeoning administrative tasks, reliance on standardized lesson plans, reduced time for preparation of lessons and correction of student work, higher face-to-face class contact time, increased demand for non-classroom contact with students, loss of opportunity for development of teaching skills, isolation from teaching colleagues, and negative feelings generated from failure to maintain previous levels of quality in classroom teaching (Densmore, 1987; Apple, 1988b; Hargreaves, 1992b).

The intensification of teaching at Appleton College has occurred for two reasons. First, teaching in general, like many other forms of educated labour, is undergoing a reorganization of work practices through deskilling, reskilling, fragmentation, and intensification as part of a labour process trend ending in the proletarianization of professional work (Derber, 1982; Harris, 1982). That this trend should also be evident, in changing patterns of work organization, at Appleton College is, therefore, not wholly unexpected. Second, the specific circumstances surrounding Appleton College at the time of this study, where the survival of the school in the face of declining enrolments was not guaranteed, created a set of local factors which accelerated processes of intensification already present. The call for teachers to take on more teaching, more duties, additional responsibilities, and extend their involvement in co-curricular activities for the good of the students and the school, through an appeal to their sense of professionalism, led to chronic work overload as documented in the work-story accounts.

On the surface, it seems strange that teachers can willingly participate in the restructure of their work practices in ways that lead to chronic work overload and the extensive degradation of quality aspects in their work. The struggle for control over teachers' work, that is implied in this apparent contradiction, suggests that teachers can be effectively co-opted into processes of rationalization leading to the degradation of their labour. Derber's (1982) analysis of ideological proletarianization, and its application to the intensification of teachers' work by Densmore (1987), indicates that professionals can identify with an employer's workplace agenda under the mystification of ideas about professional identity and status.

The primacy of an ethic of care in the professional identity of Appleton College's teachers, together with its congruence to the organizational objectives of the school in achieving financial viability, point toward some important conclusions. First, the ethic of care which clearly provides much in the way of an intrinsic value base for the purpose of teacher's day-to-day work, and of personal satisfaction and professional gratification from the performance of teaching work, may be a reaction to the alienation experienced from general trends toward the proletarianization of teachers' work. Second, the high degree of similitude between an ethic of care in teaching at Appleton College and the educational and organizational imperatives to care in the school's self-established identity suggest a locally grounded form of ideological co-option of the culture of teacher professionalism at the school. If this is the case, then their co-option in the reorganization of work patterns in teaching at the school, along with its institutional reinforcement through the appeal to care more, and more, is not accidental but evidence of the control of their labour towards greater productivity or surplus value. Third, the identification of care as a professional ethic in teachers' work can be considered a classed and gendered category (Skeggs, 1997) that plays a role in controlling the work of teaching (Acker, 1995). Also, the rapid feminization of teaching (Apple, 1988a) and the persistence of masculinist forms of management in schools (Limerick and Lingard, 1995) invites the development and appropriation of ideologies of care as gendered controls in the politics of teachers' work.

The intensified conditions of teaching work at Appleton College are real, there can be no doubt about that. They are corroborated and consensually validated through the consistent accounting of characteristics of teacher work intensification in a wide range of teacher work stories. The congruence between an organizational ethic in the teacher's professional identities and an organizational imperative in the school's self-image is also strong in the accounts presented. The work stories indicate that these teachers will strive hard, undergo self-sacrifice, and put themselves out to fulfil their professional expectations of care. The call on teachers to extend their degree of care to meet the needs of the school, through changed and more intense work practices, has led them into taking on more work, at the same time as they have experienced a loss of quality in their working conditions, in short, to the intensification of their work. Given this, it seems a reasonable conclusion that the Appleton College teachers have been co-opted in the degradation of their own work.

There are many problems for these teachers which arise from the intensification of their work. They are harassed by the burdens of time with insufficient time to complete all of their work tasks in ways that give satisfaction. They have to cut corners in their work by doing essential things first, including a host of administrative and other non-teaching duties, at the expense of creative work like lesson preparation. They face the potential atrophy of teaching skills through lack of opportunity for engagement with other teachers in professional development and participation in collaborative networks. They become socially and professionally isolated as a result of lack of time and opportunity for relaxed interaction with work peers. They are confronted with loss of work satisfaction and the consequent diminution of work-related self-esteem from the replacement of quality with quantity as outputs become the priority of their work. They face a host of emotional and physical symptoms of stress, including anxiety, guilt, and constant tiredness from the persistent presence of unmet needs in their working lives. Very importantly, they support a process of degradation in their work through the pursuit of institutional imperatives and perceived professional behaviours which lead to a snowballing presence of intensifying conditions in their work.

In testimony to their resourcefulness and insightfulness, these teachers are aware of the huge impact which changed work demands and conditions of work have made on their working lives. They resist and contest the trends in various ways. However, they do not seem to be fully aware of the mystifying role which their professional ideology of care, and its manifestation in a strong commitment to doing more, and more, for the good of the school and its pupils, plays in the continued expansion of the difficult and trying conditions of work they rail against. Indeed, it is a disturbing revelation to find that these teachers are contributing to the continued presence of oppressive and debilitating working conditions at their school through their dedicated pursuit of their professional ideal.

Intensification is happening in teaching and it is happening at Appleton College. The work of teaching intensifies when teacher's workloads increase, especially when they become overburdened with non-teaching duties, such as administrative tasks and co-curricular activities, and when they are called upon to produce more from their work. At Appleton College, increased productivity, through higher work output from teachers, is seen as the key to the financial viability, and ultimately the very survival, of the school. The characteristics of intensification in teaching are consistent with theoretical understandings about the proletarianization of professional work, and the process of ideological co-option, which lead professional workers to accommodate the lack of effective control over changing conditions in their work through identification with the goals and values of their employing organization. Through ideological co-option, teachers at Appleton College promote the interests of their employer, through their participation in professional behaviours and work practices which encourage the continuation of intensified work conditions for the teachers at the school.

6   Towards a Revitalization of a Critical Theory of Teachers' Work

In this chapter we want to draw the conceptual threads together and represent a revitalized critical theory of teachers' work as a 'constellation' of propositions. To develop a neat weave of these threads it is appropriate to pause for a moment and reflect on where the book has been so far. From the outset, we are motivated by a commitment to a socially critical view of schooling. Such a view asserts that schooling should be organized around the needs of the most disenfranchised members of society. We are trying to make sense of, with practical and emancipatory intent, the contemporary crisis in teachers' work in many post-industrial countries characterized by:

1   an impoverishing of the material conditions of teachers' work;
2   a damaging of the student–teacher relationship through the intrusion of the market;
3   a silencing of teachers in the policy development process – teachers' voices are now a 'subjugated knowledge' (Foucault, 1980); and,
4   an infecting of consciousness with discourses that undermine the possibility of critical thought/reflection (Shor, 1987).

Teachers experience all of this as a crisis of confidence. Many teachers feel increasingly demoralized, stressed, anxious, disillusioned, even burnt-out. The concept of alienation is not too strong a term to describe this experience. Alienation here refers to increasing powerlessness, and negative feelings about the self that are generated in the 'organisational economy' (Wexler, 1992, p. 8) of the school. The category 'organisational economy', names the way in which schools mediate the flow of social and cultural resources teachers and students use to create an identity. Such feelings are generated in response to an unlimited expectation of commitment – leading to chronic work overload – that requires survival responses such as cutting corners, and reducing time for preparation, diminished creativity, and 'retooling one's skills'.

This contemporary crisis requires a revitalized critical theory that emphasizes a labour process of teachers' work capable of making sense of technologies of power that have a global reach. We need theory capable of connecting globalization to the classroom. We also need a labour process theory of teachers' work that does not fall into the 'dualistic trap of pitting and polarising a voluntaristic subject [the teachers] against determining structure or object' (Knights, 1990, p. 306). This revitalization, we argue, is essential at this time, because of the need to have a robust critique of the dominating and global effects of the 'new right restoration' that is so profoundly shaping public schools. In the past, critical theories of teachers' work have often been content to make sense of teachers' work in a much more constrained 'context' (Seddon, 1995a). For example, until recently it was considered adequate to construe teachers' work in a context of state[1] bureaucracies (Seddon, 1995b). At the end of the 1990s, teachers' work is more than ever affected by technologies of power that operate globally (Taylor et al., 1997; Smyth, 1998). To develop a revitalized critical theory of teachers' work that connects globalization to the classroom requires arguing for an expansive view of globalization. As such we are keenly interested in how the political-economic, socio-cultural and technological changes that are occurring at the global level are reaching into the everyday life of schools. To stress this point, we believe that the phenomenon called global-ization has political-economic, socio-cultural and technological dimensions that are not reducible to just the political-economic. We agree with Giddens (1994) that '[g]lobalisation is not only, or even primarily, an economic phenomenon' but 'is really about the transformation of space and time' or 'action at a distance, and relate its intensifying over recent years to the emer-gence of means of instantaneous global communication and mass transportation' (p. 4).

Broadly speaking then, we believe that globalization needs to be under-stood as a complex phenomenon that involves intricate interrelationships between these three arenas. A number of terms now circulate in the discourse of globalization that recognize or represent this complex set of relationships. Aronowitz et al. (1996) use the label 'technoscience and cyber-culture': categories which carry a view of technology, science and culture in which each of these is 'permeated and penetrated by the other two' (p. 18). Johnson (1997) has coined the term 'interface culture' to concentrate our attention on the contemporary collision between technology and culture. Castells (1994) invokes the nexus between the political economy and cyber-culture with the term 'informational capitalism'. We agree with Bauman (1998) that globalization should be understood as the 'new world disorder', and might be better termed as 'glocalization' (Robertson, 1995). For Bauman, glocalization infers, 'globalization for some and localization for some others':

Glocalization is first and foremost a redistribution of privileges and deprivations, of wealth and poverty, of resources and impotence, of

> power and powerlessness, of freedom and constraint. It is, one may say,
> a process of world-wide restratification, in the course of which a new
> world-wide socio-cultural hierarchy is put together....What is free
> choice for some is cruel fate for some others.
>
> (Bauman, 1998, p. 43)

Bauman refers to those with the freedom to act as 'tourists': 'seduced by the
true or imaginary pleasures of a sensation-gatherers life' (p. 47), who 'travel
because they want to'. But globalization also has a side effect – it is the
'transformation of many others into vagabonds' (p. 47); who live a 'postmodern version of slavery' (p. 46), 'who travel because they have no other
bearable choice' (p. 47).

We began to outline some of the features of such a view of globalization
in Chapter 1. We will now continue this theorizing about globalization
within the propositions of our constellation.

This revitalization of a critical theory of teachers' work requires incor-
porating a sophisticated theory of subjectivity in the experience of the
labour process of teachers. We agree with Ezzy's (1997) thesis of the need
to 'theorise the social processes involved in the construction of subjectivity'
(p. 428) and especially to account for the way teachers 'relate to and
manoeuvre' (p. 431) around those discourses that authorize good practice
and hence are committed to normative control of teachers' work. As such
we are interested in the dynamic interplay between the structuring nature of
discourses and their acceptance, resistance and manipulation by teachers.
We are interested in theorizing about the subjectivity of teachers in terms
of:

> the middle ground between, on the one hand, a sovereign self that is
> invulnerable and impermeable to the influence of others,...and, on the
> other hand, a deconstructed self that emphasises the linguistic sources
> of the self and the influence of context 'to the point where it engulfs, if
> not annihilates, the self'.
>
> (p. 433)

We are interested in how teachers construct themselves – their
identities/subjectivities – in the experience of working.

The revitalized critical theory of teachers' work being asserted in this
book can be taken to have a constellation of propositions. The metaphor of
theory as constellation was a term Adorno, among others (Bernstein, 1991;
Jameson, 1996; Buck-Morss, 1997), borrowed from Benjamin 'to signify a
juxtaposed rather than integrated cluster of changing elements that resist
reduction to a common denominator, essential core, or generative first principle' (Jay, 1984, pp. 14–15). Building theory as constellation involves
holding ideas – as aspects of reality – 'in a reciprocally constituitive relation-

ship, and thus hinders their one-sided absolutization' (Schnädelbach, 1993, p. 298). Theory as constellation infers an 'interrelational and transactive [understanding that] is not just one way, and purely socially deterministic' (Thayer-Bacon, 1997, p. 255). Just as suns in a heavenly constellation shine on each other so do the elements of our theoretical constellation. Our constellation has the following propositions:

1   Schooling is still a significant site of social and cultural formation.
2   Schools can make a significant contribution to an egalitarian society.
3   Teachers are the most important actors in the technology called schools.
4   Teachers' own identities have to contend with the power relations that operate in schools and educational systems.
5   Teachers as workers sell their labour power in a 'globalizing' labour market.
6   The curriculum/pedagogy is the main specification of the labour process of teaching.
7   Control of teachers' work takes structural, ideological and disciplinary modes.
8   Control, as a result of globalization, has a detrimental and material effect on teachers' work.

These propositions have been developed as a consequence of a process of 'dialectical theory building' (Lather, 1986, p. 262) involving a juxtaposing of a labour process theory of teachers' work, and critical ethnographies of schools, positioned in a globalization 'context'. In this way we hope to have at least begun to write subjectivity into a labour process theory of teachers' work in the somewhat enlarged context of globalization. In sum, we hope to have begun to map the complex relationships between the subjectivity of teachers – always unstable, and trapped in a dialectic of being and becoming – and the technologies of power with a global reach. Figure 6.1 attempts to 'concept map' the key features of this theory-building process and hence also the arguments in the preceding chapters. Chapter 1 began our discussion of the globalization context. Chapter 3 is represented in the box labelled labour process theory of teachers' work. Chapters 4 and 5 have been included in the box labelled critical ethnography of schools. Perhaps the metaphor of a map is a little too outlandish for our purpose here. Perhaps more realistically we have begun to sketch out what a critical theory of teachers' work might look like that aims to revitalize labour process theory through a contemporary reading of life in schools, within a frame of globalization.

Figure 6.1

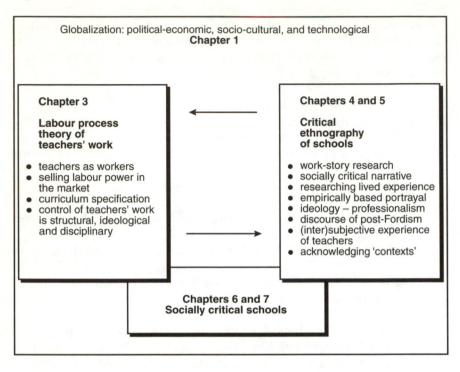

In this chapter we concentrate on a language of critique. Occasionally this spills out into a language of possibility that gives broad direction for a contemporary politics of teachers' work. It is in the next chapter that we more fully develop a language of possibility.

The first three propositions of our tentative constellation are drawn from our commitment to a socially critical view of schooling in the context of globalization.

Schooling is Still a Significant Site of Social and Cultural Formation

This is perhaps a moot point in the light of the growing impact of media culture on identity formation in contemporary societies. A poignant quote from Giroux (1994) is instructive here:

> For years, I believed that pedagogy was a discipline developed around the narrow imperatives of public schooling. And yet, my identity has been largely fashioned outside of school. Films, books, journals, videos, and music in different and significant ways did more to shape my poli-

tics and life than did formal education, which always seemed to be about somebody else's dreams.

(p. x)

Having said that, we believe that schooling as a heavily contested terrain is still worth fighting for because it significantly:

1 contributes to identity formation of young people – that is school produces individuals;
2 still acts as a gatekeeper for (re)production of economic inequality i.e. it credentials the already wealthy while simultaneously provides a smoke-screen to hide the scam (Fitzgerald, 1976) – that is school produces economic futures; and,
3 provides representational resources that the population at large uses to make sense of their lives – that is school produces culture.

We are of course making an assumption here that we will still be sending 'our' children to the neighbourhood school, at least in the future.

What is crucial to our analysis is the increasing contestation between the school and media culture for significance as a site of social and cultural formation. By media culture we mean:

[c]ultural objects like music, dance, fashion, television, movies, magazines, advertising, art and new words are influential parts of a society filled with gadgets and various pleasing and disturbing images that affect how individual and collective identities are defined, created, changed and disallowed (Aronowitz, 1992). These cultural objects have a very real existence because they are consumed by people for entertainment and information for exchange of money.

(Hattam et al., 1998a, p. 99)

The socio-cultural and technological aspects of globalization become significant when considering this contest. Transnational corporate capitalism has developed the 'informational society' (Luke, 1991) or 'society of the spectacle' (Debond, 1970; Agger, 1992) as electronically mediated consumption communities. 'Within such transnational consumption communities, the flow of goods, services and signs generates densely encoded "hyperrealities" or "mediascapes" [or virtual realities], which form new regions and sites of shared cultural consciousness...' (Luke, 1991). Those with the capital have access to television and global communications including the information superhighway (Kellner, 1995). Importantly, the convergence of technological and socio-cultural globalization involves 'monstrous media conglomerates – ABC/Disney, Time Warner/Turner, SONY/Colombia, Paramount/Viacom/ Blockbuster, CBC/Westinghouse'

(Kellner, 1995, p. 47) – that aim to commodify information and entertainment as rapidly as possible to maximize capital accumulation. Not surprisingly, in Australia, the media magnates Murdoch and Packer are the wealthiest families.

Living within these transnational consumption communities therefore has a colonizing and post-colonial dimension (During, 1992). Globalization might be understood to have two conflicting vectors – from above and from below.

'To fuel the growth of transnationalised capitalism, more and more of the everyday lifeworld must be colonised by the corporate coding system reducing autonomous non-commodified behaviour to scripted/packaged choices projected across hyperreality' (Luke, 1991, p. 18–19). As such, culture in the 1990s is being colonized/Americanized/homogenized. Deregulation of the (free) market means being opened up to the commodification of transnational corporations. Every city has the same shops, the same films, the same music, the same fashion, the same news, and the same food. If culture is understood as the way in which we make sense of our experience, then our consciousness is colonized by 'corporate capital's codes, scripts and packages' (p. 19), and we're seduced to behave as collaborators/consumers/clients in the good-life of a 'carefree utopia of cybernetic postindustrialism' (p. 2). The scripts of hyperreality aim to produce a 'particular kind of subjectivity, typically grounded upon a "possessive individualism"' (p. 13). As Kellner (1995) put it: 'Part of the downside of the computer and media society...is it masks deteriorating social conditions and crisis, challenging radical theory to deploy these very technologies to point to current problems and to propose solutions' (p. 45).

As a post-colonial dimension, the convergence of technology and culture has meant the emergence of spaces for freedom of speech that are out of reach of the censors, be they military regimes or the thought police of 'democratic countries'. As an example, at the time of writing this book, Malaysian websites are being posted daily to report on the trial of Anwar Ibrahim who is the focus for an emerging 'reformasi' movement in Malaysia. Such websites offer a space within Malaysia to carry critical comment on this important trial, comment that is censored in the mainstream press. Globalization thus means the increased possibility of living 'hybrid' lives. Hybridity is understood here to involve sustaining what Bhabha (1994) refers to as a 'third space'. In such a third space, cultural difference is not obliterated, made deviant, or considered pejorative but rather held in tension, as a quality to be sought after:

> For a willingness to descend into that alien territory [or third space]...may open the way to conceptualizing an international culture,

based not on the exoticism or multiculturalism of the diversity of cultures, but on the inscription and articulation of culture's hybridity.

(Bhabha, 1994, p. 38)

The diaspora experience as I intend it here defined, not by essence or purity, but by the recognition of a necessary heterogeneity and diversity; by a conception of 'identity' which lives with and through, not despite difference; by hybridity.

(Hall and Jacques, 1990, p. 235)

Examples include the increased interest and openness to indigenous knowledges – especially in areas such as environmental protection and the social sciences (Harding, 1998), and to eastern 'religious' ways of knowing such as a socially engaged activism based on Buddhist ethics (Eppsteiner, 1988; Jones, 1989).

Unless schools can become more attuned to the ways in which media culture is impacting on the identity formation of young people they will either become increasingly irrelevant or the already damaged relationship between teachers and students will continue to be exacerbated.

Schools Can Make a Significant Contribution to an Egalitarian Society

During most of the post-World War Two era, the practice of teaching and learning in schools has been broadly defined in terms of an 'educational settlement' (Freeland, 1986; Reid, 1998). We often name this settlement a 'general liberal' education. A settlement can be understood in this instance, as an 'unwritten social contract…[or] a bargain, a historic compromise… struck between the different conflicting social interests in society' (Hall, 1988, p. 36).

Under a welfare state settlement, public schools have been able to advance an egalitarian view of schooling. Not only has an egalitarian view of society been nurtured in public schools,[2] but public schooling has contributed to the making of a more egalitarian society. Largely worked out in schools, but supported by federal and state governments, schools have made some inroads into offering opportunities for advancement through education to an increasingly diverse group of young people. Perhaps the commitment of many teachers to an 'ethic of care' as 'care beyond the norm' (Chapter 5, p. 116) helps to make sense of this work in public schools. '[C]aring is about doing something more, about putting yourself out, in an attempt to do the best by your students and it may involve large sacrifices in time and energy' (Chapter 5, p. 122). The idea of schooling for a 'fair go', an Australian idiom for egalitarianism, has been given expression in a myriad of ways, including:

1   reforms to the post-compulsory credentials that undermine the selecting and sorting function of schools and the opening-up curriculum options for a large group of students who have been denied meaningful and credentialled educational experiences;

2   school-based reforms largely developed under the auspices of the Disadvantaged Schools Project (DSP); and the National School Network (NSN) that aim to improve student learning by providing a more meaningful curriculum;

3   programmes to improve the learning outcomes of girls, especially in areas of the curriculum that have been traditionally stereotyped as boys only;

4   revamping studies of Australian history that have promulgated a racist view and simultaneously degraded Aboriginal and Torres Strait Islander cultures;

5   taking seriously the need to develop cultural understanding and especially the learning of languages other than English, and the importance of nurturing languages for those children who have a non-English speaking background; and,

6   developing inclusive approaches to teaching and learning based on collaboration, negotiation and assessment designed to give feedback on what has been achieved rather than odium for what has not.

These reforms represent 'care beyond the norm' and have come about as a consequence of activist teachers struggling against the grain of the dominant view. Doing the extra yards has involved not only working at the classroom and school level but also engaging in political work at the state and federal level, at least in Australia. This issue will be taken up in more detail in the next chapter.

In these postmodern times (Lyotard, 1984; Jameson, 1991), or 'new times' (Hall and Jacques, 1990) the commitment to struggle for some form of egalitarian or socially just society has come under scrutiny. To be committed to a more socially just society has been pilloried by some as a 'master narrative' – and hence something to be despised. Such a view we believe is to throw the baby out with the bath water. At this time, when 'modern barbarity' (Offe, 1996) is on the rise, is not the time to retreat from the struggle to advance a more just way of arranging society. It is not the time to give up on struggling with the question – what sort of schools do we need to fulfil an egalitarian view of the world? In an emerging global village, perhaps the most dangerous form of barbarity is the rise of fundamentalism – which might be simply understood as 'tradition defended in the traditional way' (Giddens, 1994, p. 6):

> Fundamentalism tends to accentuate the purity of a given set of doctrines, not only because it wishes to set them off from other tradi-

tions, but because it is a rejection of a model of truth linked to the dialogic engagement of ideas in a public space. It is dangerous because [such a model of truth is] edged with a potential for violence.

(Giddens, 1994, p. 6)

Perhaps the most dangerous fundamentalisms include: the rise of certain religious groups including ultra-orthodox Jewish groups in Israel; or the moral majority sweeping the USA; or the 're-licensing of racism' (Perera and Pugliese, 1997) by political parties that argue for a rigid form of national identity based on a form of ethnic absolutism; and, especially economic rationalism or the neo-liberal way.

The purpose of schooling collapses under a neo-liberal way to a societal confidence trick – in which a discourse of choice and quality is used to defend an education system which is tuned to a relentless race of individuals (i.e. 'our' children) for educational credentials – a race that is 'always already' skewed in favour of the wealthy. Having a federal government like that in Australia (and its equivalent elsewhere) whose policy formulations, broadly speaking, are about letting loose in a completely unfettered way the rationality of the market into education and training, is a cause for alarm, given the effects noted in countries such as New Zealand (Gordon, 1994; Kelsey, 1995; Wylie 1995), England (Ball et al., 1996) and the United States (Apple, 1993a) – countries that have already felt the blunt end of economic fundamentalism.

It is important to contemplate this last point carefully.

Why would we want to go down the same path – or use the same 'diseased reason' (Horkheimer, 1947/1993) as the countries mentioned above when their market-driven school reforms are proving to be such a disaster? What now seems clear from those countries which have preceded Australia in hurtling towards a neo-liberal future, is that the social democratic imagining of schooling – that schooling might ameliorate economic inequalities in society – is undermined when the logic of the market is let loose on schooling. Instead, the combination of economic and cultural capital is reasserted as the significant determinant for success in schools. Under the logic of the market, schooling unabashedly reasserts itself as a site of social reproduction – schooling contributes without embarrassment to the rich getting richer and the poor getting poorer and larger in number. If all schools are forced to compete for 'market share', based on the fantasies of the level playing field and the trickle down effect, then we will end up with public schools that are funded across a gradient that reflects the socio-economics of the community – a few rich schools and lots of poor schools. Why would we want to produce such a future?

Teachers are the Most Important Actors in the Technology called Schools

Profound changes in our society unavoidably means that classroom life is becoming increasingly complex. Teachers are having to deal with increasing complexity in student lives. Poverty is on the increase. The full-time youth labour market has all but collapsed. Rural communities are suffering from micro- and macro-economic reform. Young people demand more democratic ways of relating as they present as 'aliens in the classroom' (Green and Bigum, 1998), with identities that increasingly draw on media culture. Nuclear war is still possible and so too is a collapse of the world's monetary system. Of course we could go on, but it is important to remember that these issues constitute the lived experience of those in the nation's classrooms everyday. Young people's complex lives are negotiated by teachers every minute of the school day. It is teachers who are making the crucial decisions about what is appropriate for (our) children. Unfortunately, in an era of 'an unsettling of settlements' (Carlson, 1995, p. 410), teachers are not considered 'as the most important actors in educational reform' (Zeichner, 1993, p. 5). Instead, those working in schools have two maps to work from. The one they have developed through experience – what we want to refer to as an 'educator's sensibility' and the one being imposed on them – a neo-liberal ideology that privileges individualism over community, instrumental reason over ethics, and private ownership over common wealth. Such an ideology continues to implement a school reform agenda 'through greater external prescription of school processes and outcomes' (Zeichner, 1993, p. 5) that must first of all silence teachers in the process.

As well as having to deal with a marketizing of the school, which concomitantly involves a deliberate de-authorization of the significance of teachers in the reform process, teachers are also having to contend with the impact of technoscience on their work. Green and Bigum (1998), refer to a process of 're-tooling schooling' which names the increasingly profound impact of information technology on schools. Using the metaphor of retooling Green and Bigum describe how information technology is not only changing educational work but also offering the possibility of re-imagining the school as a technology. Will the neighbourhood school survive techno-science and cyberculture and what is the role of teachers in the re-tooled school? Schools are 'caught in an increasingly expensive pattern of consumption of high-technology products' (Green and Bigum, 1998, p. 74) in which the technologizing of education through digital electronics leads some to fantasies of 'distance education' without teachers.

Technoscience also has a profound impact on the nature of the labour process. With a view to pushing his analysis to suggest a form of resistance DiFazio (1996) concludes:

1   In general, new, high-tech, production regimes are labour destroying. As a result, increasing numbers of workers are becoming permanently redundant. The wave of the future is more workers in a global labour market with fewer opportunities. Workers 'of all collars' are increasingly forced into greater competition with each other. In light of this situation, the struggle...has become a struggle for all workers in all labour processes: manual, skilled, and intellectual. That is the struggle for income independent of work.

2   Technological and scientific knowledge have become the principal productive forces in late-industrial societies. Not only has manual work been displaced, but skilled work has been displaced as well. In the new workplaces, technoscience is dominant, and skilled work is moved to the margins of production. Both skilled and industrial unionism face an increasing dilemma in view of these developments. Unions must reconceptualize their organizing strategies, with an increasing emphasis on knowledge work.

3   With more and more workers faced with the technological elimination of their work, we have at least two problems. First, the work ethic is no longer a central organizing principle for social life; and second, there is a general decline in wages. In order to address these problems, we must actively participate in the creation of a new public ethic of social responsibility around which life can now be organized. Second, the struggle for the decommodification of medicine, housing, education, food, and so on has to be initiated (pp. 202–3).

The rest of our constellation of a critical theory of teachers' work, has been developed through juxtaposing a labour process theory with critical ethnographies of schools.

Teachers' Own Identities have to Contend with the Power Relations that Operate in Schools and Educational Systems

Schools, we believe, need to be considered as 'scripted' (Gutierrez, 1994; Gutierrez et al., 1995) and 'disciplinary spaces' (Pignatelli, 1993) in which both students and the teachers are engaged in a daily project of 'becoming somebody' (Wexler, 1992). Wexler has used this term to refer to what students are up to in schools. We want to expand this to include also what teachers are up to. For teachers, schools are not places in which one can ponder the question to be or not to be. But rather there is a need to 'be somebody, a real presentable self, one anchored in the verifying eyes of' (p. 7) students, parents and the 'panoptical gaze of peer accountability' (Chapter 4, p. 81). Schools are places which demand 'identity work' (Snow and Anderson, 1987). This project of becoming somebody involves two interwoven strands for teachers: negotiating the labour market, and hence their identity as a competent 'teacher' able to sell their labour power, while simultaneously working on a (social, cultural) identity. In foregrounding the complex 'identity politics' of teachers in schools we want to highlight the following:

1   teachers generally have an already well-developed sense of self as a teacher. Unfortunately it does seem as though teachers learn about teaching in programmes that have a preference for a socially conservative ideology, as opposed to a socially transformative one. 'Consequently it is likely that many [teacher education] programs are shaped by the unexamined implicit influence of teacher educators' ideologies' (Grundy and Hatton, 1995, p. 23). Such courses tend to 'reinforce a previously unreflective orientation' (Hatton, 1997, p. 243);

2   teachers continue to negotiate identities while learning to teach (Sumara and Luce-Kapler, 1996). Not surprisingly, teachers hold on to 'old structures' and ways of doing things, especially when reforms are done to them and when little time is allowed for the reconstruction of practice;

3   teachers negotiate identities in 'territories of race, gender, class and difference' (MacPherson and Fine, 1995). Teachers are 'positioned' (Davies and Harre, 1990) in educational contexts that are always already riven with hierarchical power relations that often favour heterosexuality, men, being white, and at least moderately affluent; and

4   teachers negotiate identities with/against technologies of control.

These last two points need further elaboration.

Teachers make sense of their work through the 'repertoire of available and sanctioned stories that they can use to interpret their experiences' (Ezzy, 1997, p. 433–4). As we have already argued, teachers seem to be caught between their own 'internally persuasive' views of teaching and learning – an educators' sensibility – and the 'authoritative discourses' of contemporary school reform – the neo-liberal way. Our ethnographic work indicates that this context produces negative feelings of self for many teachers that are generated from a failure to maintain previous levels of quality in classroom teaching. Doing more with less usually means doing it less well, especially when the job is already intense and complex. The retreat of the state from a commitment to public schooling is manifested negatively in the subjective and intersubjective states of teachers. It is teachers who eventually, and on a day-to-day basis, have to live the contradictions inherent in the neo-liberal way to school reform. Post-Fordist school reform means that teachers are also having to 'relate to and manoeuvre around' in schools that expect them to speak the language of power – and it is managerialist, patriarchal, disinterested in process, is outcomes focused (fetishized?), and is upward accountability driven. Responsibility, of a rather diminished type, is devolved downward. As such, teachers are working in schools that are moving towards 'flatter management structures'. Often this means middle management without recompense. Such schools involve increased public performance of outcomes, an increased need for interpersonal competencies, and at a time in which it is increasingly difficult to maintain quality relationships with students or colleagues. In this rather schizoid context, teachers' identity work might best be described as doing more 'emotional labour' (Blackmore, 1996): of repressing negative emotions, of dealing with embarrassment, shame or guilt, while also being committed to a view of profession that values an ethic of care.

Teachers as Workers Sell their Labour Power in a 'Globalizing' Labour Market

Teachers are positioned within an always already classed society and 'share the interests of both the petty bourgeoisie and the working class' (Apple, 1986, p. 32). Teachers sell their labour power in a labour market characterized by an 'international division of labour' (Spivak, 1988, p. 287) and hence their work is being significantly affected industrially through those neo-liberal discourses that predominate in such a globalizing marketplace. The term 'industrially' usually refers to workers' pay and conditions. In teacher unions there is usually a clear delineation between industrial issues and curriculum. We think this is not only unhelpful for advancing a politics of teachers' work that is up to struggling against the deleterious effects of globalization, but is in fact also a misreading of the nature of teachers' work. We believe that curriculum is an industrial issue. In this case we have been somewhat mischievous here in our use of the word industrial and hope that the reader will see the next aspect of our constellation as a significant dimension of the 'industrial' concerns for teachers.

In this section we want to continue our analysis of the political-economic aspect of globalization that we began in Chapter 1. Political-economic globalization according to Hopkins and Wallerstein (1996) is understood in terms of the 'world-system', 'an historical social system that originated in the sixteenth century' (p. 2):

> In the modern world-system, world production[3] has been carried on by the rules of the capitalist world-economy in which the institutionalised primary consideration of those who own or control the means of production is the endless accumulation of capital.
> (Hopkins and Wallerstein, 1996, p. 3)

For Hopkins and Wallerstein the 'world-system' involves the following evolving and interrelated 'institutional domains' or 'vectors': the interstate system; the structure of world production; the structure of the world labour force; the pattern of world human welfare; the social cohesion of the states;

and, the structures of knowledge. A short sketch of each of these vectors opens up possibilities for us to connect the labour process of teachers' work to a globalizing labour market.

The interstate system

The interstate system (Reifer and Sudler, 1996), since the end of the Cold War, is still very much dominated by the US struggling to 'maintain hegemonic power in a world-economy' (Hopkins and Wallerstein, 1996, p. 3), in a 'new world order'. The US maintains its hegemony, in part, by massive military expenditures that reinforce the Cold War balance of power in Europe and Asia, enmesh US allies into a US-dominated security structure, and guarantee an open door for free enterprise in the Third World. This new world order is characterized by a world awash with weapons including a proliferation of nuclear weapons and other weapons of mass destruction, increasing economic inequality or immiseration with the growing crisis of Third World debt, and disintegration in many parts of the globe including Eastern Europe, the Middle East, parts of Africa, and Asia. Concomitant with these changes has been an ascendancy of the new right who now control the policy levers of governments in many post-industrial countries. Bourdieu (1998, p. 125) refers to this neo-conservativism as 'a sort of radical capitalism', an undisguised unrestrained capitalism, that:

> knows and recognises no purpose but the ever increasing creation of wealth and, more secretly, its concentration in the hands of a small privileged minority; and it therefore leads to a combat by every means, including the destruction of the environment and human sacrifice, against any obstacle to the maximization of profit.
>
> (p. 126)

Castells (1998) argues that to make sense of globalization we need to understand the 'rise of the fourth world'. The system of informational capitalism, understood as a 'social structure where the sources of economic productivity, cultural hegemony and political-military power depend, fundamentally, on the capacity to retrieve, store, process and generate information and knowledge' (Castells, 1994, p. 19) gives rise to 'black holes' of poverty and social exclusion.

> The Fourth World comprises large areas of the globe, such as much of Sub-Saharan Africa, and impoverished rural areas of Latin America and Asia. But it is also present in literally every country, and every city, in this new geography of social exclusion. It is formed of American inner-city ghettos, Spanish enclaves of mass youth unemployment, French banlieues warehousing North Africans, Japanese Yoseba quar-

ters, and Asian megacities' shanty towns. And it is populated by millions of homeless, incarcerated, prostituted, criminalized, brutalized, stigmatized, sick, and illiterate persons. They are the majority in some areas, the minority in others, and a tiny minority in a few privileged contexts. But, everywhere, they are growing in number, and increasing in visibility, as the selective triage of informational capitalism, and the political breakdown of the welfare state, intensify social exclusion. In the current context, the rise of the Fourth World is inseparable from the rise of informational, global capitalism.

(Castells, 1998, pp. 164–5)

The structure of world production

The structure of world production (Ikeda, 1996) is now dominated by Transnational Corporations (TNC) that sustain a 'core-periphery zonal organisation'[4] (Hopkins and Wallerstein, 1996, pp. 4–5) which entails developing commodity chains of production. The core is understood to include the post-industrial West (or North) that roughly translates as the OECD countries. The periphery are those 'developing' nations – the 'Third World', the South or 'comprador countries'. Some countries are considered as semi-periphery and might be thought of as the developed Third World. Broadly speaking, the periphery serves as the supplier of cheap raw materials and labour while the core accumulates the profit, maintains the high research and development and high technology aspects of production, and generates the principal markets. Globalizing production as a means to further the accumulation of profit by TNCs has meant 'liberalizing' trade barriers, deregulating the financial sector, the establishment of trade blocs such the EU, and a move to controlling the service sector (especially banking, financial services, transportation and telecommunications). To make this point more dramatically it is worthwhile contemplating for a moment, the extent of the 'increasing inequality and polarization in the distribution of wealth' (Castells, 1998):

> The poorest 20 percent of the world's population have seen their share of the global income decline from 2.3 percent to 1.4 percent in the past 30 years. Meanwhile, the share of the richest 20 percent has risen from 70 percent to 85 percent. This has doubled the ratio of the share of the richest over the poorest – from 30:1 to 61:1. The assets of the world's 358 billionaires (in US dollars) exceed the combined annual incomes of countries with 45 percent of the world's population.
>
> (p. 80)

In the contemporary Australian context, the relentless desire for increased productivity and efficiency by workers, including teachers, has meant 'award restructuring' and the introduction of post-Fordist workplace reforms. In schools this has meant pushing for a 'flatter management structure' and hence devolving management responsibility downward. A significant strategy for pushing through restructuring in the schooling sector has been the use of moral panics or manufactured crisis (Berliner and Biddle, 1995). Manufacturing crises generates a discourse of deviancy to deflect public attention from the broader structural questions. The deviants are the workers (especially trade unionists) who want to be paid too much, who are not productive enough, and teachers who do not teach the right things well enough. Schools have had to wear responsibility for our economic problems, the deviancy of youth and the 'literacy crisis' to name but a few manufactured crises. What does not seem to get much mention in the official rhetoric though, is the ineffectiveness of corporate management in working towards more democratic relationships in the workplace, the failure of policies on unemployment, and the fact that our present system defends economic redistribution from the poor to the already wealthy.

The structure of the labour force

A world-system that is driven by an endless desire for high profit (necessarily largely monopolized) works to sustain the uneven distribution of rewards – it is fundamental to the system. 'This requirement of unevenness has been integral to the continuing formation of the world labour force' (Hopkins and Wallerstein, 1996, p. 4). The segregated world labour force has been structured not only by multiple employers and the states, but also through syndical action, migration, and the creation of solidarities. Workers' demands have often been translated into a 'social wage' involving education, health and 'redistributive allocations' (pensions and unemployment benefits). Importantly though, globalization of the economy has meant a 'worldwide broadening of wage employment, albeit mostly part-lifetime, and a decrease in the share of the "social wage" within aggregate household income, owing to the rise in "incidental" or "casual" wage labour' (Tabak, 1996, p. 88). The world's labour market now involves a 'spectacular growth in rates of urbanization' (p. 89), an 'impressive rise in the core in the relative share of the female labour force' (p. 88), and a remarkable growth in the infra-economy – 'the informal other half of economic activity, the world of self-sufficiency and barter of goods and services', and a 'bypassing of unionized labour' (p. 95) giving rise to the establishment of subcontracting of production, and location of production in countries capable of 'coerced employment' (Hopkins and Wallerstein, 1996, p. 5).

In the Australian context the restructuring of the labour force has meant replacing a centralized wage-fixing system with enterprise bargaining, and a concomitant policy to undermine the bargaining power of trade unions. (What this means of course is a privileging of collective bargaining by employers in concert with Federal government instruments – such as Competition Policy – while undermining workers capacity to collectively bargain.)

The pattern of human welfare

The expansion of welfare, or human development (Max-Neef, 1991), has been a significant feature of policy rhetoric of states, during, and since the Cold War. In much of the core zone (with the US being an exception), ensuring increased human welfare has been sustained within the welfare state, which has involved subsidized health, improved access to education and especially growth in tertiary education, and the development of agri-business pushing the Green revolution. Welfare statism though has been under attack since the late 1960s with the onset of a fiscal crisis of the state. The new right restoration, sought to dismantle the welfare state, shifted responsibility for welfare from the state to kinship networks, religious organizations, philanthropic and other non-governmental organizations (Pelizzon and Casparis, 1996). The result has been increasing hostility towards immigrants, as scapegoats to blame, with a concomitant increase in overt racism. The hostility towards taxation as a means of redistributing income has meant a 'deepening and widening [of the] poverty gap' (p. 136), and a 'feminisation of poverty'. In the periphery states, 'welfare-statism, to the extent it ever existed, was replaced by direct repression and accompanied by economic austerity mediated by the World Bank and the IMF' (p. 137). In health there has been expanding slums in the world's cities, dumping of toxic wastes, and environmental degradation has spiralled. Educational profiles have remained unequal: 'each national system of education helped to reproduce the class structure; and class, in turn, structured the school' (p. 141), and women are as disadvantaged as ever:

> the fiscal justification has served primarily to shift the burden of schooling costs from the state onto the market and the family, and to place the blame for the school system's inability to ensure job access on the students.
>
> (p. 141)

There has been a rise in vocationalism which involves 'redefining higher education as existing to serve the economic needs of society' (p. 142). Policy on schooling is increasingly designed to marketize schools – to force schools to compete for market share. Such policy deliberately aims to undermine public schooling and hence shift responsibility for schooling to the private sector.

The social cohesion of states

In relation to state structures in the world-system, in the core zones especially, the liberal statist (Keynesian) vision became the prevailing model in the post-1945 period and served as the ideological foundation of US hegemony. Since the economic stagnation of the 1970s and the imposition of structural adjustment programmes on the developing countries, social cohesion has been on the decline (Pusey, 1996, 1998). For example, crime rates have been slowly growing: mafia-type criminal organizations have expanded; adolescent criminality has become a mark of sprawling deindustrialized areas; and large-scale crime by criminal multinational corporations[5] who trade in drugs, weaponry, and money laundering. Of course the deregulation (non-control) of international financial markets has meant that 'tax avoidance' through tax havens has become a form of legalized crime. A growing revolt by tax payers has meant pursuing policies of privatisation of public utilities:

> Liberalism as the dominant ideology of the world system is thus caught in numerous ideological and political complications that previously it could gloss over or ignore altogether. Minority rights undermine the 'one man (*sic*), one vote' principle; affirmative action contradicts meritocracy; the state is viewed by rightwingers as 'unduly meddling', and by the minorities as inadequate, untrustworthy and hypocritical.
>
> (Derlugian, 1996, p. 171)

In Australia many commentators have argued that 'economic fundamentalism' tears the social fabric. Many have begun to argue that governments need desperately to include social (cultural, environmental) considerations in their policy formulation. The importance of developing 'social capital' (Cox, 1995) has been one of the significant strands in these type of arguments, where social capital refers to such things as 'developing a durable network of more or less institutionalised relationships of mutual acquaintance and recognition' (Bourdieu, 1986, p. 248); developing trust, reciprocity, mutuality (Cox, 1995), and skills for participation in ceremonies and rituals, solidarity, civic participation and integrity (Putnam, 1993).

Structures of knowledge

To understand the world-system we also need to analyse the structure of knowledge that operates as a 'continually evolving structured framework within which social action' (Hopkins and Wallerstein, 1996, p. 2) occurs. Broadly speaking,

> [t]he single most important innovation in the structures of knowledge of the modern world system was the displacement of philosophy/theology

by science as the central organizing metaphor of knowledge, and indeed the dominance of a particular mode of scientific method.

(p. 7)

The 'prototype of "big science"…became the metaphor of material progress through rational (Western) science', which is understood as a 'universal science, empirical and positivistic, expressing the Enlightenment ideal of endless progress implemented in an ultimately law-like (Newtonian, mechanistic, and hence in principle, predicable) world' (Lee, 1996, p. 179). Most significantly has been the deepening ideological commitment by political leaders and other policy makers in the core to such a scientism. Not only has such a view of knowledge been used to understand and control the material world but it has also profoundly influenced the nature of the social sciences, giving dominance to a form of functionalism, especially in the US. Of course the hegemony of this 'instrumental rationality' has been undermined from a number of quarters. From within the social sciences, and especially the proponents of culture – critical theory, structuralism and post-structuralism – have all dented empiricism's claim to be value-free, sectioned off from politics and ethics or outside of interpretation. From within science itself, and especially by those working for a 'new science' (Capra, 1982), it is now widely recognized that a science of entities fails to properly understand the very large, the very small, and the very complex. Contemporary science struggles to develop a science of relationships based on the interrelationship between reality and consciousness, transdisciplinarity, and a metaphor of ecology rather than mechanism. This 'politics of knowing' (Lather, 1991) manifests itself in schooling as: a call for critical literacies (Lankshear and McLaren, 1993); the emergence of forms of cultural studies (Giroux, 1994; Giroux and McLaren, 1994; Hattam et al., 1998a); a gradual shift to the 'social' in science courses; and, a loud and vociferous critique of Western knowledge production around race, class, sexuality and gender.

The Curriculum/Pedagogy is the Main Specification of the Labour Process of Teaching

Curriculum for us 'names' what teachers do with students in schools. We want to be much more expansive here than simply referring to curriculum as course specification, or the intended curriculum that you can read in any syllabus text. We also want the term curriculum to carry what gets practised – the implemented curriculum. Hence the term curriculum refers to both the formal and hidden curriculum (see Chapter 3). Such an expansive view of the term curriculum overlaps with the term pedagogy, where pedagogy refers to both the theory and practice of teaching and learning. That is, pedagogy and curriculum might be considered to be equivalent.

Control of the labour process of teachers' work then is about control of the curriculum/pedagogy. In the Australian scene during the last decade or so (and its equivalents elsewhere), this control could be seen to have the following strands.

The development and implementation of the national curriculum

The development and implementation of the national curriculum (called National Statements and Profiles in Australia) could be seen as an attempt to come to some form of 'educational settlement' about the nature of the core knowledge to which every child should have access. This settlement was designed to be an alternative to implementing standardized testing in Australia, at a time when the calls for accountability measurements were growing louder. The National Statements and Profiles aimed to ensure that the judgements of teachers were central to the accountability process. In the words of Boomer (1992) who was one of the chief architects of the National Statements and Profiles:

> [C]urrent accumulating pressures for better assessing and reporting will not go away, and...it behoves educators to take the vanguard and the control in developing the best possible systems....that profile...constructive alternatives to national testing...out of a strongly teacher-centred, classroom-oriented understanding of how judgement works on a day-to-day basis in our schools...I see the [profiles] approach more in terms of an action research instigated by systems in their search for a non-toxic multipurpose method of supporting reform in education, at the same time as accounting publicly and informing themselves on how well the students and the curriculum are going.
>
> (pp. 61–4)

Many critiques though see the National Statements and Profiles as an accounting technology that is aligned with a 'corporate managerialism' (McTaggart, 1992), 'steeped in a positivist view of knowledge, a simplistic view of persons as learners, and a liberal view of progress' (Collins, 1996, p. 10) that fails to advance a concern for social justice in education (Reid, 1992). These Australian critiques resonate with those from the US (Apple, 1993b) and the UK (Bowe and Ball, 1992; Ball, 1994).

The development and implementation of the National Statements and Profiles[6] also allowed state educational bureaucracies in Australia to dismantle their advisory support services, and hence to become 'managerial husks' (Seddon, 1995b). The development of the National Statements and Profiles meant that state education bureaucracies could argue that the curriculum had been specified, the curriculum debate was over, the responsibility was now with schools and teachers to get on and implement it – just get on and do it. This has meant that the once important dialogic space between policy development and the classroom has been downsized out of existence (Bartlett, 1994) and the opportunity for teachers' voices to be a part of the ongoing process of development of policy is significantly curtailed. It also means that responsibility for the curriculum has been devolved, but such devolution is somewhat of a scam because of the overlay of 'cruel accounting' (Thomson, 1998a) that has and is still being developed in parallel with the National Statements and Profiles. The closing down of government sponsored spaces for debate in state education bureaucracies means an institutional silencing of teachers' voices. It now seems clear that educators' knowledge is ignored when developing policy on schooling (Taylor et al., 1997). It is not only teachers' voices that have been marginalized. It appears as though recent policy development on schools has been ideologically deaf to the best researchers in this country. Take for instance the recent debacle about literacy standards in Australia (Comber et al., 1998).

Perhaps even more insidious has been the blatant muting of social justice discourse (Lingard and Garrick, 1997; Luke, 1997). The category 'social justice' has all but disappeared. As examples, the Disadvantaged Schools Program has been renamed the Commonwealth Literacy Program, with its future now under a cloud, and the funding for the National Schools' Network has ceased. To undermine a commitment to equal outcomes and hence affirmative action, neo-liberal governments retreat to a 'blaming the victim' position by marshalling such arguments as the need for freedom of speech. But of course freedom of speech collapses to ridding our culture of the unnecessary constraints of 'political correctness' (Newfield, 1993; Wark, 1995) while simultaneously authorizing a discourse of derision (Kenway, 1990). The empirical evidence though, overwhelmingly supports the view (Teese et al., 1995; Dwyer, 1996) that the outcomes of schooling are still very much skewed in favour of those groups who are already advantaged in society. The already disadvantaged or disenfranchised – such as those living in poverty and Aborigines – continue to not be served well by the schooling system and the present confluence of reforms is only making things worse.

For teachers, the National Statements and Profiles are just one of many resources/policies or imperatives that need attention. For the experienced teacher the National Statements and Profiles are often used as another resource for evaluating and modifying practice. Often though, the National Statements and Profiles are an interference in implementing other reforms. As an example, in Chapter 4 we reported how, even though the National Statements and Profiles were an immediate 'priority', they were actually an interference to implementing middle schooling. The priority is imposed from above – teachers are expected to report on student achievement using the levels specified in the National Statements and Profiles. The imperative to implement the Statements and Profiles takes time away from other curriculum issues, such as devising curriculum for students that require negotiation (Chapter 4, p. 85). There is an intensification of work associated which is also allied with frustration that the Statements and Profiles will not actually improve teaching and learning, and that the requirement to assign levels is actually impossible or at least meaningless.

Marketizing/vocationalizing the curriculum

To push the market into the specification of curriculum the Australian federal government in the late 1980s pursued a policy renewal process through a series of national forums aimed at addressing 'the problem' of post-compulsory education and training. In a retrospective article on the development of key competencies, Borthwick (1993) defined 'the problem' with post-compulsory education and training as: 'attempting to grapple with the dramatic growth in Year 11 and 12 and with the changes of expectation of purposes of this phase of schooling' (p. 21). 'The problem of post-compulsory education and training' was taken up in the first instance in Finn's (1995) report which recommended, among other things, the need for a convergence of general and vocational education (Maxwell, 1996), national reform of entry level training (Carmichael, 1992), and the development of employment-related key competencies. Such recommendations are not surprising given endorsement through the logic of economic rationalism of Canberra (Pusey, 1991), the rise of a neo-liberal valorization of the free market, and the fetish within the then Federal Labour Government to solve Australia's economic problems by improving our international competitiveness through embracing the rhetoric of the 'clever country' (Australian Vice-Chancellors Committee, 1991). The need to further develop employment-related key competencies was taken up by the Mayer Committee. The Mayer Committee in its report, 'Key Competencies' (1992), not only defined a key competency, but also argued for seven key competencies 'that all young people need to be able to participate effectively in the emerging forms of work and work organisation'. An eighth area of competence, 'cultural understandings' was confirmed in July 1993 by the Australian Education Council (Centre for Workplace Communication and Culture, 1994). During 1994–6, the Federal Government funded a range of implementation projects around Australia in both the school and Vocational Education and Training (VET) sector. During 1997–8 policy has been put in place to ensure that teachers use the key competencies as a framework for curriculum design, implementation and assessment.

There have also been other less subtle methods of marketizing the curriculum. The most blatant has been the increased intrusion of the market into the everyday life of schools. Schools are increasingly being seen by businesses as sites for advertising. This includes such strategies as offering promotional material/prizes to schools, providing funds for use of the company logo, providing resources (that are heavily 'badged') for use in classrooms (Burrow, 1994; Kenway et al., 1994c) and even having post-compulsory courses approved (Kenway and Fitzclarence, 1998).

Marketizing curriculum, at the post-compulsory end of schooling now goes under the auspices of enterprise education and the emergence of VET courses (Seddon, 1994; Smyth, 1998; Smyth and Hattam, 1998a). Commitment to universal participation in a general liberal education is now very much undermined by the emergence of courses, or even schools, that are about vocational pathways and teaching enterprise skills. Such courses (and schools) are predicated on developing uncritical 'relationships' with 'industry'. Schooling is being asked to play a more important role in vocational skill formation and preparing job-ready flexible and multi-skilled workers, but at a time when the labour market is characterized by increasing levels of part-time work, creeping credentialism, almost complete decimation of the youth full-time labour market, and a large pool of unemployed labour (Spierings, 1995).

Rolling out basic skill testing and benchmarking

Not content with the national reporting possibilities of the National Statements and Profiles, many states in Australia have developed forms of basic skills testing. Such reforms have culminated in the recent attempts in Australia to foist a national testing regime on to schools. Using the national benchmarks set in the National Literacy and Numeracy Plan, such testing is being argued in terms of parental choice. The national literacy benchmarks supposedly allow parents to shop around for the best school for their children:

> Here the Government establishes itself as a champion of parents' rights. In constructing the collective 'parent' (read 'white middle-class educated literate parent with money'), the Minister's statements actively capitalise on, and galvanise, the dissatisfactions of a number of different interest groups. Missing from this rhetoric, however, are any specifications that such choice will be available to all parents. 'Choice' is presented as an unproblematic goal, but which parents can 'shop around'?
>
> (Comber et al., 1998, p. 27)

Such testing/benchmarking is ahistorical, culturally insensitive, reductive, incongruent with the practised curriculum and uninformative for teachers with a practical intent to make a difference for their students (Hattam, 1997). Perhaps even more abhorrent is the way that policy on literacy testing is being used to force schools to compete for market share. The test/benchmark now becomes a commodity to tout in the educational marketplace

(Marginson, 1995; Connell, 1996). Apple (1993a) summarizes these critiques:

> I have argued that the politics of official knowledge – in this case surrounding proposals for a national curriculum and for national testing – cannot be fully understood in an isolated way. All of this needs to be situated in larger ideological dynamics in which we are seeing an attempt by a new hegemonic bloc to transform our very ideas of the purpose of education. This transformation involves a major shift...in which democracy becomes an economic, not a political concept and where the public good withers at its very roots.
>
> (p. 236)

The marketization/globalization of schooling – or 'fast capitalist educational change' (Shacklock, 1998) – is well underway and involves a double dose of infection: public schools are being forced to compete for students (Marginson, 1995) and the school curriculum is being infected by the market (Kenway et al., 1994b). The local public school, now has to spend increasing amounts of time and resources on marketing image (rather than improving teaching and learning). The school curriculum is also now a site for commercial markets to seek out new consumers and for industry to develop employment-related and entrepreneurial (enterprise) competencies (Collins, 1996; Smyth and Hattam, 1998a).

Control of Teachers' Work takes Structural, Ideological and Disciplinary Modes

To 'wring out more effort' from teachers requires control strategies to be in place. Because this proposition has been outlined in some detail in Chapter 2, we only need to summarize here some of the important points.

Control (or power) limits 'the range of practices and relationships possible in classrooms' (Gore, 1995, p. 166). Getting consent for such limitation involves:

1   Power from above – the use of regulations, sanctions, surveillance, rewards and punishments.
2   Discursive coercion – 'distort[ing] human communication and thereby the use of human reasoning in power relationships' (Corson, 1995, p. 89). Such distortions are ideological and as Corson describes, can be of several types:
    • type 1 – the representation of sectional interests as universal, by defining interests specific to a group so that those interests are perceived as universally valid;
    • type 2 – the denial or transmutation of contradictions, for example,

by reformulating fundamental system contradictions as more superficial issues of social conduct;

- type 3 – the naturalization of the present through reification, for example, by defining present or past organizational realities as 'the way things are' and objective, so that alternatives seem unworkable or unrealistic (p. 89).

3   Control/power is productive at the level of discourse and constructs the subjectivity of teachers. Teachers speak themselves into being through variously accepting, rejecting, manipulating and transforming those sanctioned discourses that authorize good practice and hence are committed to normative control of teachers' work.

Control, as a Result of Globalization, has a Detrimental and Material Effect on Teachers' Work

The marketization of the schooling sector has a significant and deleterious effect on teachers' work. As a consequence, the contemporary scene in schools is now characterized by public school teachers who are, by and large, increasingly demoralized by what is happening to schools. Such a demoralization involves the following:

Intensification as an academic label for what is happening to teachers' work fails to properly convey the reality of the 'chronic work-overload' that characterizes contemporary teaching. The reduction of real resources – including time, and increases in class-size, means a 'physical and temporal compression' (Chapter 4, p. 73). There is just 'too little time', there are 'too many things to do in the time available' (Chapter 5, p. 131), and 'you can't relax and unwind'. Teachers report feeling continually 'work-tired'. The school as a 'greedy organization' constantly pushes teachers to the limit, forcing teachers to cut corners with preparation time and correction. The devolving of responsibility downward through the use of 'flatter management structures' means a permanent increase in administrative workload. The implementation of National Curriculum contributes to increased workload, an increase, that has very little recompense in terms of time or resources available for professional development. The system exacerbates the problem by instituting forms of 'cruel accounting'.

Associated with intensification is a *deskilling* or redefining of teachers' work, not in terms of being educated professionals or intellectuals but as competent practitioners or technicians (Ball, 1995; Knight et al., 1995). Rather than promoting an upskilling of teachers' work involving a continuation of the school-based curriculum movement of the 1980s, teachers are now expected to implement imposed curriculum frameworks, and increasingly teach to the test. Of course this analysis is rather simplistic. Some schools have managed to use the present situation as an opportunity to upskill teachers. The move to 'flatter management structures' has a positive outcome for teachers' work in some instances. Schools that can manage to sustain democratic cultures and continue to pursue more collaborative ways of teaching provide opportunities for a range of 'upskilling' (Hattam et al., 1997a; Smyth et al., 1997; McInerney et al., 1998). The commitment to sustain democratic school cultures means learning how to: promote student voice, work in teams with other teachers, enhance the dialogue with the community, and critically reflect on teaching and learning. (See the next chapter for a more sophisticated description of such a democratic imagining of schools.)

Deskilling is also promoted by increasing levels of imposed *surveillance*, often referred to as 'accountability measures'. Examples include: having to provide levels for students using the National Statements and Profiles; standardized testing (or Basic Skills Testing and 'benchmarking') that have little relevance to best teaching/learning practice and curriculum development; being evaluated by external 'quality assurance' teams that provide schools with ways of measuring students' outcomes for public consumption; the 'peer assessment' of Advanced Skills Teachers using external peers (Smyth and Shacklock, 1998); and the tightening of line management of school principals by superintendents to ensure compliance of department policies (Starr, 1998).

Educational leadership has become damaged. Leadership in this case refers to not only the institutional forms of leadership, such as school principals and other administrative leaders but also to others in the school who get to show leadership. With regards to the institutional leadership, globalization/marketization has meant that collegiate relationships with teachers are now increasingly difficult to sustain. The post-Fordist notions of flattened hierarchy/collaborative teams are undermined by the needs of the system for accountability. The practice of accountability has been devolved downward and into the principal's office with a concomitant shift of power to the 'central management', as 'major decision making and involvement in policy development or systematic planning is largely denied them' (Starr, 1998). Educational leaders are now also required to spend increasing amounts of time on 'impression management'. Having to compete with the neighbouring school also undermines the collegiate relationships with other schools. The neighbouring school, which was once an ally, a space for professional dialogue about the work, is now 'the enemy'. Having to manage image also undermines the possibility of actually working on 'problems'. Schools can no longer admit to having a 'problem' because this undermines the reputation of the school. How can a school admit to working on literacy problems, of working on issues related to the poverty of the school community, to racism or sexism when they have to compete for market share?

Towards a Contemporary Politics of Teachers' Work

Certainly teachers and students and (most) educational researchers are now silenced in the policy development process. Such an ideological and institutional deafness though should not deter us from contesting the policy formulations being done to schools by those touting the advantages of marketization and privatization. Rather than have policy that is about an ongoing dialogic encounter with teachers, that writes with teachers, and that has the educative relationship between the teacher and the student at the centre of its concerns, we now have policy that is not even educative in nature (Thomson, 1998b) and that is outrightly oppositional to teachers. Just because there is no longer a democratic and dialogic process for the development of educational policy in Australia does not mean the end of a politics of teachers' work (Ginsburg, 1995; Connell, 1996; Thomson and Reid, 1998). As such it is essential to continue to speak back, and to work on developing and sustaining 'counter-publics' (Smyth and Hattam, 1998b) that support teachers in schools who struggle to realize an egalitarian view of schooling.

In this book we want to argue that school reform needs to be a process that strongly articulates with the concerns of teachers and as such needs to be framed in those terms. Importantly, schools do have some level of autonomy – there is space to work against the grain. What might be possible in this space is a key consideration for the next chapter. How might a critical theory of teachers' work resonate and continue to nurture an educator's sensibility in schools committed to the struggle for socially just schooling? What might a pragmatic 'resistance within' (Mac an Ghaill, 1988; Troman, 1996) look like? These are questions we will struggle with.

Notes

1   In Australia this refers to the division into the various states. For example, South Australia has its own state education department responsible for a publicly funded system of schools.
2   We might add, against the selfish individualism that is so valued in Australian elite private schools. What always seems to go unmentioned when considering schooling's role in making our society is the role of elite private schools. It is always Australian public schools that get a battering for not being good enough. For being in crisis. For letting the standards slip. Of course elite private schools have no interest in making a contribution to Australia as egalitarian. Elite private schools unabashedly promote themselves as places to get the best credentials for university entrance, into the most sought-after courses. Elite private schools as a consequence are significant protagonists in the ongoing struggle over what gets to be understood as good schooling. In this struggle, the elite schools are always on the side of keeping it like it is. They have yet to make one significant contribution to the debate in Australia which argues for change that is based on an egalitarian sensibility. Rather they make claims to the arguments based on quality and choice, arguments that resonate only with those who have freedom to choose.

3   'World production' refers to the existence of a network of commodity chains which link production activities across multiple jurisdictions, 'such that almost never could any single state place under its jurisdiction all the processes of production needed that are integral to any of the major economic activities located within its borders' (Hopkins and Wallerstein, 1996, p. 3).

4   A number of terms are called upon to describe this division, some old, some new, each reducing global difference to a bare binary opposition – West and non-West, North and South, First World and Third World, core and periphery, developed and under-developed. Each of these terms possesses its own limits and politics, but all presuppose that they don't actually name – a European world hegemony lasting from about 1760 to about 1960, and its deeply problematic, very partial breakdown. (During, 1992, p. 339)

5   Castells (1998) discusses what he calls the 'global criminal economy'.

6   From the outset, the states rights issue in Australia undermined the possibility of ever implementing a national curriculum. Most states at least tinkered with the content of the nationally developed curriculum and have begun to put in place alternatives. See Watt (1998) for an update of developments in this area.

7 Struggling with 'Global Effects'

Teachers as Pedagogical-Political Workers

Towards a Politics of Possibility for Teachers' Work

To make sense of what is happening to teachers' work with practical and emancipatory intent requires a critical theory capable of connecting globalization to the everyday life of the classroom. In the last chapter we began to draw our conceptual threads together and started to sketch out a critical theory of teachers' work that emphasized a labour process of teachers' work capable of making sense of technologies of power with a global reach. But the last chapter is only half of the story. A critical theory of teachers' work should be thought of as social theory 'combining the discourses of both critique and possibility' (Giroux, 1985a, p. xviii), involving a 'critique of domination and a theory of liberation' (Kellner, 1989, p. 1). Critical theory can be understood to involve a 'dialectical sensibility' (Agger, 1977a; Agger, 1977b), or a 'dialectical imagination which refuses to separate thought and action' (Agger, 1977a, p. 2). Foucault captures the spirit of such a sensibility in his meditation on Kant's 'way of philosophizing' when he asserts that:

> it has to be considered as an attitude, an ethos, a philosophical life in which critique of what we are is at one and the same time the historical analysis of the limits that are imposed on us and experiment with the possibility of going beyond them.
>
> (Foucault, 1984, p. 50)

This chapter then involves such an ethos and begins to sketch out how we might experiment with the possibility of going beyond the present.

Benhabib (1986) offers a somewhat more elaborate version of critical theory that speaks of interconnecting moments of critique, norm and utopia. Critique as we use the term means 'to demystify the apparent objectivity of social processes by showing them to be constituted by the praxis of knowing and acting subjects' (Benhabib, 1986, p. 9). It is worth quoting Benhabib at length on what she means by norm and utopia:

> Norm and Utopia are concepts referring to two visions of politics which I also name the 'politics of fulfilment' and the 'politics of transfiguration.' The politics of fulfilment envisages that the society of the future attains more adequately what present society has left unaccomplished. It is the culmination of the implicit logic of the present. The politics of transfiguration emphasizes the emergence of qualitatively different needs, social relations, and modes of association, which burst open the utopian potential within the old. Within a critical social theory the articulation of norms continues the universalist promise of bourgeois revolutions – justice, equality, civil rights, democracy, and publicity – while the articulation of utopia continues the tradition of early socialist, communitarian, and anarchist movements – the formation of community needs and solidarity, and qualitatively transformed relations to inner and outer nature. In short, while norms have the task of articulating the demands of justice and human worthiness, utopias portray modes of friendship, solidarity, and human happiness. Despite their essential tension, a critical social theory is only rich enough to address us in the present, insofar as it can do justice to both moments.
>
> (Benhabib, 1986, p. 13)

The notion of 'critique, norm and utopia' represents an historical exposition of the lineage of critical theory as 'formulated by members and associates of the Institut für Sozialforschung [known as the Frankfurt School] in the 1930s', which 'from the beginning rejected the demarcation between ethics and politics and the new science of society as drawn up by the young Durkheim' (Benhabib, 1986, p. 2). In that sense Benhabib offers an understanding of critical theory as an attempt to not only understand the human condition but also 'allying itself with the struggles of those for whom the hope of a better future provides the courage to live in the present' (Benhabib, 1986, p. 15). As a continuation of the project begun by Marx, critical theory is an expression of his famous aphorism, the eleventh 'Theses on Feuerbach' – 'the philosophers have only interpreted the world, in various ways: the point, however is to change it' (Marx, 1978, p. 145). This struggle for liberatory or emancipatory knowledge, or 'making hope practical' (Kenway et al., 1994d) is the topic for this chapter.

Translating norm and utopia into languages of possibility for teachers involves developing a dual politics – a politics of struggle with the present and a politics of a democratic (re)imagining of school. At a time in which both the material conditions of schools and our imaginations are being saturated with a marketizing view of schooling it is essential to not only struggle against the grain but also to keep alive an alternative vision for schooling. For socially critical teachers, and their supporters, this means acting politically in pedagogical ways outside of schools and practising pedagogy that is openly political inside of them.

Acting Politically Globally / Locally

Our critique in this book has aimed at making sense of how globalization affects teachers' work. So too must our theory of liberation be developed in this globalizing 'context'. It is no longer adequate to frame a politics of teachers' work in a context of the state. Instead, we need to be acting politically in ways that are responsive to 'global effects'. If we see a dialectical relationship between the global and the local then our politics might be understood, as both 'think global and act local' and 'think local and act global'. In other words, a politics of teachers' work needs to involve both responding to the global effects in local contexts and also attempting to act globally to defend the local. As with the last chapter, we can only hope to sketch out some possibilities here. In that chapter, we began to outline in broad terms, what the terrain of struggle looks like. Under each of our propositions we began to outline a contemporary politics of teachers' work that involved the following:

1   Schooling is still a significant site of social and cultural formation.
    * Becoming more attuned to the ways in which media culture impacts on the identity formation of young people.

2   Schools can make a significant contribution to an egalitarian society.
    * Resisting the forms of self-managing schools that might more accurately be called self-damaging schools that involve a wholesale dismantling of the public education system that leaves schools as stand-alone entities competing for market share in anything but a level playing field.

3   Teachers are the most important actors in the technology called schools.
    * Responding to an outright opposition to teachers by neo-liberal governments.
    * Reasserting the importance of teachers in educational reform.
    * Struggling for income independent of work because of the impact of digital electronics on the labour market.
    * Participating in the reinvigoration of the public sphere especially the debate about the type of society we want.
    * Struggling for the de-commodification of schooling.

4   Teachers' own identities have to contend with the power relations that operate in schools and educational systems.
    * Struggling with a politics of the personal and avoiding the detrimental effects of having to do increased emotional labour in schools.

5   Teachers-as-workers sell their labour power in a 'globalizing' labour market.
   * Resisting forms of award restructuring that compel workers to abandon union solidarity.
   * Taking cognisance of the trajectory of moving increasingly to a global labour market that forces workers to undercut each others' wages and conditions.
   * Making a din about the dismantling of the welfare state through scapegoating the most disenfranchised groups in society.
   * Connecting with groups that argue for a somewhat more expansive definition of living a good life, rather than the economic imperative of being a compliant worker.
   * Joining in the politics of knowing that struggles to weaken the hold that positivism still has on how we live, and make sense of our lives. For teachers this specifically means working for critical literacies.
   * Joining the loud and vociferous critique of knowledge production around race, class, sexuality and gender.

6   The curriculum/pedagogy is the main specification of the labour process of teaching.
   * Reasserting the importance of the educative relationship between the teacher and the student.
   * Resisting 'caging teachers' in elaborate, centrally dreamed-up curriculum frameworks (Collins, 1996, p. 11).
   * Continuing to reassert a discourse about social justice in schooling.
   * Minimizing the damage due to the introduction of testing/benchmarking that is ahistorical, culturally insensitive, reductive, incongruent with the practised curriculum and uninformative for teachers with a practical intent to make a difference for their students.
   * Struggling to have curriculum/pedagogy considered as an 'industrial' issue.

7   Control of teachers' work takes structural, ideological and disciplinary modes.
   * Responding to the institutional deafness of policy to teachers, most educational researchers', as well as students' voices.
   * Reclaiming the spaces to debate the nature of good teaching and learning, and to re-institute a well-funded dialogue between classrooms and the policy development process.
   * Working to have the professional development of teachers properly funded.

8   Control, as a result of globalization, has a detrimental and material effect on teachers' work.

- •   Responding to the contemporary crisis in teachers' work, or to invoke Adorno (1974), responding to the fact that teachers are now living an increasingly 'damaged life'.
- •   Becoming more sophisticated in reading and responding to the ways in which the media is used to manufacture crises or moral panics about what is happening in schools.

How is it possible to enact such a complex and seemingly overwhelming politics?

Of course many teachers are acting, individually and collectively, to resist the degradation of their work. However, it is becoming even more difficult to contest the seemingly endless stream of educational reforms let alone chart new possibilities. The most common approach has been 'resistance through accommodation': to accept the imposed initiatives and try to shape them to fit already established practices. Turning one's back on the policy avalanche and focusing on the classroom may appear to be the 'professional' thing to do, but it can surely only confirm teachers as technicians. If educators do not engage in a more sophisticated struggle against the onslaught of economic rationalism into schooling, then we are doomed to become increasingly dependent on the ideas and directions of 'experts' far removed from school communities.

So what can be done? A contemporary politics of teachers' work, we believe, involves a struggle to develop and sustain 'counter-publics' (Smyth and Hattam, 1998) that not only speak back to the 'potentially devastating social effects of untrammelled market forces' (Pusey, 1998, p. 42) on schooling, but also keep alive an 'egalitarian sensibility' (Hattam et al., 1998b, p. 1).

Struggling with a Politics of Identity – Rejecting the Role of Clerk or Technician

Before outlining the possibilities for such counter-publics it is essential to recognize that contemporary reforms in schooling involve a struggle over what it means to be a teacher. At the very centre of the contemporary struggle over the purposes of schooling is a contest over the consciousness of teachers. In Chapter 5 we mapped this struggle using a discourse of professionalism. Alternatively, Giroux (1986) argues that we are witnessing a 'disappearance of a form of intellectual labour central to the nature of critical pedagogy itself' (p. 33). He goes on to argue that contemporary educational policy aims to: 'reduce teachers to either high level clerks implementing the orders of others within the school bureaucracy or to the status of specialized technicians...' (p. 33).

Teachers are having to counteract a marketizing discourse which seeks to reduce teaching to that of a technical enterprise based on sets of competencies and skills rather than practices informed by ethical frameworks. But teachers are not automatons, that simply implement the authoritative discourse of government policy pronouncements (Ball, 1994). Rather, they struggle to make sense of – and hence to unite into a coherent practice – the interrelationships, contradictions and profound differences between the authoritative discourse (government policy) and their own internally persuasive discourse. Teachers engage in their work with intent to put into practice their internally persuasive discourses. Such intent though is forced to struggle with other available (and competing) verbal and ideological points of view, approaches and directions. A number of critical scholars (Giroux, 1988; Ball, 1995; Smyth, 1996b) have attempted to (re)imagine teachers as transformative intellectuals as an alternative construal of teachers to that of 'technicians' or 'clerks of the empire' (Giroux, 1985b, p. 27).

In trying to understand the role of teachers as intellectuals we return to Gramsci (1971) for advice. This quote has been edited in response to the sexist nature of the original:

> All men [and women] are intellectuals...but not all have in society the function of intellectuals.... Each [person]...outside of [their] professional activities, carries on some form of intellectual activity, that is, [s]he is a 'philosopher', an artist, a person of taste, [s]he participates in a particular conception of the world, has a conscious line on moral conduct, and therefore contributes to sustain a conception of the world or to modify it, that is, to bring into being new modes of thought.
>
> (p. 9)

Transformative intellectuals theorize with 'practical intent' (Bernstein 1978; Alway 1995), and hence aim to 'keep simultaneously in view the distinct standpoints of the theorist and of the political agent...and insisting on holding new theoretical paradigms accountable to the demands of political practice; at the same time...to access the viability of alternative forms of practice in light of the results of theoretical reflection' (Fraser, 1989, p. 2). Transformative or 'resisting' (Giroux, 1986) intellectuals cannot be reduced to simply:

> being a faceless professional, a competent member of a class just going about her/his business...but rather whose place it is publicly to raise embarrassing questions, to confront orthodoxy and dogma (rather than to produce them), to be someone who cannot easily be coopted by governments or corporations, and whose raison d'être is to represent all

those people and issues that are routinely forgotten or swept under the rug.

(Said, 1994, p. 9)

Central to our politics of counter-publics, is a politics of identity for teachers. We agree with both Aronowitz (1994) and Calhoun (1994) that a politics of identity has to be understood as a form of collective action, committed to 'to make class identities count' (p. 182) as well as to work against a number of other oppressions including patriarchy, racism and homophobia. The teacher as transformative intellectual, or 'cultural worker' (Giroux and Trend, 1992) amounts to the teacher as pedagogical-political worker; a term that infers both a political pedagogy and a pedagogical politics.

Making the Political Pedagogical – Sustaining Counter-publics

To be working on such an identity, to be nurturing an alternative to the marketized/commodified subject of globalized capitalism, requires that teachers struggle to sustain some critical and political agency in their work – that is, to sustain a view of teachers as critically reflective practitioners. But a struggle over agency cannot be constrained to hiding in the classroom or even working tirelessly on the culture of a school. A contemporary politics of teachers' work requires a struggle to reinsert teachers' voices into the policy process and hence requires spaces to speak (back) from. Teachers need to connect with 'sites of resistance' (Miyoshi, 1995) and hope, counter-publics that aim to find 'ways of democratizing the state and civil society' (Whitty et al., 1998, p. 135). The point of contemporary politics is the 'absence of democracy itself' (Rogers, 1995, p. 16). Important 'counter-publics' already exist but require ongoing nurturing and building of democratic capacity itself (Rogers, 1995, p. 17). We want to very briefly highlight four of these: unions, under-graduate teacher education programmes, postgraduate teacher education programmes, and university research.

Unions

Teacher unions are still the most important counter-public space within which teachers can struggle for a more socially just system of education. In Australia, teacher unions are still very active and have managed to sustain their membership despite the demographic fall in union membership in general. What seems most important in these unsettling times is to ensure that union activism does not collapse to a struggle over wages. As we have already outlined in Chapter 2, the labour process of teaching is most importantly specified in terms of the curriculum. As such, unions need to become more involved in struggles over curriculum/pedagogy. To put this most bluntly, the curriculum is an industrial issue. Another important challenge for unions is how to forge international relationships capable of struggling against Transnational Corporations and neo-liberal governments, and develop campaigns to defend public education globally. Globalizing capitalism requires globalizing unions.

Under-graduate teacher education programmes

Teacher education programmes are an important space for the struggle over the consciousness of teachers. In these programmes, there is the possibility that student teachers can be inducted into the identity work of a pedagogical-political worker. Reid et al. (1998, p. 252) outline a model for such a programme based on this rationale: '[t]eachers will have to fight for the right to determine key aspects of their labour process. To conduct this fight successfully, all teachers need highly developed political skills' (p. 252). The under-graduate programme alluded to by Reid et al. aims to develop 'political sensibilities' that will enable teachers:

> [T]o struggle in the various arenas where policy is determined, to wrest back and then maintain some greater degree of autonomy in their curriculum work. This will require the capacity to recognise the ways in which curriculum control operates, the critical skills to uncover hegemonic constructions of teaching as an apolitical activity, and the will to work collectively, through union and professional associations, to do something about it. It also requires political understandings including knowledge about how and where educational policy is shaped, who to target in political campaigns, and how education unions and political parties work. And it demands a significant array of political skills, including the capacity to negotiate, advocate, lobby, communicate and organize in the wider political arena.
>
> (p. 252)

Postgraduate teacher education programmes

Within the context of the demoralizing onslaught of structural reforms to teachers' work, postgraduate programmes for teachers can be seen as significant sites for professional regeneration (Hattam et al., 1997b). To not be seriously implicated, compromised or accommodated by the ideology of marketization requires that these sites offer teachers the 'representational resources' (New London Group, 1996) to examine what is happening to their working conditions, solace in knowing that others too have not abandoned commitments to a viable public education system, and the opportunity to redesign and reconstruct their practices in the light of their 'resistant reading' (Janks and Ivanic, 1992). We think it is appropriate to invoke Michael Welton's (1993) description of new social movements – that is, 'sites of revolutionary learning', as a metaphor for such programmes. As such they offer a means to: 'resuscitate social relations, opposition, defiance, struggle and hope whenever they have been crushed, distorted or stifled by order, which is always the order of the state' (Touraine, 1985, p. 55).

University research

Even though positivist forms of knowing are very much in vogue with neo-liberal governments in the name of accountability, many educational researchers are struggling to practise emancipatory forms of knowledge production. Such research is overtly concerned with social injustice and aims to give voice to 'subjugated knowledges'. It has a strong commitment to reflexive engagement with the reality of schools, and rejects a blame the victim or individualizing view of the world being promoted by those wishing to deny the existence of society. Smyth and Hattam (1998) give an example of how a research institute does research against the grain of the marketization of both teachers' and academics' work.

Our analysis here is of course far from complete and would require a further chapter on its own to do justice to the topic. In such a chapter we would also need to refer to other social movements as important counter-publics. We must not forget about feminism, the environment movement, and anti-racism groups to name a few. It would not be possible for a teacher to be involved with all of the counter-publics we have briefly outlined here; that it is not the point of our politics. What we believe to be most important is for teachers to participate in those spaces that nurture critical discourses and that enliven debate and political action in the public sphere about the sort of society we want to live in. The point is to be involved somehow:

> Whether we wish to form unions, organize communities, create producers' co-ops, launch feminist solidarity councils, 'green' the use of federal lands, limit corporate abuses, hold politicians accountable to promises, mobilize our own scattered resources in economic reconstruction, get our views expressed in the media, or do almost anything else that's worthwhile, some increase in our capacity to do democratic organizing would obviously be welcome.
>
> (Rogers, 1995, p. 17)

Such a view of community development defines how teachers might also practise a contemporary politics inside of schools.

Making Pedagogy Political

At this point it might be asserted that our vision of the socially critical school represents a fanciful ideal which is beyond the reach of school communities. We do not want to downplay the formidable nature of the barriers to school-based reform, but some teachers and school communities are working to sustain a broader view of teaching and learning – a view with a more expansive horizon – with a more courageous vision than being provided by neo-liberal education policy.[1] In a context of devolution some schools are managing to work against the grain of marketization and the concomitant effects of intensification. Some Australian schools have managed to sustain a 'culture of innovation' (Kress, 1993) through applying strategies of 'whole school reform' (Connell and White, 1989) developed through such programmes as the Disadvantaged Schools Program (Connell et al., 1991) and the National Schools Network (Ladwig et al., 1994). Taking 'whole school reform' seriously means the school is viewed as a site for an 'actually existing democracy' (Fraser, 1997) – places which are about 'teaching democracy democratically' (Worsford, 1997). Some schools continue to struggle to enact a vision of a school as a site of negotiation of interests. Teachers in such schools reject the view that the interests of their school communities have been incorporated into the policy formulations of outside experts. Instead, such schools maintain a view that curriculum making is largely worked out locally. These schools are committed to a struggle to actively involve the whole school community, including groups who have been constantly marginalized or silenced, in the curriculum-making process and to ensure all students are actively engaged in learning and decision making. The socially critical school, we believe, has the potential to function as a genuine public sphere where students (citizens) can come together to deliberate and construct alternative visions of society.

Struggling for Socially Critical Schools

What is recognized in those schools still struggling for a socially critical alternative to the shallow and marketized school on offer by neo-liberal policy, is that teachers are the most important actors in educational reform and it is their efforts which ultimately determine the success of any moves to change schooling practices (Zeichner, 1993). In such schools an educator's sensibility is nourished rather than silenced or denuded. Pragmatically what this means is supporting a school culture that nurtures teachers' learning for the following constellation of features.

Pursuing a courageous educational vision with the school community

We are using the term socially critical to name a courageous educational vision, but others sometimes refer to such a vision by terms such as democratic schooling (Goodman, 1992). Such a vision is courageous because it means working with the 'tension between individuality and community' (Goodman, 1989, p. 41) – that individualistic goals are balanced by values of compassion (Greene, 1991) and civic responsibility. Such a view 'implies a moral commitment to promote values of economic and social justice and actively inhibit racism, sexism, classism, ethnocentrism and other forms of oppression' (p. 41). 'Living dangerously' (Giroux, 1993) against the grain of contemporary educational policy based on a selfish individualism, socially critical teachers struggle to realize a:

> connectionist pedagogy. In addition to cultivating each child's unique individuality, this education makes a conscious effort to help children understand the ways that life on this planet is deeply interconnected and interdependent. It represents a pedagogy that places one's connection to the lives of all human beings and other living things on this planet at the center of the educational process.
>
> (Goodman and Kuzmic, 1997, p. 81)

Sustaining a culture of debate in which teachers can (continually) test the adequacy of their theories about teaching and learning that also develops collaboration

Would you continue to send your children to a school if you found out that most of the teachers were not reflective about their teaching? or if the school sustained a culture that frowned on rigorous examination of teaching practice? What might a rigorous examination of teaching and learning look like? A socially critical version – critical reflection or action research – has these three key elements: a research spiral, a critical community and critical reflection. As an example of a research spiral, Smyth (1989) recommends these elements:

1   Describe…what is it that you do as a teacher?
2   Inform…what does this mean?
3   Confront…how did I come to be like this?
4   Reconstruct…how might I do things differently?

Working on 'critical incidents' (Tripp, 1992) forms the basis for further investigation and improvement. Ideally, critical reflection is sustained with other interested teachers, forming a community of critical learners to develop some clearer understandings about: how people talk about and categorize teaching and students; what counts as learning and participation; and, how people relate to each other (the nature of power and authority relations) (Kemmis and McTaggart, 1988). In the contemporary scene, teachers are having to struggle to incorporate moral and ethical criteria into their practice of reflection. Critically reflective teachers ask:

> which educational goals, experiences, and activities lead toward forms of life which are mediated by concerns for justice, equity, and concrete fulfilment and whether current arrangements serve important human needs and satisfy important human purposes. Here both the teaching (ends and means) and the contexts which surround the teaching are viewed as problematic, as value-governed selections from a larger universe of possibilities.
>
> (Zeichner and Liston, 1986, p. 6–7)

Promoting a dialogue with the local community with a view to incorporating the existential struggles of the local community into curriculum

Democratic schools promote a dialogic relationship (Shor and Freire, 1987) with the local community. What this means is a commitment to having a two way interchange:

> One begins with the assumption that the other has something to say to us and to contribute to our understanding. The initial task is to grasp the other's position in the strongest possible light. One must always be responsive to what the other is saying and showing…. There is a play, a to-and-fro movement in dialogic encounter, a seeking for a common ground in which we can understand our differences. The other is not an adversary or an opponent but a conversational partner.
>
> (Bernstein, 1991, p. 337)

Not only is the (socially critical) school keen to ensure the community knows what is happening in the school, but the school is also keen to know about the local community. It is essential to recognize the need to craft a curriculum that is responsive to the context – that it takes into consideration the nature of the local community. Knowing about the local community involves understanding the political economy, and the cultural geography, and especially having a clear understanding of the significant issues that the community is struggling with. In dialogue with the local community, the school can learn the most significant aspects of their students' 'present, existential, concrete situation' (Freire, 1972, p. 68), those situations 'most weighted with existential meaning (and thus the greatest emotional content),…[that]…"reveal longings, disbeliefs, hopes, and an impetus to participate"' (Freire, 1974, p. 49). Dialogue with the community can reveal 'generative themes' that are unresolved social problems in the community, good for generating curriculum based on the integration of the 'personal concerns of students and their communities and the larger issues facing our world' (Beane, 1990, p. 40).

Promoting 'student voice' capable of integrating their personal concerns and the larger issues facing our world

> Why is it, in spite of the fact that teaching by pouring in, learning by passive absorption, are universally condemned, that they are still entrenched in practice?
>
> (Dewey, 1966/1916, p. 38)

More that 80 years hence, and didactic teaching is still prevalent even though most educators agree that 'new knowledge is produced (constructed) through a process of cognitive change and self-regulation' (Kincheloe, 1993, p. 107), that is, a constructivist view of learning is now well regarded. Such a view 'maintains that the knower personally participates in all acts of knowing and understanding' (p. 107). Against a banking concept of education, in which students are treated as 'receptacles to be filled' with 'contents which are detached from reality, disconnected from the totality that engendered them and could give them significance' (Freire, 1972, p. 45) socially critical teachers promote 'student voice' in the curriculum-making process of the school. Promoting student voice in the classroom is often referred to as 'negotiating the curriculum' (Boomer et al., 1992) or 'critical teaching' (pedagogy) (Shor, 1987, 1992, 1996). Schools might incorporate student voice in the school's development plan in designing curriculum from generative themes, or assisting students develop a 'critical sensibility' 'as in the ability to critique a system and its relations to other systems on the basis of the workings of power, politics, ideology, and values' (New London Group, 1996, p. 85).

Promoting debate about the content of the curriculum that is responsive to concern for social injustice and that encourages the development of critical literacies (Fairclough, 1992)

> Critical literacy education pushes the definition of literacy beyond the traditional decoding or encoding of words in order to reproduce the meaning of the text and society until it becomes a means for understanding one's own history and culture, and for fostering an activism toward equal participation for all the decisions that affect and control our lives.
>
> (Shannon, 1991, p. 518)

Socially critical teachers reject approaches to the curriculum that treat knowledge as deposits or as sanitized and non-controversial. Society is not assumed to be fair and just. Instead, socially critical teachers devise a curriculum that opens up a space for students to develop 'resistant reading' (Janks and Ivanic, 1992) positions that encourage students to 'check and criticise the history [they] are told against the [one they are living]' (Inglis, 1985, p. 108).

Towards a Politics for Democratic Schooling

It is usual in the conclusion to a book to make some form of recommendation for policy development. In the present context, we can only predict that such recommendations will fall on deaf ears, as educational policy is being developed by neo-liberal governments that care little for a democratic imagining of schooling. Now is not the time, however, to be silent. Rather, it is necessary to find ways to support teachers in schools and other counter-publics who are struggling to realize an egalitarian view of schooling. Those teachers need to be supported to:

1   resist the worst of devolution – of giving away a centrally funded and supported public school system to produce a user-pays system that relies on the economic capital of the local community;
2   minimize the damage due to the introduction of testing/benchmarking that is ahistorical, culturally insensitive, reductive, incongruent with the practiced curriculum, and uninformative for teachers with a practical intent to make a difference for their students;
3   reclaim the spaces to debate the nature of good teaching and learning, and to re-institute a well funded dialogue between classrooms and the policy development process;
4   resist 'caging teachers in elaborate, centrally dreamed-up curriculum frameworks' (Collins, 1996, p. 11); and
5   properly fund the professional development of teachers.

If you believe that schooling plays a role in the formation of our society, then it follows that it is also essential to support the struggle to sustain a socially critical educator's sensibility in schools.

Note

1   The Teachers' Learning Project is an Australian Research Council funded project involving the Department for Education Training and Employment (DETE) and the Flinders Institute for the Study of Teaching (FIST). The Research Team consists of Professor John Smyth, Associate Professor Michael Lawson, Peter McInerney (DETE) and Robert Hattam (FIST). The major aims of the project are to:

- develop a detailed account of the supportive conditions and structures to facilitate the professional development of teachers;
- identify and develop strategies which can be used in schools to promote and support teachers' learning;
- develop and trial materials which schools could use to enhance teacher learning; and
- evaluate the implementation of trial materials and strategies concerned with teachers' learning.

The special focus of this research has been on teacher managed forms of learning and the research team has published the following case studies of teachers' learning at eight public schools in South Australia.

Lawson, M., McInerney, P., Hattam, R. and Smyth, J. (1997) *Learning about Reporting: The Student Progress Conference at Ingle Farm East School.* Adelaide: Flinders Institute for the Study of Teaching.

Hattam, R., McInerney, P., Lawson, M. and Smyth, J. (1997a) *Sustaining a School as a Learning Community: Teachers' Learning at Hackham West Schools.* Adelaide: Flinders Institute for the Study of Teaching.

Smyth, J., McInerney, P., Hattam, R. and Lawson M. (1997) *Sustaining Teacher Learning as a Dialogical Encounter: Conversing with the Pieces of the Puzzle at the Pines School.* Adelaide: Flinders Institute for the Study of Teaching.

Lawson, M., McInerney, P., Hattam, R. and Smyth, J. (1998) *Learning to Teach the Virtual Class: Teachers' Learning in the Open Access College Senior Secondary School of Distance Education.* Adelaide: Flinders Institute for the Study of Teaching.

Lawson, M., McInerney, P., Hattam, R. and Smyth, J. (1998) *Sustaining a Vibrant Senior Secondary Curriculum in Rural South Australia: Teachers' Learning in the Mid North Senior Secondary School Cooperative (MNSEC).* Adelaide: Flinders Institute for the Study of Teaching.

McInerney, P., Hattam, R., Smyth, J. and Lawson, M. (1998) *Middle Schooling From the Ground Up: Teachers' Learning at Seaford 6–12 School.* Adelaide: Flinders Institute for the Study of Teaching.

Smyth, J., McInerney, P., Hattam, R. and Lawson, M. (1998) *Placing Girls at the Centre of the Curriculum: Teachers' Learning and School Reform at Gepps Cross Girls High School.* Adelaide: Flinders Institute for the Study of Teaching.

McInerney, P., Smyth, J., Hattam, R. and Lawson, M. (1999) *Maintaining a Rigorous Curriculum in an Isolated Community: Teachers' Learning at Indulkana Aboriginal School.* Adelaide: Flinders Institute for the Study of Teaching.

References

Acker, S. (1992) 'Creating Careers: Women Teachers at Work'. *Curriculum Inquiry* 22(2), 141–63.

—— (1995) 'Carry on Caring: the Work of Women Teachers'. *British Journal of Sociology of Education* 16(1), 21–36.

Adorno, T. (1974) *Minima Moralia: Reflections from Damaged Life*. London, New Left Books.

Agger, B. (1977a) 'Dialectical Sensibility 1: Critical Theory, Scientism and Empiricism'. *Canadian Journal of Political and Social Theory* 1(1), 1–30.

—— (1977b) 'Dialectical Sensibility 2: Towards a New Intellectuality'. *Canadian Journal of Political and Social Theory* 1(2), 47–57.

—— (1992) *Cultural Studies as Critical Theory*. London, Falmer Press.

Alvesson, M. and Willmott, H. (1996) *Making Sense of Management: A Critical Introduction*. Thousand Oaks, CA, Sage.

Alway, J. (1995) *Critical Theory and Political Possibilities: Conceptions of Emancipatory Politics in the Works of Horkheimer, Adorno, Marcuse, and Habermas*. London, Greenwood Press.

Anderson, G. (1989) 'Critical Ethnography in Education: Origins, Current Status and New Directions'. *Review of Educational Research* 59(3), 249–70.

Anyon, J. (1998) 'Rank Discriminations: Critical Studies of Schooling and the "Mainstream" in Educational Research. A Review of Ladwig'. *Educational Researcher* 27(3), 32–3.

Apple, M. (1982) *Education and Power*. New York, Routledge and Kegan Paul.

—— (1986) *Teachers and Texts: A Political Economy of Class and Gender Relations in Education*. New York, Routledge and Kegan Paul.

—— (1988) 'Redefining Equality: Authoritarian Populism and the Conservative Restoration'. *Teachers College Record* 90(2), 167–84.

—— (1988a) 'Work, Class and Teaching'. In Ozga, J. (ed.), *Schoolwork: Approaches to the Labour Process of Teaching*. Milton Keynes, Open University Press, pp. 99–115.

—— (1988b) *Teachers and Texts: A Political Economy of Class and Gender Relations in Education*. New York, Routledge.

—— (1993a) *Official Knowledge: Democratic Education in a Conservative Age*. New York, Routledge.

—— (1993b) 'The Politics of Official Knowledge: Does a National Curriculum Make Sense?' *Teachers College Record* 95(2), 224–41.

—— (1996a) *Cultural Politics and Education*. Buckingham, Open University Press.

Apple, M.W. (1996b) 'Power, Meaning and Identity: Critical Sociology of Education in the United States'. *British Journal of Sociology of Education* 17(2), 125–44.

Apple, M. and Jungck, S. (1992) 'You Don't Have to Be a Teacher to Teach this Unit: Teaching, Technology and Control in the Classroom'. In Hargreaves, A. and Fullan, M. (eds), *Understanding Teacher Development*. Cassell, London, pp. 20–42.

Apple, M. and Oliver, A. (1996) 'Becoming Right: Education and the Formation of Conservative Movements'. *Teachers College Record* 97(3), 419–45.

Apple, M. and Teitelbaum, K. (1986) 'Are Teachers Losing Control of their Skills and Curriculum?' *Journal of Curriculum Studies* 18(2), 177–84.

Appleton College (1993) 'Marketing Appleton College – Whose Responsibility?' Unpublished Staff Discussion Paper, Appleton College.

Applied Psychology Research Group, Department of Psychology, University of Melbourne (1989) *Teacher Stress in Victoria: A Survey of Teachers' Views Summary and Recommendations*. Melbourne, Office of Schools Administration, Ministry of Education, Victoria.

Aronowitz, S. (1973) *False Promises: The Shaping of American Working Class Consciousness*. New York, McGraw Hill.

—— (1994) *The Politics of Identity: Class, Culture and Social Movements*. New York, Routledge.

Aronowitz, S. and Giroux, H. (1985) *Education Under Siege: The Conservative. Liberal and Radical Debate Over Schooling*. South Hadley, Bergin and Garvey.

Aronowitz, S., Martinson, B. and Menser, M. (1996) *Technoscience and Cyberculture*. London, Routledge.

Ashenden, D. (1989) 'The Future of the Teaching Profession'. Text of a public lecture given in Melbourne, 2 November 1989, under the auspices of the State Board of Education of Victoria.

Austin, A. and Baldwin, R. (1994) 'Faculty Collaboration: Enhancing the Quality of Scholarship and Teaching'. *ERIC Digest*.

Australian Teaching Council (ATC) (1995) *What Do Teachers Think?* Sydney, Australian Teaching Council.

Australian Vice-Chancellors Committee (1991) 'Foundations of the Clever Country: Report for the 1992–1994 Triennium'. Canberra.

Baldwin, G. (1994) 'The Student as Customer: the Discourse of "Quality" in Higher Education'. *Journal of Tertiary Educational Administration* 16(1), 125–34.

Ball, S. (1988) 'Staff Relations During the Teachers Industrial Action: Context, Conflict and Proletarianisation'. *British Journal of Sociology of Education* 9(3), 289–305.

—— (1992) 'Changing Management and the Management of Change: Educational Reform and School Processes, an English Perspective'. Paper presented to American Education Research Association symposium 'National Educational Reforms and School Processes: International perspectives', San Francisco.

—— (1993) 'Education Policy, Power Relations and Teachers Work'. *British Journal of Educational Studies* 4(2), 106–21.

—— (1994) *Education Reform: A Critical and Post-structural Approach*. Buckingham, Open University Press.

References

—— (1995) 'Intellectuals or Technicians? The Urgent Role of Theory in Educational Studies'. *British Journal of Educational Studies* 43(3), 255–71.

Ball, S., Bowe, R. and Gewirtz, S. (1996) 'School Choice, Social Class and Distinction: the Realization of School Advantage in Education'. *Journal of Education Policy* 11(1), 89–122.

Ball, S.J. (1990) *Politics and Policy Making in Education: Explorations in Policy Sociology*. London and New York, Routledge.

Barnard, M. (1992) 'Teachers in a State of Intellectual Undress'. *The Age*. 27 October, Melbourne, p.13.

Barone, T. (1992) 'Beyond Theory and Method: a Case of Critical Story Telling'. *Theory into Practice* 31(2), 142–6.

Bartlett, L. (1994) 'Qualitative Research in Australia'. *Qualitative Studies in Education* 7(3), 207–25.

Barton, L., Barrett, E., Whitty, G., Miles, S. and Furlong, J. (1994) 'Teacher Education and Teacher Professionalism in England: Some Emerging Issues in England'. *British Journal of Sociology of Education* 15(4), 529–43

Bauman, Z. (1998) 'On Glocalization: or Globalization for Some and Localization for Some Others'. *Thesis Eleven* 54 (August), 37–49.

Beane, J. (1990) *A Middle School Curriculum: from Rhetoric to Reality*. Columbus, OH, National Middle School Association.

Benhabib, S. (1986) *Critique, Norm and Utopia: A Study of the Foundations of Critical Theory*. New York, Columbia University Press.

Bergen, B. (1988) 'Only a Schoolmaster: Gender, Class and the Effort to Professionalize Elementary Teaching in England, 1870–1910'. In Ozga, J. (ed.), *Schoolwork: Approaches to the Labour Process of Teaching*. Milton Keynes, Open University Press, pp. 39–60.

Berliner, D. and Biddle, B. (1995) *The Manufactured Crisis: Myths, Fraud, and the Attack on America's Public Schools*. Reading, MA, Addison-Wesley.

Bernstein, B. (1971) *Class, Codes and Control*, 1. London, Routledge.

—— (1990) *The Structure of Pedagogic Discourse*. New York, Routledge.

—— (1991) *The New Constellation*. Cambridge, MA, MIT Press.

Bernstein, R. (1978) *The Restructuring of Social and Political Theory*. Philadelphia, PA, University of Pennsylvania Press.

Bhabha, H. (1994) *The Location of Culture*. London, Routledge.

Bigelow, W. (1990) 'Inside the Classroom: Social Vision and Critical Pedagogy'. *Teachers College Record* 91(3), 359–67.

Blackmore, J. (1993) 'In the Shadow of Men: the Historical Construction of Educational Administration as a "Masculinist" Enterprise'. In Blackmore, J. and Kenway, J. (eds), *Gender Matters in Educational Administration and Policy*. Geelong, Victoria, Deakin Press, pp. 27–48.

—— (1996) 'Doing "Emotional labour" in the Education Market Place: Stories from the Field of Women in Management'. *Discourse* 17(3), 337–49.

Blase, J. (1986) 'A Qualitative Analysis of Sources of Teacher Stress: Consequences of Performance'. *American Educational Research Journal* 23(1), 13–40.

Blase, J. and Anderson, G. (1995) *The Micropolitics of Educational Leadership*. New York, Teachers College Press.

Bluer, R. (1991) 'Reforming Schools – the Australian Way'. *Unicorn* 17(2), 67.

Boomer, G. (1992) 'The Advent of Standards in Australian Education'. *Curriculum Perspectives* 12(1), 61–6.

Boomer, G., Laster, N., Onore, C. and Cook, J. (eds) (1992) *Negotiating the Curriculum: Educating for the 21st Century*. London, Falmer Press.

Borthwick, A. (1993) 'Key Competencies – Uncovering the Bridge Between General and Vocational'. In Collins, C. (ed.), *Competencies: The Competencies Debate in Australian Education and Training*. Canberra, Australian College of Education, pp. 21–34.

Bourdieu, P. (1986) 'The Forms of Capital'. In Richardson, J. (ed.), *Handbook of Theory and Research for the Sociology of Education*. New York, Greenwood Press, pp. 241–58.

—— (1998) 'A Reasoned Utopia and Economic Fatalism'. *New Left Review* 227, 125–30.

Bowe, R. and Ball, S. (1992) *Reforming Education and Changing Schools: Case Studies in Policy Sociology*. London, Routledge.

Braverman, H. (1974) *Labour and Monopoly Capital*. London, Monthly Review Press.

Britzman, D.P. (1991) *Practice Makes Practice*. Albany, NY, State University of New York Press.

Broadfoot, P., Osborn, M., Gilly, M. and Paillet, A. (1988) 'What Professional Responsibility Means to Teachers: National Contexts and Classroom Constants'. *British Journal of Sociology of Education* 9(3), 265–87.

Buck-Morss, S. (1997) *The Dialectics of Seeing: Walter Benjamin and the Arcades Project*. Cambridge, MA, MIT Press.

Burawoy, M. (1979) *Manufacturing Consent: Changes in the Labour Process under Monopoly Capitalism*. Chicago, IL and London, University of Chicago Press.

—— (1985) *The Politics of Production*. London, Verso.

Burgess, R. (1988) 'Conversations with a Purpose: the Ethnographic Interview in Educational Research'. *Studies in Qualitative Methodology* 1, 137–55.

Burrow, S. (1994) 'McDonald's in the Classroom'. In Deakin Centre for Education and Change (eds), *Schooling What Future? Balancing the Education Agenda*. Geelong, Deakin Centre for Education and Change, pp. 13–20.

Bush, T., Coleman, M. and Glover, D. (1993) *Managing Autonomous Schools: the Grant-Maintained Experience*. London, Paul Chapman.

Buswell, C. (1980) 'Pedagogic Change and Social Change'. *British Journal of Sociology of Education* 1(3), 293–306.

Calhoun, C. (1994) 'Postmodernism as Pseudohistory: Continuities in the Complexity of Social Action'. In Sztompka, P. (ed.), *Agency and Structure: Reorienting Social Theory*. Amsterdam, Gordon and Breach Science Publishers, pp. 167–96.

Capra, F. (1982) *The Turning Point: Science, Society and the Rising Culture*. London, Flamingo.

Carchedi, G. (1977) *On the Economic Identification of Social Classes*. London, Routledge and Kegan Paul.

Carlson, D. (1992) *Teachers and Crisis: Urban School Reform and Teachers' Work*. New York, Routledge.

—— (1995) 'Constructing the Margins of Multicultural Education and Curriculum Settlements'. *Curriculum Inquiry* 25(4), 407–31.

References

Carmichael, L. (Chair) (1992) *The Australian Vocational Certificate Training System*. Employment and Skills Formation Council. Canberra, National Board of Employment, Education and Training.

—— (1993) 'Workplace Imperatives for Education and Competence'. In Collins, C. (ed.), *Competencies: The Competencies Debate in Australian Education and Training*. Canberra, Australian College of Education, pp. 15–20.

Carnoy, M. and Levin, H. (1985) *Schooling and Work in the Democratic State*. Stanford, CA, Stanford University Press.

Carr, W. and Hartnett, A. (1996) *Education and the Struggle for Democracy*. Buckingham, Open University Press.

Carspecken, P. and Apple, M. (1992) 'Critical Qualitative Research: Theory, Methodology, and Practice'. In LeCompte, M., Millroy, W. and Preissle, J. (eds), *The Handbook of Qualitative Research in Education*. San Diego, Academic Press, pp. 507–53.

Castells, M. (1989) *The Information City: Information Technology, and the Urban-Regional Process*. Oxford, Blackwell.

—— (1994) 'European Cities, the Informational Society, and the Global Economy'. *New Left Review* 204, 18–32.

—— (1998) *Information Age: Economy, Society, and Culture – Volume 3, End of Millennium*. Oxford, Blackwell.

Centre for Workplace Communication and Culture (1994) *Cultural Understanding as the Eighth Key Competency*. Final report to the Queensland Department of Education and the Queensland Vocational Education, Training and Employment Commission. University of Technology, Sydney.

Ceroni, K. (1995) 'Promises Made, Promises Broken: a Literary Criticism of the Pennsylvania Lead Teacher Experience'. Unpublished Doctoral Dissertation, University of Pittsburgh.

Ceroni, K. and Garman, N. (1994) 'The Empowerment Movement: Genuine Collegiality or Yet Another Hierarchy?' In Grimmett, P. and Neufeld, J. (eds), *Teacher Development and the Struggle for Authenticity: Professional Growth and Restructuring in the Context of Change*. New York and London, Teachers College Press, pp. 141–61.

Clifford, J. (1981) 'On Ethnographic Surrealism'. *Comparative Studies in Society and History* 23(4), 539–64.

Cole, M. and Walker, S. (eds) (1989) *Teaching and Stress*. Milton Keynes, Open University Press.

Collins, C. (1993) 'Competencies: For and Against'. Paper presented at the Curriculum in Profile: Quality or Inequality Conference, Brisbane.

—— (1994) *Curriculum and Pseudo-science: Is the Australian National Curriculum Built on Credible Foundations*. Belconnen, Australian Capital Territory, Australian Curriculum Studies Association, Occasional Paper No. 2.

—— (1996) 'What Teachers Need to Know? The Competencies Debate'. *South Australian Educational Leader* 7(4), 1–12.

Comber, B., Green, B., Lingard, B. and Luke, A. (1998) 'Literacy Debates and Public Education: A Question of 'Crisis'?' In Reid, A. (ed.), *Going Public: Education Policy and Public Education in Australia*. Deakin West, ACT, Australian Curriculum Studies Association, pp. 18–36.

Connell, R. (1985) *Teachers' Work*. Sydney, Allen and Unwin.

—— (1990) 'The State, Gender and Sexual Politics'. *Theory and Society* 19(4), 507–44

—— (1995) 'Transformative Labour: Theorizing the Politics of Teachers' Work'. In Ginsburg, M. (ed.), *The Politics of Educators' Work and Lives*. New York and London, Garland, pp. 91–114.

Connell, R. and White, V. (1989) 'Child Poverty and Educational Action'. In Edgar, D., Keane, D. and McDonald, P. (eds), *Child Poverty*. Sydney, Allen and Unwin, pp. 104–22.

Connell, R., White, V. and Johnston, K. (eds) (1991) *Running Twice as Hard: the Disadvantaged Schools Program in Australia*. Geelong, Victoria, Deakin University Press.

Connell, R.W. (1996) 'Schools, Markets, Justice: Education in a Fractured World'. Inaugural Lecture at the University of Sydney, Faculty of Education.

Considine, M. (1988) 'The Corporate Management Framework as Administrative Science: A Critique'. *Australian Journal of Public Administration* 47(1), 4–18.

Conti, R. and Warner, M. (1993) 'Taylorism, New Technology and Just-in-time Systems in Japanese Manufacturing'. *New Technology, Work and Employment* 8(1), 32–42.

Cookson, P. and Lucks, C. (1997) 'The New Politics of Teaching'. In Biddle, B., Good, T. and Goodson, L. (eds), *International Handbook of Teachers and Teaching*, Vol. II, Dordrecht, Kluwer Academic Publishers, pp. 971–84.

Cornbleth, C. (1995) 'Controlling Curriculum Knowledge: Multicultural Politics and Policy Making'. *Journal of Curriculum Studies* 27(2), 165–85.

Corson, D. (1995) 'Discursive Power in Educational Organisations: An Introduction'. In Corson, D. (ed.), *Discourse and Power in Educational Organisations*. Cresskill, NJ, Hampton Press, pp. 3–15.

Cortazzi, M. (1991) *Primary Teaching. How It Is: A Narrative Account*. London, David Fulton.

Court, M. (1994) 'Removing Macho Management: Lessons from the Field of Education'. *Gender, Work and Organisation* 1(1), 33–49.

Cox, E. (1995) *A Truly Civil Society*. Sydney, ABC Books.

Cox, R. (1980) 'Social Forces, States and World Orders: Beyond International Relations Theory'. *Millennium: Journal of International Studies* 10(2), 126–55.

Cross, J. (1995) 'Report of the Junior Secondary Review: Exposition and Critique'. *South Australia Educational Leader* 4(3), 1–5.

Dale, R. (1989) *The State and Education Policy*. Milton Keynes, Open University Press.

Danylewycz, M. and Prentice, A. (1986) 'Revising the History of Teachers: A Canadian Perspective'. *Interchange* 17(2) 135–46.

Darling-Hammond, L. (1988) 'Policy and Professionalism'. In Lieberman, A. (ed.), *Building a Professional Culture in Schools*. New York, Teachers College Press, pp. 55–77.

Davies, B. and Harre, R. (1990) 'Positioning: The Discursive Production of Selves'. *Journal for the Theory of Social Behaviour* 20(1), 43–63.

Dawkins, J. (1990) *Quality of Teaching – An Issue for All*. Canberra, Australian Government Publishing Service.

Debond, G. (1970) *The Society of the Spectacle*. Detroit, Black and Red Press.

References

Deetz, R. and Kersten, M. (1983) 'Critical Modes of Interpretive Research'. In Putnam, L. and Pacanowsky, M. (eds), *Communication and Organizations*. London, Sage, pp. 147–71.

Delbridge, R., Turnbull, P. and Wilkinson, B. (1992) 'Pushing Back the Frontiers: Management Control and Work Intensification under JIT/TQM Factory Regimes'. *New Technology, Work and Employment* 7(2), 97–106.

Denscombe, M. (1995) 'Teachers as an Audience for Research: the Acceptability of Ethnographic Approaches to Classroom Research'. *Teachers and Teaching: Theory and Practice* 1(2), 173–91.

Densmore, K. (1985) 'An Interpretation of Teaching: Two Case Studies on Beginning Teachers'. Unpublished Doctoral Dissertation, The University of Wisconsin, Madison.

—— (1987) 'Professionalism, Proletarianization and Teachers Work'. In Popkewitz, T.S. (ed.), *Critical Studies in Teacher Education: Its Folklore, Theory and Practice*. London, Falmer Press, pp. 130–60.

Department for Education and Children's Services (DECS) (1994) *Action Plan for the Middle Schooling Years*. Adelaide, Department for Education and Children's Services.

Derber, C. (1982) 'Managing Professionals: Ideological Proletarianization and Mental Labor'. In Derber, C. (ed.), *Professionals as Workers: Mental Labor in Advanced Capitalism*. Boston, MA, G.K. Hall and Co., pp. 167–208.

Derlugian, G. (1996) 'The Social Cohesion of the States'. In Hopkins, T. and Wallerstein, I. (eds), *The Age of Transition: Trajectories of the World-System – 1945–2025*. New York, Zed Books.

Dewey, J. (1966/1916) *Democracy and Education*. New York, Free Press.

DiFazio, W. (1996) 'Technoscience and the Labour Process'. In Aronowitz, S., Martinson, B. and Menser, M. (eds), *Technoscience and Cyberculture*. London, Routledge, pp. 195–204.

Donmoyer, R. (1990) 'Generalizability and the Single-case Study'. In Eisner, E. and Peskin, A. (eds), *Qualitative Inquiry in Education*. New York, Teachers College Press, Colombia University, pp. 175–200.

Dow, A. (1996) 'Collaboration and Resistance at Gallipoli High School: The Work of Teaching in a Post-Fordist Era'. Unpublished doctoral dissertation, Flinders University.

Dreeben, R. (1988) 'The School as a Workplace'. In Ozga, J. (ed.), *Schoolwork: Approaches to the Labour Process of Teaching*. Milton Keynes, Open University Press, pp. 21–36.

Dunham, J. (1992) *Stress in Teaching*, 2nd edn. London, Routledge.

During, S. (1992) 'Postcolonialism and Globalization'. *Meanjin* 51(2), 339–53.

Dwyer, P. (1996) *Opting Out: Early School Leavers and the Degeneration of Youth Policy*. Hobart, National Clearinghouse for Youth Studies and Youth Research Centre.

Edelwich, J. and Brodsky, A. (1980) *Burn-Out: Stages of Disillusionment in the Helping Professions*. New York, Human Science Press.

Edwards, R. (1979) *Contested Terrain: The Transformation of the Workplace in the Twentieth Century*. London, Heinemann.

Eisner, E. (1991) *The Enlightened Eye: Qualitative Inquiry and the Enhancement of Educational Practice*. London, Macmillan.

Elliott, B. and Maclennan, D. (1994) 'Education, Modernity and Neo-conservative School Reform in Canada, Britain and the US'. *British Journal of Sociology of Education* 15(2), 165–85.

Eppsteiner, F. (ed.) (1988) *The Path of Compassion: Writings on Socially Engaged Buddhism.* Berkeley, CA, Parallax.

Eyers, V. (1992) *The Education of Young Adolescents in South Australian Government Schools (1).* South Australian Department for Education and Children's Services.

Ezzy, D. (1997) 'Subjectivity and the Labour Process: Conceptualising "Good Work"'. *Sociology* 31(3), 427–44.

Fairclough, N. (ed.) (1992) *Critical Language Awareness.* London, Longman.

Farber, B. (1984) 'Stress and Burnout in Suburban Teachers'. *Journal of Educational Research* 77(6), 325–31.

Fay, B. (1977) 'How People Change Themselves: The Relationship between Critical Theory and Its Audience'. In Ball, T. (ed.), *Political Theory and Praxis: New Perspectives.* Minneapolis, MN, University of Minnesota Press, pp. 200–33.

Finn, B. (Chair) (1991) *Young People's Participation in Post-Compulsory Education and Training: Report of the Australian Education Council Review Committee.* Canberra, Australian Government Printer.

Fitzgerald, R.T. (1976) *Poverty and Education in Australia: Commission of Inquiry into Poverty*, 5th Main Report. Canberra, Australian Government Printing Service.

Flinders, D. (1988) 'Teacher Isolation and the New Reform'. *Journal of Curriculum and Supervision* 4(1), 17–29.

Foucault, M. (1977) *Discipline and Punish.* Harmondsworth, Penguin.

—— (1980) *Power and Knowledge: Selected Interviews and Other Writings.* New York, Pantheon.

—— (1984) 'What is Enlightenment?' In Rabinow, P. (ed.), *The Foucault Reader: An Introduction to Foucault's Thought.* London, Penguin, pp. 32–50.

Franzway, S., Court, D. and Connell, R. (1989) *Staking a Claim: Feminism, Bureaucracy and the State.* Sydney, Allen and Unwin.

Fraser, N. (1989) *Unruly Practices: Power, Discourse and Gender in Contemporary Social Theory.* Minneapolis, MN, University of Minnesota Press.

—— (1997) *Justice Interruptus: Critical Reflections on the Postsocialist Condition.* New York, Routledge.

Freedman, S. (1990) 'Weeding Women out of "Women's True Profession": The Effects of the Reforms of Teaching and Teachers'. In Biklen, S. and Antler, J. (eds), *Changing Education, Women as Radicals and Conservatives.* Albany, NY, State University of New York Press, pp. 239–56.

Freeland, J. (1986) 'Australia: the Search for a New Educational Settlement'. In Sharp, R. (ed.), *Capitalist Crisis and Schooling: Comparative Studies in the Politics of Education.* Sydney, Macmillan, pp. 212–36.

—— (1991) 'Quality of What, and Quality for Whom?' In Chapman, J., Burke, G. and Wilkinson, V. (eds), *Improving the Quality of Australian Schools.* Hawthorn, Victoria, Australian Council for Educational Research, pp. 60–82.

Freire, P. (1972) *Pedagogy of the Oppressed.* New York, Penguin.

—— (1974) *Education: The Practice of Freedom.* London, Writers and Readers Publishers Cooperative.

References

Friedman, A. (1977) 'Responsible Autonomy versus Direct Control over the Labour Process'. *Capital and Class* (1), 43–57.

Fritzell, C. (1987) 'On the Concept of Relative Autonomy in Educational Theory'. *British Journal of Sociology of Education* 8(1), 23–36.

Fullan, M. and Hargreaves, A. (1991) *What's Worth Fighting For?* Toronto, Ontario Public School Teachers' Federation.

Game, A. and Pringle, R. (1983) *Gender at Work*. Sydney, George Allen and Unwin.

Garman, N. (1994a) 'Qualitative Inquiry. Meaning and Menace for Educational Researchers'. Adelaide, Flinders Institute for the Study of Teaching. Unpublished conference paper.

Garman, N.B. (1994b) 'Beyond the Reflective Practitioner and Toward Discursive Practice'. *Teaching and Teachers' Work* 2(4), 1–7.

Gee, J. and Lankshear, C. (1995) 'The New Work Order: Critical Language Awareness and "Fast Capitalism" Texts'. *Discourse: Studies in the Cultural Politics of Education* 16(1), 5–20.

Gewirtz S., Ball, S. and Bowe, R. (1995) *Markets, Choice and Equity in Education*. Buckingham, Open University Press.

Giddens, A. (1979) *Central Problems of Social Theory: Action, Structure and Contradiction in Social Analysis*. London, Macmillan.

—— (1994) *Beyond Left and Right: The Future of Radical Politics*. Cambridge, Polity Press.

Ginsburg, M. (1987) 'Reproduction, Contradiction and Conceptions of Professionalism'. In Popkewitz, T. (ed.), *Critical Studies in Teacher Education: Its Folklore, Theory and Practice*. London and Philadelphia, Falmer Press, pp. 86–129.

—— (1988) 'Educators as Workers and Political Actors in Britain and North America'. *British Journal of Sociology of Education* 9(3), 359–67.

—— (ed.) (1995) *The Politics of Educators' Work and Lives*. New York and London, Garland Publishing.

Ginsburg, M., Cooper, S., Raghu, R. and Zegarra, H. (1990) 'National and World-systems Explanations of Educational Reform'. *Comparative Education Review* 34(4), 474–99.

Giroux, H. (1985a) 'Introduction'. In Freire, P., *The Politics of Education: Culture, Power, and Liberation*. Massachusetts, Bergin and Garvey, pp. xi–xxv.

—— (1985b) 'Critical Pedagogy, Cultural Politics and the Discourse of Experience'. *Journal of Education* 167(2), 22–41.

—— (1986) 'Curriculum, Teaching, and the Resisting Intellectual'. *Curriculum and Teaching* 1(1&2), 33–42.

—— (1988) *Teachers as Intellectuals: Towards a Critical Pedagogy of Learning*. New York, Bergin and Garvey.

—— (1993) 'Living Dangerously: Identity Politics and the New Cultural Racism: Towards a Critical Pedagogy of Representation'. *Cultural Studies* 7(1), 1–27.

Giroux, H. and McLaren, P. (eds) (1994) *Between Borders: Pedagogy and the Politics of Cultural Studies*. New York and London, Routledge.

Giroux, H. and Trend, D. (1992) 'Cultural Workers, Pedagogy and the Politics of Difference: Beyond Cultural Conservatism'. *Cultural Studies* 6(1), 51–73.

Giroux, H.A. (1994) *Disturbing Pleasures: Learning Popular Culture*. New York and London, Routledge.

Gitlin, T. (1980) *The Whole World is Watching: Mass Media in the Making and Unmaking of the New Left.* Berkeley, CA, University of California Press.

Glaser, B. and Strauss, A. (1967) *The Discovery of Grounded Theory.* New York, Aldine Publishing Company.

Goodman, J. (1989) 'Student Participation and Control for Democratic Schooling: Towards a Connectionist Power Structure'. *Curriculum and Teaching* 4(2), 39–59.

—— (1992) *Elementary Schooling for Critical Democracy.* Albany, NY, State University of New York Press.

Goodman, J. and Kuzmic, J. (1997) 'Bringing a Progressive Pedagogy to Conventional Schools: Theoretical and Practical Implications from Harmony'. *Theory into Practice* 36(2), 79–86.

Goodwin, N. (1996) 'Governmentality in the Queensland Department of Education: Policies and the Management of Schools'. *Discourse* 17(1), 65–74.

Gordon, L. (1994) 'Rich and Poor Schools in Aotearoa'. *New Zealand Journal of Educational Studies* 29(2), 113–25.

Gore, J. (1995) 'On the Continuity of Power Relations in Pedagogy'. *International Studies in Sociology of Education* 5(2), 165–88.

—— (1998) 'Disciplining Bodies: On the Continuity of Power Relations in Pedagogy'. In Popkewitz, T. and Brennan, M. (eds), *Foucault's Challenge: Discourse, Knowledge and Power in Education.* New York, Teachers College Press, pp. 231–51.

Gospel, H. (1992) *Markets, Firms and the Management of Labour in Modern Britain.* Cambridge, Cambridge University Press.

Gough, J. (1979) *The Political Economy of the Welfare State.* London, Macmillan.

Grace, G. (1978) *Teachers, Ideology and Control: A Study in Urban Education.* London, Routledge and Kegan Paul.

—— (1985) 'Judging Teachers: the Social and Political Context of Teacher Evaluation'. *British Journal of Sociology of Education* 6(1), 3–16.

—— (1987) 'Teachers and the State in Britain: A Changing Relation'. In Lawn, M. and Grace, G. (eds), *Teachers: The Culture and Politics of Work.* London, Falmer Press, pp. 193–228.

Gramsci, A. (1971) *Selections from the Prison Notebooks.* London, Lawrence and Wishart.

Green, B. and Bigum, C. (1998) 'Re-tooling Schooling? Information Technology, Cultural Change and the Future(s) of Australian Education'. In Smyth, J., Hattam, R. and Lawson, M. (eds), *Schooling for a Fair Go.* Sydney, Federation Press, pp. 71–96.

Greene, M. (1991) 'Retrieving the Language of Compassion: the Education Professor in Search of Community'. *Teachers College Record* 92(4), 541–55.

Grossi, V. (1981) 'Socio-political Implications of Participatory Research'. *Convergence* 14(3), 43–51.

Grundy, S. and Hatton, E. (1995) 'Teacher Educator's Ideological Discourses'. *Journal of Education for Teaching* 21(1), 7–24.

Gutierrez, K. (1994) 'How Talk, Context, and Script Shape Contexts for Learning: A Cross-case Comparison of Journal Sharing'. *Linguistics and Education* 5, 335–65.

Gutierrez, K., Larson, J. and Kreuter, B. (1995) 'Cultural Tensions in the Scripted Classroom; the Value of the Subjugated Perspective'. *Urban Education* 29(4), 410–42.

Habermas, J. (1971) *Towards a Rational Society.* London, Heinemann.

References

—— (1976) *Legitimation Crisis*. London, Heinemann.

Hall, C. and Millard, E. (1994) 'The Means of Correct Training? Teachers, Foucault and Disciplining'. *Journal of Education for Teaching* 20(2), 153–60.

Hall, S. (1988) 'The Toad in the Garden: Thatcherism among the Theorists'. In Grossberg, L. and Nelson, C. (eds), *Marxism and the Interpretation of Culture*. Urbana and Chicago, IL, University of Illinois Press, pp. 35–73.

—— (1990) 'Cultural Identity and Diaspora'. In Rutherford, J. (ed.), *Identity*. London, Lawrence and Wishart, pp. 222–37.

—— (1996) 'The Meaning of New Times'. In Morley, D. and Kuan-Hsing Chen (eds), *Stuart Hall: Critical Dialogues in Cultural Studies*. London, Routledge, pp. 223–37.

Hall, S. and Jacques, M. (1990) 'From the Manifesto for New Times: The New Times'. In Hall, S. and Jacques M. (eds), *New Times: the Changing Face of Politics in the 1990s*. New York, Verso, pp. 23–37.

Hannaway, J. and Carnoy, M. (1993) *Decentralisation and School Improvement*. San Francisco, CA, Jossey-Bass.

Harding, S. (1998) *Is Science Multicultural? Postcolonialisms, Feminisms, and Epistemologies*. Bloomington, IN, Indiana University Press.

Hargreaves, A. (1990) 'Contrived Collegiality: A Sociological Analysis'. Paper presented at the XIIth meeting of the International Sociological Association, Madrid.

—— (1992a) 'Cultures of Teaching: A Focus for Change'. In Hargreaves, A. and Fullan, M. (eds), *Understanding Teacher Development*. New York, Teachers College Press, pp. 216–40.

—— (1992b) 'Time and Teachers' Work'. *Teachers College Record* 94(1), 87–108.

—— (1993) 'Collaboration: A Key to Leadership for Quality in Education'. *The Practising Administrator* 15(3), 16–18.

Hargreaves, A. and Dawe, R. (1989) 'Pathways of Professional Development: Contrived Collegiality, Collaborative Culture and the Case of Peer Coaching'. Unpublished manuscript. Toronto, Ontario Institute for Studies in Education.

Hargreaves, A. and Wignall, R. (1989) *Time for the Teacher: A Study of Collegial Relations and Preparation Time Use*. Toronto, Ontario Institute for Studies in Education.

Harris, K. (1982) *Teachers and Classes: A Marxist Analysis*. London, Routledge and Kegan Paul.

—— (1990a) 'Teachers and Proletarianisation: a Reply to Lauder and Yee'. *Australian Journal of Education* 34(2), 192–203.

—— (1990b) 'Teachers: Really Taking Control of Schools'. *Education Links* (38), 21–5.

—— (1994) *Teachers: Constructing the Future*. London, Falmer Press.

Hartley, D. (1994) 'Mixed Messages in Education Policy: Sign of the Times?' *British Journal of Educational Studies* 42(3), 230–44.

Hartsock, N. (1983) *Money, Sex and Power: Towards a Feminist Historical Materialism*. New York, Longman.

Harvey, L. (1990) *Critical Social Research*. London, Allen and Unwin.

Hattam, R. (1997) 'Howard's Way, Diseased Reason and Literacy in Schools'. *Flinders Institute for the Study of Teaching – Research Quarterly* (2), 5–9.

Hattam, R., McInerney, P., Smyth, J. and Lawson, M. (1997a) *Sustaining a School as a Learning Community: Teachers' Learning at Hackham West Schools*. Adelaide, Flinders Institute for the Study of Teaching.

Hattam, R., Shacklock, G. and Smyth, J. (1997b) 'Towards a Practice of Critical Teaching about Teachers' Work'. *Teaching in Higher Education* 2(3), 225–41.

—— (1998a) 'Doing Critical Cultural Studies: an Antidote to Being Done to'. In Smyth, J., Hattam, R. and Lawson, M. (eds), *Schooling for Fair Go*. Sydney, Federation Press, pp. 97–114.

Hattam, R., Smyth, J. and Lawson, M. (1998b) 'Schooling for a Fair Go: (Re)Making the Social Fabric'. In Smyth, J., Hattam, R. and Lawson, M. (eds), *Schooling for a Fair Go*. Sydney, Federation Press, pp. 1–14.

Hatton, E. (1988) 'Teachers' Work as Bricolage: Implications for Teacher Education'. *British Journal of Sociology of Education* 9(3), 337–57.

—— (1997) 'Teacher Educators and the Production of Bricoleurs: an Ethnographic Study'. *Qualitative Studies in Education* 10(2), 237–57.

Helsby, G. and McCulloch, G. (1996) 'Teacher Professionalism and Curriculum Control'. In Goodson, I. and Hargreaves, A., *Teachers Professional Lives*. London, Falmer Press, pp. 56–74.

Hopkins, T. and Wallerstein, I. (1996) 'The World-System: Is there a Crisis?' In Hopkins, T. and Wallerstein, I. (eds), *The Age of Transition: Trajectory of the World-System 1945–2025*. London, Zed Books, pp. 1–12.

Horkheimer, M. (1947/1993) 'Reason Against Itself: Some Remarks on the Enlightenment'. *Theory, Culture and Society* 10, 79–88.

Ikeda, S. (1996) 'World Production'. In Hopkins, T. and Wallerstein, I. (eds), *The Age of Transition: Trajectory of the World-System 1945–2025*. London, Zed Books, pp. 38–86.

Inglis, F. (1985) *The Management of Ignorance*. London, Blackwell.

Jackson, N. (1993) 'Competence: a Game of Smoke and Mirrors?' In Collins, C. (ed.), *Competencies: The Competencies Debate in Australian Education and Training*. Canberra, Australian College of Education, pp. 154–61.

Jameson, F. (1991) *Postmodernism, or the Cultural Logic of Late Capitalism*. Durham, NC, Duke University Press.

—— (1996) *Late Marxism: Adorno and the Persistence of the Dialectic*. London and New York, Verso.

Janks, H. and Ivanic, R. (1992) 'Critical Language Awareness and Emancipatory Discourse'. In Fairclough, N. (ed.), *Critical Language Awareness*. London, Longman, pp. 305–31.

Jay, M. (1984) *Adorno*. Cambridge, MA, Harvard University Press.

Jessop, B. (1989) 'Conservative Regimes and the Transition to Post-Fordism: The Cases of Great Britain and West Germany'. In Gottdiener, M. and Komninos, N. (eds), *Capitalist Development and Crisis Theory: Accumulation, Regulation and Spatial Restructuring*. London, Macmillan.

Johnson, S. (1997) *Interface Culture: How New Technology Transforms the Way we Create and Communicate*. San Francisco, CA, Harper Edge.

Jones, K. (1989) *The Social Face of Buddhism: An Approach to Political and Social Activism*. London, Wisdom.

References

Jones, K. and Hatcher, R. (1994) 'Educational Progress and Economic Change: Notes on Some Recent Proposals'. *British Journal of Educational Studies* 42(3), 245–60.

Kainan, A. (1992) 'Themes of Individualism, Competition and Cooperation in Teachers' Stories'. *Teaching and Teacher Education* 8(5/6), 441–50.

Kellner, D. (1989) *Critical Theory, Marxism and Modernity*. Baltimore, MD, John Hopkins University Press.

—— (1995) 'Marxism, the Information Superhighway, and the Struggle for the Future'. *Humanity and Society* 19(4), 41–56.

Kelsey, J. (1995) *Economic Fundamentalism: New Zealand Experiment – A World Model for Structural Adjustment*. London, Pluto Press.

Kemmis, S. and McTaggart, R. (1988) *The Action Research Planner*. Geelong, Victoria, Deakin University Press.

Kenway, J. (1990) 'Education and the Right's Discursive Politics: Private versus State Schooling'. In Ball, S. (ed.), *Foucault and Education: Disciplines and Knowledge*. London, Routledge, pp. 167–206.

—— (1995) *Marketing Education: Some Critical Issues*. Geelong, Victoria, Deakin University Press.

Kenway, J., Bigum, C., Fitzclarence, L. and Collier, J. (1994a) 'Educationally and Socially Responsible Marketing'. Paper presented to Australian Secondary Principal's Association National Conference, Melbourne.

Kenway, J., Bigum, C., Fitzclarence, L. and Collier, J. (1994b) 'New Education in New Times'. *Journal of Education Policy* 9(4), 317–33.

Kenway, J., Collier, J. and Tragenza, K. (1994c) 'Schools as Commercial Free Zones'. In Deakin Centre for Education and Change (eds), *Schooling What Future? Balancing the Education Agenda*. Geelong, Deakin Centre for Education and Change, pp. 21–34.

Kenway, J. and Fitzclarence, L. (1998) 'Consuming Children? Public Education as a Market Commodity'. In Reid, A. (ed.), *Going Public: Education Policy and Public Education in Australia*. Deakin West, Australian Capital Territory, Australian Curriculum Studies Association, pp. 47–56.

Kenway, J., Willis, S., Blackmore, G. and Rennie, L. (1994d) 'Making "Hope Practical" rather than "Despair Convincing": Feminist Post-structuralism, Gender Reform and Educational Change'. *British Journal of Sociology of Education* 15(2), 187–210.

Keyman, E. (1997) *Globalization, State, Identity/Difference: Toward a Critical Social Theory of International Relations*. Atlantic Highlands, New Jersey, Humanities Press.

Kincheloe, J. (1993) *Towards a Critical Politics of Teacher Thinking: Mapping the Postmodern*. Westport, CT and London, Bergin and Garvey.

Kitney, G. (1999) 'Global backlash'. *The Age* 6 February, pp. 19 and 22.

Knight, J., Lingard, B., Bartlett, L. and Porter, P. (1995) 'Hogging and Coagulating the Australian Education Agenda'. Paper delivered to the Annual Conference of Australian Association of Research in Education, Hobart.

Knights, D. (1990) 'Subjectivity, Power and the Labour Process'. In Knights, D. and Wilmott, H. (eds), *Labour Process Theory*. London, Macmillan, pp. 297–35.

Knights, D. and Willmott, H. (1989) 'Power and Subjectivity at Work: From Degradation to Subjugation in Social Relations'. *Sociology* 23(4), 535–58.

Kress, G. (1993) 'Participation and Difference: the Role of Language in Producing a Culture of Innovation'. In Luke, A. and Gilbert, P. (eds), *Literacy in Contexts: Australian Perspectives and Issues*. Sydney, Allen and Unwin.

Ladwig, J. (1991) 'Is Collaborative Research Exploitative?' *Educational Theory* 41(2), 111–20.

Ladwig, J., Currie, J. and Chadbourne, R. (1994) *Towards Rethinking Australian Schools. The National Schools Network*. Ryde, NSW, National Schools Network.

Lankshear, C. and McLaren, P. (eds) (1993) *Critical Literacy: Politics, Praxis, and the Postmodern*. Albany, NY, State University of New York Press.

Larson, M. (1977) *The Rise of Professionalism*. Berkeley, CA, University of California Press.

—— (1980) 'Proletarianisation and Educated Labour'. *Theory and Society* 9(2), 131–75.

Lather, P. (1986) 'Research as Praxis'. *Harvard Educational Review* 56(3), 257–77.

—— (1991) 'Deconstructing/Deconstructive Inquiry: the Politics of Knowing and Being Known'. *Educational Theory* 41(2), 153–73.

Lauder, H. and Yee, B. (1987) 'Are Teachers being Proletarianised? Some Theoretical, Empirical and Policy Issues'. In Walker, S. and Barton, L. (eds), *Changing Policies, Changing Teachers*. Milton Keynes, Open University Press, pp. 58–71.

Lawn, M. (1987) *Servants of the State: The Contested Control of Teaching, 1900–1930*. London, Falmer Press.

—— (1989) 'Being Caught in Schoolwork: the Possibilities of Research in Teachers' Work'. In Carr, W. (ed.), *Quality in Teaching: Arguments for a Reflective Profession*. Lewes, Falmer Press, pp. 147–62.

—— (1991) 'The Social Construction of Quality in Teaching'. *Evaluation and Research in Education* 5(1–2), 67–8.

—— (1996) *Modern Times? Work, Professionalism and Citizenship in Teaching*. London, Falmer Press.

Lawn, M. and Mac an Ghaill, M. (1996) 'Primary Teaching in a Restructuring Public Service'. Unpublished Report for the Economic and Social Research Council.

Lawn, M. and Ozga, J. (1986) 'Unequal Partners: Teachers Under Indirect Rule'. *British Journal of Sociology of Education* 7(2), 225–38.

—— (1988) 'The Educational Worker? A Reassessment of Teachers'. In Ozga, J. (ed.), *Schoolwork: Approaches to the Labour Process of Teaching*. Milton Keynes, Open University Press, pp. 81–98.

Lee, R. (1996) 'Structures of Knowledge'. In Hopkins, T. and Wallerstein, I. (eds), *The Age of Transition: Trajectory of the World-System 1945–2025*. London, Zed Books, pp. 178–208.

Lesko, N. (1996) 'Past, Present, and Future Conceptions of Adolescence'. *Educational Theory* 46(4), 453–72.

Levinson, B.A. (1993) 'Accommodating Voices: Notes for a Critical School Ethnography'. *Critical Pedagogy Networker* 6(4), 1–10.

Lewis, M. (1990) 'Interrupting Patriarchy: Politics, Resistance, and Transformation in the Feminist Classroom'. *Harvard Educational Review* 60(4), 467–88.

Lewis, M. and Simon, R. (1986) 'A Discourse Not Intended for Her: Learning and Teaching within Patriarchy'. *Harvard Education Review* 36(4), 457–72.

References

Limerick, B. and Lingard, B. (eds) (1995) *Gender and Changing Educational Management*. Rydalmere, NSW, Hodder Education.

Lingard, B. and Garrick, B. (1997) 'Producing and Practicing Social Justice Policy in Education: A Policy Trajectory Study from Queensland'. Paper for the International Sociology of Education Conference, Sheffield, UK.

Little, J. (1987) 'Teachers as Colleagues'. In Richardson-Koehler, V. (ed.), *Educator's Handbook: A Research Perspective*. New York, Longman, pp. 491–518.

—— (1992) 'Opening the Black Box of Professional Community'. In Lieberman, A. (ed.), *The Changing Contexts of Teaching*. Chicago, IL, University of Chicago Press, pp. 157–78.

—— (1993) 'Professional Community in Comprehensive High Schools: the Two Worlds of Academic and Vocational Teachers'. In Little, J. and McLaughlin, M.W. (eds), *Teachers' Work: Individuals, Colleagues, and Contexts*. New York, Teachers College Press, pp. 137–63.

—— (1995) 'Subject Affiliation in High Schools that Restructure'. In Siskin, L.S. and Little, J. (eds), *The Subjects in Question: Departmental Organization and the High School*. New York, Teachers College Press, pp. 172–200.

Lortie, D. (1975) *School Teacher: A Sociological Study*. Chicago, IL, University of Chicago Press.

Luke, A. (1996) 'Genres of Power? Literacy Education and the Production of Capital'. In Hason, R. and Williams, R. (eds), *Literacy in Society*. London, Longman, pp. 308–38.

—— (1997) 'New Narratives of Human Capital: Recent Redirections in Australian Educational Policy'. *Australian Educational Researcher* 24(2), 1–22.

Luke, T. (1991) 'Touring Hyperreality: Critical Theory Confronts Informational Society'. In Wexler, P. (ed.), *Critical Theory Now*. London, Falmer Press, pp. 1–26.

Lyotard, J.F. (1984) *The Postmodern Condition: A Report on Knowledge*. Manchester, Manchester University Press.

Mac an Ghaill, M. (1988) *Young, Gifted and Black*. Milton Keynes, Open University Press.

—— (1991) 'State-school Policy: Contradictions, Confusions and Contestation'. *Journal of Education Policy* 6(3), 299–313.

MacPherson, P. and Fine, M. (1995) 'Hungry for an Us: Adolescent Girls and Adult Women Negotiating Territories of Race, Gender, Class and Difference'. *Feminism and Psychology* 5(2), 181–200.

Marginson, S. (1992a) 'Education as a Branch of Economics: The Universal Claims of Economic Rationalism'. In Stockley, D. (ed.), *Rationalising Education: Melbourne Studies in Education 1992*. Melbourne, LaTrobe University Press, pp. 1–14.

—— (1992b) 'Education after Finn: Shifting the Emphasis'. *Independent Education* 22(1), 4–8.

—— (1995) 'Markets in Education: A Theoretical Note'. *Australian Journal of Education* 39(3), 294–312.

Martinez, Y., Scott, J., Cranston-Gringras, A. and Platt, J. (1994) 'Voices from the Field: Interviews with Students from Migrant Farmworker Families'. *Journal of Educational Issues of Language Minority Students* 14(Winter), 333–48.

Marx, K. (1978) 'Theses on Feuerbach'. In Marx, K. and Engels, F., *The Marx-Engels Reader*. London, W.W. Norton.

Maslen, G. (1994) 'Education Cutbacks: the Right Wing Sting'. *Australian Educator* (Autumn), 22–5.

Max-Neef, M. (1991) *Human Scale Development*. New York, Apex Press.

Maxwell, G. (1996) 'Forum: Convergence of General and Vocational Education – Overview and Critique'. *Unicorn* 22(2), 4–13.

Mayer, E. (chair) (1992) *Putting General Education to Work: the Key Competencies Report* (Report of the committee to advise the Australian Council and Ministers for Vocational Education, Employment and Training on the employment-related key competencies for post-compulsory education and training), Melbourne, The Australian Council for the Ministers for Vocational Education, Employment and Training.

McGuiness, P. (1993) 'Education Sinking in a Sea of Mediocrity'. *The Australian*. 2 June, Sydney, p. 15.

McInerney, P., Hattam, R., Smyth, J. and Lawson, M. (1998) *Middle-Schooling From the Ground Up*. Adelaide, Flinders Institute for the Study of Teaching.

McTaggart, R. (1989) 'Bureaucratic Rationality and the Self-educating Profession: The Problem of Teacher Privatism'. *Journal of Curriculum Studies* 21(4), 345–61.

—— (1992) 'Confronting "accountability": Resisting Transnational Corporate Ideology'. *Curriculum Perspectives* 12(1), 72–8.

Miller, J. (1990) *Creating Spaces and Finding Voices: Teachers Collaborating for Empowerment*. Albany, NY, State University of New York Press.

Mishler, E. (1986) *Research Interviewing. Context and Narrative*. Cambridge, MA, Harvard University Press.

Miyoshi, M. (1995) 'Sites of Resistance in the Global Economy'. *Boundary 2*, 22 (1), 61–84.

National Schools Network (1996) *What is the National Schools Network? Rethinking our Work and Schools for a Changing World*. National Schools Network Brochure.

Natriello, G. (1997) 'Dropouts, School Leavers, and Truants'. In Saha, L. (ed.), *International Encyclopedia of the Sociology of Education*. London, Pergamon Press, pp. 577–81.

Newfield, C. (1993) 'What about Political Correctness? Race, the Right, and the Managerial Democracy in the Humanities'. *Critical Inquiry* 19(Winter), 308–36.

New London Group (1996) 'A Pedagogy of Multiliteracies: Designing Social Futures'. *Harvard Educational Review* 66(1), 60–92.

Nias, J. (1989) *Primary Teachers Talking: A Study of Teaching as Work*. London and New York, Routledge.

Nias, J., Southworth, G. and Yeomans, R. (1989) *Staff Relationships in the Primary School: A Study of Organizational Cultures*. London, Cassell.

Noddings, N. (1984) *Caring: A Feminine Approach to Ethics and Moral Education*. Berkeley, CA, University of California Press.

—— (1988) 'An Ethic of Caring and its Implications for Instructional Arrangements'. *American Journal of Education* 96(2), 215–30.

—— (1992) *The Challenge to Care in Schools: An Alternative Approach to Education*. New York, Teachers' College Press.

Oakley, A. (1981) 'Interviewing Women: A Contradiction in Terms'. In Roberts, H. (ed.), *Doing Feminist Research*. London, Routledge and Kegan Paul, pp. 30–61.

O'Connor, J. (1973) *The Fiscal Crisis of the State*. New York, St. Martins Press.

—— (1984) *Accumulation Crisis*. Oxford, Blackwell.

References

Offe, C. (1984) *Contradictions of the Welfare State*. London, Hutchinson.
—— (1985) *Disorganised Capitalism*. Oxford, Polity Press.
—— (1996) 'Modern Barbarity: A Micro-state of Nature?' *Constellations* 2(3), 354–77.
Ozga, J. (ed.) (1988) *Schoolwork: Approaches to the Labour Process of Teaching*. Milton Keynes, Open University Press.
—— (1993) 'Teacher De-professionalisation: Hard Lessons from England'. Paper presented at the Annual Conference of the Australian Association for Research in Education, Fremantle, 22–5 November.
Ozga, J. and Lawn, M. (1981) *Teachers, Professionalism and Class: A Study of Organised Teachers*. Lewes, Falmer Press.
Pelizzon, S. and Casparis, J. (1996) 'World Human Welfare'. In Hopkins, T. and Wallerstein, I. (eds), *The Age of Transition: Trajectories for the World-System – 1945–2025*. New York, Zed Books, pp. 117–47.
Perera, S. and Pugliese, J. (1997) '"Racial suicide": the Re-licensing of Racism in Australia'. *Race and Class* 39(2), 1–19.
Perrenoud, P. (1996) 'The Teaching Profession between Proletarianization and Professionalization: Two Models of Change'. *Prospects* 26(3), 509–29.
Pignatelli, F. (1993) 'What Can I Do? Foucault on Freedom and the Question of Teacher Agency'. *Educational Theory* 43(4), 411–32.
Platt, J. (1981) 'On Interviewing One's Peers'. *British Journal of Sociology* 32(1), 75–91.
Popkewitz, T. (1984) *Paradigm and Ideology in Educational Research*. Lewes, Falmer Press.
—— (1994) 'Professionalisation in Teaching and Teacher Education: Some Notes on its History, Ideology and Potential'. *Teaching and Teacher Education* 10(1), 1–14.
Popkewitz, T. and Lind, K. (1989) 'Teacher Incentives as Reforms: Teachers' Work and the Changing Control Mechanism in Education'. *Teachers College Record* 9(4), 578–85.
Prentice, A. (1975) 'The Feminization of Teaching'. *Histoire Sociale* 8, 5–20.
Prillaman, R., Eaker, D. and Kendrick, D. (eds) (1994) *The Tapestry of Caring: Education as Nurturance*. Norwood, NJ, Ablex Publishing Corporation.
Pusey, M. (1991) *Economic Rationalism in Canberra: A Nation-building State Changes its Mind*. New York, Cambridge University Press.
—— (1996) 'Economic Rationalism and the Contest for Civil Society'. *Thesis Eleven* 44, 69–86.
—— (1998) 'Australia: Once the Lighthouse Social Democracy of the World. The Impact of Recent Economic Reforms'. *Thesis Eleven* 55(November), 41–59.
Putnam, R. (1993) 'The Prosperous Community: Social Capital and Public Life'. *The American Prospect* 13 (Spring), 35–42.
Quantz, R. and O'Connor, T. (1988) 'Writing Critical Ethnography: Dialogue, Multivoicedness, and Carnival in Cultural Texts'. *Educational Theory* 38(1), 95–109.
Rabinow, P. (ed.) (1984) *The Foucault Reader*. London, Penguin Books.
Redclift, N. and Sinclair, M.T. (eds) (1991) *Working Women: International Perspectives on Labour and Gender*. London, Routledge.
Reekie, W. (1984) *Market, Entrepreneurs and Liberty*. Brighton, Wheatsheaf.
Reid, A. (1992) 'Social Justice in Education'. *Curriculum Perspectives* Newsletter Edition (November), 14–21.

—— (1993) 'Controlling Australia's Teachers: An Agenda for the Next Decade'. In Reid, A. and Johnson, B. (eds), *Critical Issues in Australian Education*. Adelaide, Painters Prints, pp. 125–37.

—— (1997) 'Controlling Teachers' Work: A Labour Process Analysis of Teachers' Work'. Unpublished doctoral thesis, Flinders University of South Australia, July.

—— (1998) 'Regulating the Education Market: The Effects on Public Education Workers'. In Reid, A. (ed.), *Going Public: Education Policy and Public Education in Australia*. Deakin West, Australian Capital Territory, Australian Curriculum Studies Association, pp. 57–68.

Reid, A., McCallum, F. and Dobbins, R. (1998) 'Teachers as Political Actors'. *Asia-Pacific Journal of Teacher Education* 26(3), 247–59.

Reifer, T. and Sudler, J. (1996) 'The Interstate System'. In Hopkins, T. and Wallerstein, I. (eds), *The Age of Transition: Trajectory of the World-System – 1945–2025*. New York, Zed Books, pp. 13–37.

Richards, C. (1994) 'Many Teachers Academically Weak: Pennington'. *The Age*. 28 July, Melbourne, p. 1.

Robertson, H. (1998) *No More Teachers, No More Books: the Commercialization of Canada's Schools*. Toronto, McClelland and Stewart.

Robertson, R. (1995) 'Glocalization: Time-space and Homogeneity-Heterogeneity'. In Featherstone, M., Lash, S. and Robertson, R. (eds), *Global Modernities*. London, Sage, pp. 25–44.

Robertson, S. (1994) 'Teachers' Labour and Post-Fordism: an Exploratory Analysis'. In Kenway, J. (ed.), *Economising Education: the Post-Fordist Directions*. Geelong, Deakin University Press, pp. 105–51.

Rogers, D. (1994) 'Conceptions of Caring in a Fourth-grade Classroom'. In Prillaman, R., Eaker, D. and Kendrick, D. (eds), *The Tapestry of Caring: Education as Nurturance*. Norwood, NJ, Ablex Publishing Corporation, pp. 33–47.

Rogers, J. (1995) 'How Divided Progressives Might Unite'. *New Left Review*, 210, 3–32.

Roof, J. and Wiegman, R. (eds) (1995) *Who can Speak? Authority and Critical Identity*. Chicago, IL and Urbana, University of Illinois Press.

Said, E. (1994) *Representations of the Intellectual: The 1993 Reith Lectures*. London, Vintage.

Sakolsky, R. (1992) 'Disciplinary Power and the Labour Process'. In Sturdy, A., Knights, D. and Wilmott, H. (eds), *Skill and Consent: Contemporary Studies in the Labour Process*. London and New York, Routledge, pp. 235–54.

Sayer, A. (1986) 'New Developments in Manufacturing: the Just In Time System'. *Capital and Class* 30, 43–72.

Schnädelbach, H. (1993) 'Max Horkheimer and the Moral Philosophy of German Idealism'. In Benhabib, S., Bonss, W. and McCole, J. (eds), *On Max Horkheimer: New Perspectives*. London and Cambridge, MA, MIT Press, pp. 281–308.

Schools Council (1990) *Australia's Teachers: An Agenda for the Next Decade*. Canberra, Australian Government Publishing Service.

Seddon, T. (1990) 'Who Says Teachers Don't Work?' *Education Links* 38, 4–9.

—— (1994) 'Reconstructing Social Democratic Education in Australia: Versions of Vocationalism'. *Journal of Curriculum Studies* 26(1), 63–83.

—— (1995a) 'Defining the Real: Context and Beyond'. *Qualitative Studies in Education* 8(4), 393–405.

References

—— (1995b) 'Educational Leadership and Teachers' Work'. Paper presented at Conference: Educational Leadership: Political, Cultural, Critical and Gendered Perspectives, Proceedings of a conference at Flinders University, July. Adelaide, Flinders Institute for the Study of Teaching.

—— (1997) 'Education: Deprofessionalised? or Re-regulated, Reorganised and Reauthorised?' *Australian Journal of Education* 41(3), 228–46.

Sewell, G. and Wilkinson, B. (1992) ' "Someone to watch over me": Surveillance, Discipline and the Just-In-Time Labour Process'. *Sociology* 26(2), 271–89.

Shacklock, G. (1995) 'A Socially Critical, Ethnographic, Work-Storied Account of Teachers' Work'. Unpublished doctoral dissertation, Flinders University.

—— (1998) 'Fast Capitalist Educational Change: Personally Resisting the Images of School Reform'. *Discourse* 19(1), 75–88.

Shacklock, G. and Smyth, J. (eds) (1998) *Being Reflexive in Critical Educational and Social Research*. London, Falmer Press.

Shanker, A. (1989) 'Reform and the Teaching Profession'. In Weis, L., Altbach, P., Kelly, G., Petrie, H. and Slaughter, S. (eds), *Crisis in Teaching: Perspectives on Current Reforms*. Albany, NY, State University of New York Press.

Shannon, P. (1991) 'Questions and Answers: Critical Literacy'. *The Reading Teacher* 44(7), 518.

Sheridan, G. (1988) 'Time to Fight Crisis in the Classroom'. *The Australian* 26 November, Sydney.

Shor, I. (1987) *Critical Teaching and Everyday Life*. Chicago, IL, University of Chicago Press.

—— (1992) *Empowering Education: Critical Teaching for Social Change*. Chicago, IL, University of Chicago Press.

—— (1996) *When Students have Power: Negotiating Authority in a Critical Pedagogy*. Chicago, IL, Chicago University Press.

Shor, I. and Freire, P. (1987) 'What is the Dialogical Method of Teaching?' *Journal of Education* 169(3), 11–31.

Simon, R. (1992) *Teaching Against the Grain: Texts for a Pedagogy of Possibility*. New York, Bergin and Garvey.

Skeggs, B. (1997) *Formations of Class and Gender: Becoming Respectable*. London, Sage.

Smetherham, D. (1978) 'Insider Research'. *British Educational Research Journal* 4(2), 97–102.

Smyth, J. (1980) 'Functional Aspects of Control in Schools'. In Smyth, J. (ed.), *Educational Leadership in Schools (Study Guide 1)*. Geelong, Deakin University Press, pp. 59–76.

—— (1989) 'A Critical Pedagogy of Classroom Practice'. *Journal of Curriculum Studies* 21(6), 483–502.

—— (1991) 'International Perspectives on Teacher Collegiality: a Labour Process Discussion Based on the Concept of Teachers' Work'. *British Journal of Sociology of Education* 12(3), 323–46.

—— (1992) 'Teachers' Work and the Politics of Reflection'. *American Educational Research Journal* 29(2), 267–300.

—— (ed.) (1993a) *A Socially Critical View of the Self Managing School*. London, Falmer Press.

—— (1993b) *Schooling for Democracy in Economic Rationalist Times.* Adelaide, Flinders Institute for the Study of Teaching.

—— (1993c) *Economic Rationalism in Education: Have We Lost Our Way?* Adelaide, Inaugural Professorial Lecture, The Flinders University of South Australia.

—— (1994) 'Critical Educational Research for New Educational Times'. *New Zealand Journal of Educational Administration* 9 (November), 2–12.

—— (1995a) 'Teachers' Work and the Labour Process of Teaching: Central Problematics in Professional Development'. In Guskey, T. and Hargreaves, A., *Professional Development in Education: New Paradigms and Practices.* New York, Teachers College Press, Columbia University, pp. 69–91.

—— (1995b) 'What's Happening to Teachers' Work in Australia?' *Educational Review* 47(2), 189–97.

—— (1996a) 'Evaluation of Teacher Performance: Move over Hierarchy here comes Collegiality!' *Journal of Education Policy* 11(2), 185–96.

—— (1996b) 'Developing Socially Critical Educators'. In Boud, D. and Miller, N. (eds), *Working with Experience: Animating Learning.* London, Routledge, pp. 41–57.

—— (1998) 'Economic Forces Affecting School Supervision'. In Firth, G. and Pajak, E. (eds), *Handbook of Research on School Supervision.* New York, Macmillan, pp. 1173–83.

Smyth, J. and Hattam, R. (1998a) 'Enterprise Education and the Construction of Teachers' Work: Exploring the Links'. Paper presented at the Australian Association for Research in Education Conference, Adelaide.

Smyth, J. and Hattam, R. (1998b) 'Intellectual as Hustler: Researching Against the Grain of the Market'. In Hunt, I. and Smyth, J. (eds), *Ethos of the University: West and Beyond.* Adelaide, Flinders University Press, pp. 145–78.

Smyth, J., McInerney, P., Hattam, R. and Lawson, M. (1997) *Sustaining Teacher Learning as a Dialogic Encounter: Conversing with Pieces of the Puzzle at the Pines School.* Case Study No. 4, Adelaide, Flinders Institute for the Study of Teaching.

Smyth, J. and Shacklock, G. (1998) *Remaking Teaching: Ideology, Policy and Practice.* London, Routledge.

Snow, D. and Anderson, L. (1987) 'Identity Work Among the Homeless: the Verbal Construction and Avowal of Personal Identities'. *American Journal of Sociology* 92, 1337–71.

Soder, R. (1991) 'The Ethics of the Rhetoric of Teacher Professionalism'. *Teaching and Teacher Education* 7(3), 295–302.

Soucek, V. (1993) 'Is There a Need to Redress the Balance Between Systems Goals and Lifeworld-Oriented Goals in Public Education in Australia?' In Collins, C. (ed.), *Competencies: The Competencies Debate in Australian Education and Training.* Canberra, Australian College of Education, pp. 162–81.

Spierings, J. (1995) *Young Australians in the Working Nation. A Review of Youth Unemployment Policies for the 1990s.* Adelaide, Social Justice Research Foundation.

Spivak, G. (1988) 'Can the Subaltern Speak?' In Grossberg, L. and Nelson, C. (eds), *Marxism and the Interpretation of Culture.* Urbana and Chicago, IL, University of Illinois Press, pp. 271–313.

References

Starr, K. (1998) 'Power and Production in Site-based Management: the Responses of Women Secondary Principals in South Australian Education'. *South Australian Educational Leader* 9(4), 1–12.

Sumara, D. and Luce-Kapler, R. (1996) '(Un)Becoming a Teacher: Negotiating Identities While Learning to Teach'. *Canadian Journal of Education* 21(1), 65–83.

Tabak, F. (1996) 'The World Labour Force'. In Hopkins, T. and Wallerstein, I. (eds), *The Age of Transition; Trajectories of the World-System – 1945–2025*. New York, Zed Books, pp. 87–116.

Taylor, F.W. (1911) *The Principles of Scientific Management*. New York, Harper and Brothers.

Taylor, S., Rizvi, F., Lingard, B. and Henry, M. (1997) *Educational Policy and the Politics of Change*. London and New York, Routledge.

Teese, R., Davies, M., Charlton, M. and Polesel, J. (1995) *Who Wins at School? Girls and Boys in Australian Secondary Schools*. Melbourne, University of Melbourne Department of Education Policy and Management.

Thayer-Bacon, B. (1997) 'The Nurturing of Relational Epistemologies'. *Educational Theory* 47(2), 239–60.

Theobald, M. (1996) *Knowing Women: Origins of Women's Education in Nineteenth Century Australia*. Melbourne, Cambridge University Press.

Thompson, E. (1963) *The Making of the English Working Class*. London, Victor Gollancz Ltd.

—— (1979) 'Folklore, Anthropology and Social History'. *Indian Historical Review* 3(2), 20–1.

Thomson, P. (1998a) 'Thoroughly Modern Management and Cruel Accounting: The Effects of Public Sector Reform on Public Education'. In Reid, A. (ed.), *Going Public: Education Policy and Public Education in Australia*. Deakin, Australian Capital Territory, Australian Curriculum Studies Association, pp. 37–46.

—— (1998b) 'Back on the Borderline: The Marginalisation of Equity in Federal Schools Policy'. *South Australian Educational Leader* 9(1), 1–11.

Thomson, P. and Reid, A. (1998) 'Towards an Agenda for Political Action. In Reid, A. (ed.), *Going Public: Education Policy and Public Education in Australia*. Deakin, Australian Capital Territory, Australian Curriculum Studies Association, pp. 105–12.

Torres, C.A. (1989) 'The Capitalist State and Public Policy Formation: A Framework for a Political Sociology of Educational Policy Making'. *British Journal of Sociology of Education* 10(1), 81–102.

Touraine, A. (1985) 'An Introduction to the Study of Social Movements'. *Social Research* 52(4), 749–87.

Tripp, D. (1992) *Critical Incidents in Teaching: the Development of Professional Judgement*. London, Routledge.

Troman, G. (1996) 'The Rise of the New Professionals? The Restructuring of Primary Teachers' Work and Professionalism'. *British Journal of Sociology of Education* 17(4), 473–87.

Wallace, J. and Louden, W. (1991) 'Qualities of Collaboration and the Growth of Teachers' Knowledge'. Paper presented at the Annual Meeting of American Educational Research Association, Chicago.

Wark, M. (1995) 'The Price is Right'. *21C* 2, 20–4.

Waters, M. (1995) *Globalization*. London, Routledge.

Watkins, P. (1992) *Class, the Labour Process and Work: Focus on Education.* Geelong, Victoria, Deakin University Press.

—— (1993) 'Work, Skill and Teachers'. *Unicorn* 19(3), 65–74.

Watt, M. (1998) 'National Curriculum: the State of Reform in the States and Territories'. *Curriculum Perspectives* 18(1), 21–34.

Weiler, K. (1995) 'Women and the Professionalization of Teaching'. In Anderson, L. (ed.), *International Encyclopedia of Teaching and Teacher Education.* New York, Pergamon, pp. 76–80.

Welton, M. (1993) 'Social Revolutionary Learning: the New Social Movements as Learning Sites'. *Adult Education Quarterly* 43(3), 152–64.

Wexler, P. (1992) *Becoming Somebody: Towards a Social Psychology of the School.* London, Falmer Press.

White, R. (1983) 'On Teachers and Proletarianisation'. *Discourse* 3(2), 45–57.

Whitty, G., Power, S. and Halpin, D. (1998) *Devolution and Choice in Education: The School, the State and the Market.* Melbourne, Australian Council for Educational Research.

Whyte, W.F., Greenwood, D.J. and Lazes, P. (1991) 'Participatory Action Research'. In Whyte, W.F. (ed.), *Participatory Action Research.* London, Sage Publications.

Willinsky, J. (1990) *The New Literacy: Redefining Reading and Writing in the Schools.* London, Routledge.

Witherell, C. and Noddings, N. (1991) *Stories Lives Tell.* New York, Teachers College Press.

Wolcott, H. (1977) *Teachers Versus Technocrats: An Educational Innovation in Anthropological Perspective.* Oregon, University of Oregon Press.

Woods, P. (1985) 'Conversations with Teachers: Some Aspects of Life History Method'. *British Educational Research Journal* 11(1), 13–26.

—— (1995) *Creative Teachers in Primary Schools.* Buckingham, Open University Press.

Worsford, V. (1997) 'Teaching Democracy Democratically'. *Educational Theory* 47(3), 395–410.

Wright, E. (1985) *Class.* London, New Left Books/Verso.

—— (1996) 'The Continuing Relevance of Class Analysis – Comments'. *Theory and Society* (25), 693–716.

Wylie, C. (1995) 'Contrary Currents: the Application of the Public Sector Reform Framework in Education'. *New Zealand Journal of Educational Studies* 30(2), 149–64.

Wyn, J. and Holden, E. (1994) *Early School Leavers: Young Women and Girls at Risk.* Parkville, Victoria, University of Melbourne Youth Research Centre.

Yeatman, A. (1990) *Bureaucrats, Technocrats, Femocrats; Essays on the Contemporary Australian State.* Sydney, Allen and Unwin.

Zeichner, K. (1993) 'Connecting Genuine Teacher Development to the Struggle for Social Justice'. *Journal of Education for Teaching* 19(1), 5–20.

Zeichner, K. and Liston, J. (1986) 'An Inquiry-oriented Approach to Student Teaching'. *Journal of Teaching Practice* 6(1), 5–24.

Index

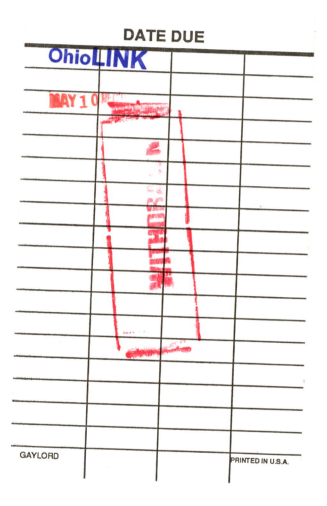